Victor Grayson

'Victor Grayson was a socialist firebrand and trailblazer. The leftist equivalent of a spectacular firework, he blazed gloriously, but briefly, before falling to earth – and from grace. This is a gripping account of his spectacular political rise, challenge to the cosy Labour establishment, bizarre ideological volte-face and sudden, never solved, disappearance.'

—Peter Tatchell, human rights defender

'Wonderful.'

—Jeremy Corbyn, former leader of the Labour party

'Remarkable ... cuts through the mystery and fabrication that has surrounded Grayson's tumultuous life and brings us a step closer to the true story of one of the most renowned socialist politicians of his generation.'

—Dan Carden MP

'Casts a new light on its fascinating subject.'

—Dr Kevin Hickson, Senior Lecturer in British Politics, University of Liverpool

'A fresh and lively portrait of Victor Grayson built on sound research and archival discoveries.'

—David Clark (Lord Clark of Windermere), former Colne Valley MP and author of *Victor Grayson: The Man and the Mystery*

'Delves into Labour's most fascinating cold case to produce a lively and compelling story of a working class hero.'

—Paul Mason, author of *How to Stop Fascism*

Victor Grayson

In Search of Britain's
Lost Revolutionary

Harry Taylor

Foreword by Jeremy Corbyn

First published 2021 by Pluto Press
345 Archway Road, London N6 5AA

www.plutobooks.com

British Library Cataloguing in Publication Data
A catalogue record for this book is available from the British Library

ISBN   978 0 7453 4398 3   Hardback
ISBN   978 0 7453 4401 0   PDF
ISBN   978 0 7453 4399 0   EPUB
ISBN   978 0 7453 4400 3   Kindle

This book is printed on paper suitable for recycling and made from fully managed
and sustained forest sources. Logging, pulping and manufacturing processes are
expected to conform to the environmental standards of the country of origin.

Typeset by Stanford DTP Services, Northampton, England

Simultaneously printed in the United Kingdom and United States of America

Contents

List of Illustrations

1. A young Victor Grayson before his election to Parliament holding a copy of the *Clarion* under his arm.
2. Victor Grayson's Colne Valley by-election address.
3. Just a section of the huge crowd waiting to hear the result from the by-election count.
4. The Colne Valley Labour League after the by-election victory in 1907.
5. Artist's impression of Grayson's protest which saw him suspended from the House of Commons.
6. When he could find no audience in the House of Commons, Grayson toured the country preaching 'Socialist Unity'. Newcastle, 1909.
7. Grayson places the Labour crown on his head as MacDonald, Glasier, Snowden and Hardie exit the stage.
8. Grayson with admirers in 1909. He was always well dressed, whatever the occasion.
9. Grayson giving a fiery speech at the London demonstration against the execution of Spanish educationist, Ferrer.
10. No Right to Work – No Right to Live. A rare surviving election leaflet from Grayson's January 1910 General Election campaign in Colne Valley.
11. Grayson speaking from a Clarion van at the opening of his last-minute campaign in Kennington during the freezing December 1910 General Election.
12. The card which Grayson's small but dedicated band of supporters handed to voters on polling day.
13. The classic portrait of Victor Grayson.
14. The actress, Ruth Grayson, adopting her husband's standard salutation 'thine fraternally'.

Foreword

Victor Grayson, his life, his speeches, his inspiration and his apparent disappearance are the stuff of Labour movement legends. Almost 120 years after the Colne Valley by-election, the stirrings and importance of that campaign are still alive in the Labour movement's rich lexicon of great achievements.

Grayson, born into poverty in Liverpool, worked in factories and later enrolled into Church missionary work. Despite an early speech impediment, he learned to speak and hold a crowd for street Christianity, and later for socialism. In Grayson's eyes he saw them as part of the same story.

His life passage saw so many similarities to that of Keir Hardie, who was a Church and temperance orator and later trade union and Labour organiser. Victor Grayson and Hardie were never close and had a tense and difficult relationship. However, their lives were so similar, both born into wrenching poverty, then embracing religion, temperance, trade unionism, Labour movement and eventually Parliament.

Grayson based his life in Manchester where he was studying theology for a religious career but was increasingly in demand as a socialist speaker. His travels all around the North of England gave him a unique basis of support in Colne Valley. When a long-predicted by-election took place in 1907, Grayson should have been the Labour candidate, but a bureaucratic and very typical Labour argument over rules and interference from the Independent Labour Party national office resulted in him not being the official candidate but supported by Labour. Keir Hardie lent his support, but was always critical. The argument between local selection of candidates and national interference by the Party machine is not new.

Grayson's dashing style, endless arguments with trade union leaders – who preferred to deal with the Liberals – and ability to excite popular support, won him a place in the hearts of the people of Colne Valley and the eternal jealousy of the then leading lights of the movement. His famous campaign embraced the cause of women's right to vote and a clear and straightforward socialist message. He used methods of community organising that made the official Labour machinery nervous as his appeal was the street meeting with the enthusiasm of music and presence. Massive meetings of people, many of whom were disenfranchised by being women or lacking the qualification to vote, meant that he won, very narrowly, in July 1907.

His first foray after the historic election was to go not to London, but Belfast, with Jim Larkin to support the dock strike and then raise the cause in Parliament. Parliamentary life had its ups and downs. The Parliamentary Labour Party never accepted him and his disruption of Parliament in support of the unemployed did not bring him friendship or support in the Tea Room or in the House. But it did make him a big name in the Labour movement and his amazing capacity for popular writing gave him a unique advantage over the dour, establishment-leaning, Labour figures.

As with many a famous and sought after figure, his cheery facade was hiding a lonely person. His stupendous energy sent him on a never-ending round of trains and meetings and urgently written articles, but he never had the time or support to develop any kind of theoretical basis for his socialism.

Human frailties increasingly affected him as he became a prolific whisky drinker. This and the refusal of the Labour Party to fully embrace him meant he fought a less effective defence of Colne Valley in 1910 and lost.

Only three years in Parliament still made him a legend. Children, including the later TUC General Secretary, Vic Feather, were named after him. There was genuine and huge love for him. The dashing young orator whose lips could bring such messages of joy to grotesquely exploited people in mills and factories. Grayson had made a huge impact but always seemed, somehow, to miss the boat, in creating the kind of socialist movement he dreamt of. The arguments during 1907 in Colne Valley undoubtedly robbed Labour of a future leader whilst his refusal to challenge the Independent Labour Party leaders in 1909 left him an outsider.

At a distance of over a century, the intensity of debate about the Labour Party and its very existence in the period up to the First World War seems odd. Grayson helped form the British Socialist Party (which a decade later was the basis of the Communist Party), but played no part in it as he was outmanoeuvred. He was still a much sought after speaker, essentially without a party, but always preaching socialism and political trade unionism.

The First World War changed everything. Hardie was against war and was destroyed by it. Grayson, then an outcast, became a different figure in the eyes of the movement, and the previously very hostile media. He supported the war and became a recruiting sergeant. His use of a clever mixture of class rhetoric and demand for better working conditions after the war helped to gain working-class support for the war. His old adversary, Churchill, saw the value of his oratory and sent him to Australia and New Zealand. He joined the New Zealand forces in response to a challenge at a public meeting to his pro-war credentials. He duly served and was badly injured in Passchendaele. Despite the sight of death and destruction he became a useful tool of the establishment alongside the former suffragette, Emmeline Pankhurst.

How, one asks, could a man born into poverty, who was such a brilliant and revolutionary speaker, who could challenge the very structures of society, become seduced into the very heart of the British War Machine? At his last public meeting, in Hull, in the intense industrial activity of 1918, he attacked those who were taking strike action for wages and rights.

Harry Taylor has written a wonderful book, building on previous books by Reg Groves and David Clark in bringing Grayson's story to life. His research is painstaking and extensive. However, a degree of mystery remains. Grayson disappeared and various sightings right up to the 1940s never really told the whole story.

The ever-secretive British state knows the answer, somewhere in some files from Scotland Yard or the Home Office, the truth is known. And why it is still a secret is at one level strange, but at another, very obvious. His power of oratory frightened the establishment, the fear of socialist unity and industrial success meant its best voices needed to be silenced. If they could not be silenced they had to be used, and at the end of his known life he had become a tool of the establishment he so hated.

However, his voice and energy gave thousands a vision of how their lives could be changed by their empowerment, and the way socialism could be built. That vision he gave people never went away, and although he was only three years in Parliament, Grayson will always be remembered and revered for giving that precious message of hope. In his memory, we should fight to mould the Labour movement into one of hope, that shapes the lives of generations to follow.

Jeremy Corbyn
MP Islington North
8 March 2021

Introduction

In the midst of a wartime London still under constant threat of aerial bombardment from the Luftwaffe, journalist and future Labour Party candidate, Reg Groves, was called in to Scotland Yard for questioning by the Metropolitan Police. Groves was at first perplexed. To his knowledge, he had committed no crime and he was not involved in any subversive activities. He had been the founder of the small London-based Trotskyist Balham Group but this had scarcely been more than an irrelevance. There was only one thing it could be. For the past few years Groves had been chasing a man who had once made headlines across the world, who had once shaken the British political establishment and had once inspired fear in the hearts of Europe's capitalist class. But Albert Victor Grayson, better known as Victor, had been missing for 20 years. Why were the police so interested in Grayson and why now, when the outcome of the war was still in the balance?

Reg Groves was a young member of the Independent Labour Party (ILP) when he first heard the name Victor Grayson. Older members of Groves' ILP branch spoke of Victor (there was never any need for the surname) as the greatest orator they had heard, a maverick who had put the cause of socialism before all others, and the lost hero of their generation. At that time, in 1924, it was taken for granted by Groves' comrades that Grayson was alive and well but had simply retired from public life. In fact, Grayson had hurriedly left his plush London apartment with two official-looking men one September evening in 1920 and, despite a string of credible sightings, had officially been missing ever since.

As Hitler's armies swept into Czechoslovakia in mid-March 1939, Groves had heard a whisper amongst several of his Labour comrades that Victor was living and working under an assumed name in London. By that time several public attempts had been made to find the missing former politician, not least by his dying mother. All were unsuccessful, but sightings were regularly reported in the national media. It seems that Groves was now let into a secret that had been kept for nearly two decades; that Grayson had renounced the socialism of his youth as well as the alcohol that had so nearly killed him, had married a wealthy younger woman and was working in business (possibly banking) around the Chelsea area. No one seemed willing or able to go into any more detail, but Groves was captivated and determined to find the truth and document Grayson's adventurous life. Throughout 1939 and into the first years of the war, Groves pursued Grayson relentlessly. As war with Germany became increasingly certain, he visited the scenes of Grayson's youthful success in Manchester and the Colne Valley in Yorkshire, and scoured the streets and apartments of London that Grayson was now rumoured to frequent. Just three months later in June, Sidney Campion, who now worked in the parliamentary press gallery but who as a youth had known Grayson, reported to his colleagues that he had just seen him on the District Line of the London Underground. Grayson and a younger, glamorous woman had boarded the train at Sloane Square. Campion was dumbstruck, he had assumed Grayson was dead. Further, the younger woman referred to the man as 'Vic'. Campion alighted after six minutes in the carriage with the couple. He had been so taken aback that he had found himself unable to quiz the man he was certain to be Grayson, but when he reported the incident to his press colleagues the story made international news. The incident seemed to confirm the rumours Groves had been hearing for some weeks and he continued his search for the next 18 months. But just as Groves felt he was getting nearer to the truth, and having possibly identified Grayson's female partner, the trail abruptly went cold. Rumours circulated that Grayson had been killed in a German air-raid on Chelsea and sightings of him came to an abrupt end. It was the following year, 1942, that the Metropolitan Police called upon Groves. An unnamed but senior figure in the wartime government had ordered the Met to carry out a full and thorough search for Grayson and wanted to find out what Groves knew. The latter co-operated and handed over some of his papers (which were never returned) but was nevertheless surprised that Britain's stretched security services were being employed to look for a man who had left Parliament more than 30 years earlier. After all, this was a period in Britain's history which the Prime Minister Winston Churchill himself later referred to as 'The Hinge of Fate'. The investigation appeared thorough: archives were scoured and public appeals made for information relating to Grayson. A mass of papers, from his school reports to personal letters, were collected (and in some instances stolen), but no outcome was forthcoming, at least publicly.

In retrospect, the 1942 investigation seems very odd. What was so important about Grayson to Britain's wartime coalition government that warranted such an investigation? Why did the Metropolitan Police spend decades denying it had ever taken place, despite their own public appeals for information at the time? When confronted with the evidence that they had carried out an investigation, the Met said all records had been passed to the National Archives (formerly known as the Public Record Office). When the National Archives confirmed they had never received such documents the Met then claimed the documents had been destroyed (when or by whom they could not say). We now know that police officers had scoured wartime Britain for any documents relating to Grayson's life, no matter how small or insignificant. The mass of papers collected during the police investigation was said to resemble several large telephone directories, but no one seems sure exactly what happened to them.

Whatever the oddities of the police investigation, Reg Groves was able to have a book published as *The Mystery of Victor Grayson* (Pendulum Publication) in 1946 which, though unadvertised and poorly produced, sold its entire print run of 10,000 copies in twelve weeks. It was never reprinted, probably owing to paper restrictions in the immediate post-war years in Britain. The biography collected first-hand accounts of Grayson's life and speculated on his fate with the possibility that he could still be alive. After all, Grayson was just three years older than Clement Attlee who had been Deputy Prime Minister in the wartime coalition and who, just the previous year, had become Prime Minister when Labour swept to power. The book's real legacy, however, was to kick-start more searches and memory-racking. The surviving documentary evidence was slim. Victor had destroyed most of his private papers prior to 1920 and his surviving family appeared less than forthcoming in Groves' quest for answers. However, following the publication, Groves received a steady stream of correspondence from those who knew Grayson. Some of it was genuinely helpful whilst others warned him off continuing his search for Grayson. Augusta Grayson, Grayson's younger sister, had launched a legal case against Groves for his suggestion that Victor might not have been born in the slums of Liverpool, but could actually have been the illegitimate child of an aristocrat. Although the case was dropped, the solicitor instructed by Augusta, Reginald de Mornay Davies, felt there was an attempt by elements of the British establishment to cover up the true story of Victor Grayson. A search through Reg Groves' papers shows that de Mornay Davies worked secretly with Groves to crack the riddle of the missing politician once and for all. Throughout the early 1950s they scoured death, burial and immigration records in Britain and Ireland. By this time, they expected Victor to be dead from cirrhosis of the liver, resulting from his years of alcoholism, which was recorded in his army medical records. Yet a thorough search of all records to March 1953 revealed no death or burial record for Albert Victor Grayson. The pair concluded that this was surely proof that Victor had assumed a new identity.

The investigation carried out in the early 1950s by Groves and de Mornay Davies differed from the 1942 police investigation in one important respect. Whilst Groves (and the police) was entirely open about his mission in the 1940s, this time around he kept his search secret. The solicitor de Mornay Davies wrote to Groves, 'Yes, great care must be taken to keep our enquiries as secret as possible as one small slip and the whole of our mutual exertions will be completely ruined.' It was also clear that Groves was blocked from making any contact with Victor's surviving daughter Elaine, for whom his sister Augusta would not pass on the address.

Groves made no mention of the extensive 1950s investigation in his second Grayson biography, *The Strange Case of Victor Grayson* (Pluto Press, 1975), nor did he make any reference to de Mornay Davies and the many obstacles that had been put in their way. If he had done so, he might have received better reviews at the time and a kinder treatment from those historians who saw it as a lost opportunity to track down the few remaining individuals who might have been able to solve the mystery. Rather bizarrely, Groves abandoned much of his last three decades of research – leaving large portions unpublished – and threw in his lot with the journalist and crime writer Donald McCormick who had written *Murder by Perfection* (John

Long, 1970). McCormick was a prolific author who specialised in writing sensationalist books on unsolved crimes and mysteries, usually claiming to have discovered key information others had missed that proved the break-through in long-debated cases, including that of Jack the Ripper. In *Murder by Perfection* McCormick described the murders of Victor Grayson and Edith Rosse by J. Maundy Gregory. Gregory was an Edwardian conman and political fixer who raised money for the Conservative and Liberal Parties through dubious means, including the selling of honours. The first half of the book dealt with Grayson's disappearance and the reader familiar with his story would have been amazed by the amount of new informa-tion McCormick brought to light, mostly from individuals long dead, in describing Grayson's life after the Great War. It read like a spy-fiction thriller with Grayson as the handsome, rebellious hero who uncovered serious political corruption involving the Prime Minister, David Lloyd George, and his fixer, Gregory. In McCormick's account, Grayson is last seen on a boat on the Thames heading to Gregory's house by the painter, George Flemwell, who recognised Grayson so unhesitatingly, having painted his portrait some years previously. Gregory, we are told, murdered Grayson because he was threatening to expose his corrupt practices. The story seemed to fit together so well that it convinced a generation of journalists and historians, and to some extent still does. Television documentaries and books are still being released parroting McCormick's 50-year-old theory, but, unfortunately, it was all pure fiction. Privately, Groves seemed to have his doubts too. Not only did McCormick's theory contradict much of the research he had latterly carried out, but he was very guarded when Groves wrote to him questioning some of his assertions. McCormick informed Groves that he had disposed of most of his papers and was therefore unable to help his investigations. Despite these misgivings, Groves went along with McCormick and his decision to do so would radically alter the public memory of Victor Grayson.

When David Clark, a former Colne Valley MP himself, came to write the first scholarly biography of Victor Grayson, he contacted Donald McCormick to probe further some of the more surprising aspects of *Murder by Perfection*. Whilst McCormick had told Groves in 1974 that he had disposed of his Grayson/Gregory notes, he now (in 1980) told

Clark that he had made a full search through his Grayson notes but was unable to answer any of his specific questions. Clark had his doubts, but McCormick was convincing and his theory was given another airing. Nevertheless, Clark's *Victor Grayson: Labour's Lost Leader* (Quartet, 1985) revived interest in Grayson in the 1980s and two television documentaries followed. Of particular interest was the fact that Clark had tracked down some of Grayson's surviving family who suggested that their missing relative was preparing to disappear. This seemed to chime with Groves' earlier investigations which had suggested Grayson was preparing for a new life.

In the three decades which followed *Victor Grayson: Labour's Lost Leader*, interest in Grayson never abated. He continued to be mentioned in television documentaries dealing with unsolved missing persons and to appear in histories of the Labour movement as the great lost hero of Edwardian England. Interest in Grayson and his political significance in the history of the Labour Party found a new, younger audience when Jeremy Corbyn was elected leader of the Labour Party in 2015. Corbyn's surprise victory coupled with his unashamedly socialist approach renewed interest in Labour's history of internal ideological struggle. Grayson's name appeared frequently on social media, and whereas he had previously been synonymous with unsolved mysteries, he was now becoming the focal point of discussion for a young generation of socialists. Twitter users pointed to his great by-election victory as evidence that Labour could win on a socialist ticket, whilst others pointed to his inconsistent parliamentary performances and the limitation of spellbinding oratory with little practical application to back it up. Rather surprisingly, internet searches for Grayson far outnumbered those for his contemporaries such as Keir Hardie, Ramsay MacDonald and Philip Snowden. To meet this renewed interest David Clark's 1985 biography was revised and re-released in 2016 as *Victor Grayson: The Man and the Mystery* (Quartet, 2016). The book brought to light new information on Grayson's personal life and gave more colour to his final years. However, in many respects Grayson remained just as much a mystery as before.

So why write about Grayson now? In 2007 I went to my university library to find a book about Hugh Gaitskell. The book was not there but next to its empty space on the shelf was a copy of Clark's *Victor Grayson: Labour's Lost Leader*. I knew nothing of the subject but sat and read the book from cover to cover late into the evening. Being a student in Liverpool, I knew some of the streets where the young Grayson had grown up and I found his life an exciting but ultimately a cautionary tale. There were no other books about Grayson in the library and the ones I searched for were long out of print. That was that, or so I thought. Five years later I was canvassing in the dismal Police and Crime Commissioner elections in Warwickshire, held in November that year. After a day of particularly fruitless campaigning in the rain, we retired to the warm home of two elderly Labour Party members. The conversation came round to the history of the Labour Party and one of the members, Ann, mentioned an MP who had disappeared. She could not remember his name so I asked whether it was Victor Grayson. Indeed it was, and we had a brief discussion about Grayson and that period of politics. A few weeks later I received a call from Ann who was moving house and had found two boxes of Grayson papers that had belonged to her husband which were going to be thrown in the skip. I gratefully saved them from destruction and spent the next few days going through the mass of information. The papers were in fact a collection of research into the life of Victor Grayson carried out in the very early 1960s by Derek Forwood, himself a Labour politician who had sadly died in 2007. Amongst the bundles of papers were letters from key Labour luminaries such as Clement Attlee and Herbert Morrison with their memories of Grayson, together with detailed letters from dozens of people who knew Grayson personally, including those who had seen him alive after his disappearance. The papers by themselves represented a significant mine of information that existed nowhere else, especially since many of the authors had died before David Clark began his serious research into Grayson's life. In addition to these papers are my own findings – the culmination of more than a decade's research – which finally uncover the true life and legacy of Victor Grayson, Britain's lost revolutionary.

History may well repeat itself and in the aftermath of Labour's 2019 General Election defeat we see again the struggle for the soul of the Labour Party in which Victor Grayson was the principal player from 1907 until the outbreak of the Great War. With the defeat of Jeremy Corbyn's

Labour, many of his supporters are looking outside the party for avenues to achieve socialism in Britain. They look, as Grayson did, to the primacy of extra-parliamentary action over the slow, creeping progress down the parliamentary road to socialism. We see in Grayson's story that in Britain, with its first-past-the-post electoral system, it is, to paraphrase Aneurin Bevan, the Labour Party or nothing.

If history repeats itself then so do historians. So much nonsense about the life and career of Victor Grayson has been blithely repeated in newspaper articles, biographies and history books in the last century that he has been side-lined as a principal player in the story of the Labour movement and of British politics in the Edwardian age. This biography will try to set the record straight.

I

The Boy from Liverpool

The life of Victorian England was an intolerable life, and ought not to be borne by human beings.

E.P. Thompson[1]

I have known much poverty and many of its suicidal horrors ...

Victor Grayson's sister, Augusta[2]

If Victor Grayson's life was shrouded in mystery, then that of his parents was no clearer. In fact, Victor should not have had the last name Grayson at all. His father was born William Dickinson in Ecclesfield, Yorkshire, in 1849. William was the son of a carpenter but was temperamentally ill-suited to work and authority. Eager to escape a life of drudgery and seeking adventure, William enlisted for the 51st Regiment of Foot of the British Army in 1866. Like many young men he lied about his age and, just 17 years old, he claimed to be 20. He was paid £1 as a bounty and joined the regiment in Sheffield, but the army failed to change his ways and within four months of enlisting William had his pay withheld for indiscipline and to recompense the government for destruction of army property.

Throughout 1867 William spent most of his time in army prison cells awaiting trial, conviction and further imprisonment for repeatedly going absent from duty without leave. The following year saw a slight improvement in his behaviour and he was rewarded with one month's leave. But William once again found himself incarcerated over Christmas 1869, just before his regiment sailed for Ireland. After a period of extended leave William returned to his unit as it moved from Curragh to Athlone, about 50 miles west of Dublin. Here, he was again repeatedly punished for poor behaviour and in 1872, when his regiment moved to Fermoy, in the south of Ireland, to embark at Queenstown (renamed Cobh in 1920) for passage to India, William deserted. This was an era when desertion and persistent bad conduct could still result in branding and flogging before a dishonorable discharge. But William managed to make good his escape and he likely stowed away to Liverpool, leaving all record of his life as William Dickinson behind him.

Victor Grayson's mother, Elizabeth, had a similarly mysterious past. In separate census records she claimed to have been born in both Scotland and Ireland around the year 1852. It is likely she was born in Scotland and later worked in service in Ireland. No exact match for Elizabeth Craig (or Creag) can be found in the Scottish records, though there are several possibilities, but compulsory registration of births did not become law in Scotland until 1855. Therefore, we cannot be certain she was registered at all. The young Elizabeth would have been entitled to a comparatively good standard of education in Victorian Scotland, so it is strange that on the birth certificates of all her children she marks her name with a simple cross denoting 'The mark of Elizabeth Grayson'. Biographers and historians have pointed to the cross on Victor Grayson's birth certificate as evidence that the devout Elizabeth could not bring herself to sign a fraudulent document, thereby questioning Victor's true parentage. However, all of Elizabeth's children have the cross in common on their birth certificates. Her illiteracy, coupled with her birth not being registered, suggests her family was amongst the very poorest. A common occurrence for a Scottish girl whose family was financially unable to keep her was to be sent to Ireland to work in service, which is what happened. However, we cannot be certain which family she worked for, though there is enduring speculation that it was the Marlborough family.

An old Grayson family legend has it that when Elizabeth was working in service she met the wayward soldier, William Dickinson. Whether Elizabeth ran away to Liverpool with William or joined him later we cannot be sure, though the two are later recorded as being married as William and Elizabeth Grayson. Yet no actual marriage certificate exists for the couple which suggests they were not legally married. Although nowadays we would not think twice about an unmarried couple cohabiting and starting a family, in mid-to-late Victorian England there was an enormous stigma attached to such an arrangement. It was not uncommon for unmarried couples to be evicted by their landlords and for social support to be limited, so the couple would have been careful not to leave a paper trail and they probably found life easier to simply say they were married. This might explain why the couple regularly moved from rented properties around several districts of central and north Merseyside. Further, as the couple were not married, all the Grayson children were born out of wedlock – socially scandalous at a time when families went to extreme lengths to cover up such a secret. Indeed, the lack of a marriage certificate and dates not adding up on existing records are strong indicators to today's family historians that children had been born out of wedlock and that the family attempted to cover their tracks. Records for the nineteenth century show that half of all murder victims were babies; the shame and stigma of an illegitimate child was so great that mothers would kill their own children. In this atmosphere, it is not surprising that the Grayson family guarded their secret so desperately.

Family secrets aside, life in late Victorian Liverpool was far from easy. The kind of homes the Grayson family lived in had no electricity or central heating and relied on gas lamps and coal fires. There would be no indoor toilet and no running water. If children survived birth, they had incurable tuberculosis, measles, whooping cough, chicken pox and scarlet fever to deal with. If they made it to school age unaffected, they were likely to find two or three children in their class knock-kneed, bow-legged or hump-backed.[3] Despite poverty in large swathes of the city, Liverpool had become a major world port in the lifetime of William and Elizabeth Grayson. With the development of artificial waterways like the Leeds-Liverpool canal, Liverpool became the main distribution centre for many of the goods produced in Britain's northern industrial heartlands. It was perfectly situated to export South Lancashire coal and Cheshire rock salt whilst receiving West Indian sugar and Virginian tobacco. As ever-growing industrial demand brought with it economic expansion, Liverpool needed an ever-increasing army of workers and it became a magnet for those seeking a better life from Ireland, Wales and Scotland. But the boom in population growth was not matched by increased housing provision. Already existing poor social conditions were exacerbated by the influx of workers, particularly for unskilled and casual work. Unscrupulous landlords, landowners and builders simply crammed as many of these desperate souls as possible into the court and cellar dwellings which came to dominate the poorer areas of the city. A Liverpool historian described the living conditions in detail:

> these court areas, a small area of ground of about thirty to forty feet wide, [were] wholly or partly surrounded by walls or buildings of appreciable height, which served to shut out the very light of day for most residents. With this cul de sac arrangement, access to the court was gained through a narrow passage with usually one communal water tap in the middle and one or two communal toilets at the end of the court. Often toilets would be in disrepair or choked for lack of water supply, making the conditions and atmosphere both noxious and very unhealthy.[4]

Whilst other cities of Victorian Britain were little better and 'displayed a facade that concealed some of the most appalling social and environmental conditions imaginable', Liverpool was the worst example of the hideousness of Victorian city life. It was on Merseyside that 'Poverty was more desperate, housing more squalid, the state of public health more shocking and social distinctions more cruel than perhaps anywhere else in the country.'[5] The Unitarian Rev. Richard Acland Armstrong arrived in Liverpool in 1885. He recalled:

> I came to Liverpool as a stranger … to take up my residence in the second city of the mightiest Empire the world has ever seen. I admired its public buildings, its vast docks, its stately shipping, its splendid shops, its lovely parks … But after the first glance I was appalled by one aspect of things … The contiguity of immense wealth and abysmal poverty forced itself upon my notice … the superb carriages of the rich, with their freights of refined and elegant ladies, threaded their way among sections of the population so miserable and squalid that my heart ached at the sight of them. I had seen wealth. I had seen poverty. But never before had I seen the two so jammed together.[6]

It was into this Liverpool that Albert Victor Grayson was born on 5th September 1881 at 8 Taliesin Street in the Everton district of the city. Within weeks of his birth the family packed up and moved a mile or two to 15 Elbow Street, Kirkdale. The new addition was William and Elizabeth's third son and he joined William Henry Grayson (nicknamed Harry), born 16th December 1876 and John Dickinson Grayson (whose middle name preserved his father's real identity), born 5 May 1879. Whilst the eldest son William had been born in Liverpool, for reasons unknown the Grayson family moved for a few months to 12 Hill Street Place, Poplar, in East London where John was born. Possibly they tried to start a new life in the capital or moved short term to escape debt or questions about William senior's past. Some historians have imaginatively suggested that the London episode was an excuse for Elizabeth to either give birth to Victor (as an illegitimate son) or to take delivery of Victor from a poor maid who had succumbed to the charms of a wealthy aristocrat. However, it was Victor's elder brother John Grayson who was born there and the family returned to Liverpool shortly afterwards. Nevertheless, William and Elizabeth waited until 1 February 1884, some two-and-a-half years later, to have Victor baptised. Though some also point to this as further evidence of conspiracy regarding Victor's true origins, it is clear that the parents were at best quite disorganised in their stewardship of the family and that William senior spent more time drinking than he did working. Some of the Grayson children were baptised within months, others the following year but it is true that Victor took the longest. When he was eventually baptised, it took place at the same time as his younger brother, Frederick, born a few weeks before on 6 January 1884. But Frederick was a sickly child and died shortly before his second birthday. The death of Frederick was followed by happier news and two daughters, Augusta and Florence, were born. Augusta would remain a constant friend to her favourite brother, Victor, throughout his life and dedicate her final years to publicising his disappearance and appealing for information about him. A further mystery surrounds just how many children William and Elizabeth did have. All the records indicate six in total, yet in later years Victor claimed to have been one of seven. Still later, his sister Augusta wrote that 'Victor was the seventh son of William and Elizabeth Grayson' which would mean they had at least ten (not unusual for that time). It has been suggested that Elizabeth lost children during pregnancy, but this would not have been recorded. More likely Elizabeth had several still-births and/or children who died not long after birth, in which case they would probably have been named by the family, but not recorded in birth, baptism or census records.

It is an irony of history that Albert Victor Grayson, who became the fearsome face of revolutionary socialism in Britain and whom the Americans dubbed 'Britain's greatest mob orator', was in fact born tongue-tied and potentially incapable of speech. According to his sister Augusta, Victor's father William 'set out in great alarm and brought the doctor from his bed to cut the baby's tongue'. It was a simple procedure that released the tongue, rooted to the base of the mouth, with a small cut of the doctor's knife. This anecdote reinforces what we know of the family's social status; there were no medically trained staff present at the home birth, standard fare for a working-class family at the time. But the release of the baby's tongue did not immediately ensure Grayson's ability to speak or his future as a great orator. During his early years he suffered from a pronounced stammer and the family are said to have scrimped to provide elocution lessons which helped the boy overcome his speech impediment but also removed any trace of a Liverpool accent.

Though the Graysons were acutely aware of their surroundings, there is no indication that either William or Elizabeth was politically active. In contrast to their son's future as a leader of the socialist movement, they were considered quite conservative and respectable. But in truth William had changed little from his army days. He was generally idle, described as having a 'colourless' personality, a drinker, though a subdued one, at least outside the home. It was noted by a family friend that he only worked when he absolutely had to and even then his skills as a carpenter were not always in high demand. Elizabeth was described as 'a good transparent woman' who was 'quick and interesting in her speech' and knew the Bible thoroughly. It was noted by those who knew the family that Victor got his best qualities from her.

With a work-shy father, money was tight. It was the Grayson children who earned the wages which kept the family from destitution, whilst

Elizabeth supplemented her children's income by taking in lodgers. Victor's older brothers William and John worked as a docker and clerk, respectively, before both joining the Grenadier Guards. Victor aged ten worked as a weekend boy in a greengrocer's shop on Great Homer Street. A Mrs E. Nelson, whose father employed Victor, wrote to the *Liverpool Echo* in 1954 to describe the young man:

> He was a pale faced lad, about 10 years old, and not very sociable. He got his gift of being able to talk from his mother, and she had a keen sense of humour. My eldest sister managed the shop and Mrs. Grayson spent many hours in there. Her husband was the type that went to work when he was broke. It was a sordid life for Mrs. Grayson. There were three sons and two daughters to be provided for. Many a time I have taken a large dish of stew and soup my mother made for them. She used to say to me, 'Take this to the Graysons'. They just lived around the corner.[7]

Next door to the greengrocers was a boot shop which housed the Mission Hall of a Plymouth Brethren group in the rooms above. Victor took an interest in this, particularly the open-air meetings the group held. Though described as a shy, quiet but kind-hearted young man, he was born with the spirit of an adventurer.

As a child Victor found his family home a crowded place, but he tucked himself away and spent much of his early life obsessively reading stories of the Wild West and his fictional childhood hero, Deadwood Dick. Dick was a Robin Hood type based in the Black Hills of Dakota who kept the American Indians at bay. He was created by Edward L. Wheeler, the brains behind a string of such heroes who populated cheap fiction, known as Penny Dreadfuls. The 'Dreadfuls' were booklets, usually eight pages long, cheap and mass-produced with illustrations. Such works were marketed to young working-class audiences and sold at newsstands across Britain. The middle classes looked on in horror as working-class youths consumed tales of bandits, thieves and murderers. One such working-class boy, Thomas Okey, who later became a Calvinistic Methodist Minister, recalled the childhood joy of the 'Dreadfuls:

It introduced me to a romantic world when pennies were scarce, and
libraries seemed far beyond my reach. We read the badly printed booklets
in all sorts of places, even in church; they gave us glimpses of freedom,
abandon, and romance, heroism and defiance of fate, whilst we chafed
at restrictions and shut doors. True, our heroes ... were outlaws. But
what boy is not a bandit, a rebel, a pirate at heart![8]

It was not long before Grayson's imagination and sense of adventure would
come together in a plan to meet his hero Deadwood Dick. The six-year-
old Grayson and schoolfriend Billy Adams attempted to walk to the Wild
West to do just that. Not knowing which way was West they made their
way to the local church to consult the weathercock. From there they headed
West in high spirits with Billy tucking his father's revolver – stolen for the
adventure – into his belt. The two child adventurers remained in high
spirits until sunset ushered in the darkness of night. Under hazy moonlight
the two boys' bravery evaporated and they quickly decided to return home
to their parents. Grayson returned full of guilt for any worry he had caused
his mother and father. The parents were pleased to have their tired, untidy
boy back, though his handkerchief, stained with crushed blackberries
foraged for the journey West, looked for a moment like blood.

A second and more dramatic incident happened when Grayson was 14
and about to finish school. It is a story that became a legend and Grayson
frequently repeated it in later life. As a young teenager he regularly wandered
around the Liverpool docks, just a short walk from the family home and
where his older brother William worked. Like many teenagers he dreamed
of adventure and escaping a certain life of servitude in the factory. Although
both his older brothers had joined the army in their youth, Victor was considered sickly and suffered from epilepsy. Perhaps because of this stigma
and the lack of understanding towards it, he felt this option was not open
to him. Liverpool was awash with tales of the adventures of stowaways and
in later years the historian Emmet O'Connor noted that '[d]aring tramps
and salty tales were not unusual among waterfront socialists of the time.
The best of them all had their stories.'[9] Victor's story was as epic as they
came. He frequently met his brother and Attilio Verona, an Italian bosun
friend at the docks, to listen to their seamen's tales and join in the singing

of shanties. One morning, dressed in his school uniform Eton-collared shirt, he departed from his usual route to St Matthews School and headed down to the docks with a plan to stow away and go out to sea. He spotted Verona and told him he wanted to stow away. Verona tried to dissuade the boy, but Grayson was insistent. If he was going to stow away, then he would be safer with someone he knew, thought Verona, so the Italian decided Grayson should go with him. Verona smuggled the boy aboard the *Ardendee* – his vessel – and concealed him in the sailors' quarters. The blonde-haired pale-faced boy could not have stood out more distinctively from the worldly collection of seamen crewing the vessel, but his sheer courage won them over and under their playful curses they kept 'young whitey' fed and hidden for three days. On the stormy third night at sea, Verona thought it safe enough to send Grayson and another stowaway to see the Welsh, rosy-cheeked Captain Clay. Clay had a mate hold a lantern to the two lads' faces while he inspected and questioned them. Although clearly displeased, Captain Clay eventually called to Verona to give the two a proper meal and send them back below.[10]

However, the two were no longer with the sailors but amongst the rats. As Grayson recalled: 'the sailors warned me against interfering with the rats, and though I suffered unspeakable agony they traversed my body and nibbled my toenails with impunity'. The pair were woken with a whip from a thick rope from a ship's mate with a brutish reputation who, Verona had warned Grayson, was a thug universally loathed on board. Grayson and his companion were given duties of pumping and carrying water for the sailors whilst they swabbed the decks of the *Ardendee*. But Victor's seafaring aspirations were cut short almost immediately. Three more ragged and dirty young men had been discovered and brought before the captain from the ship's bowels. Their appearance and hunger betrayed the fact they had not enjoyed the care and protection that Victor had during three days at sea. Captain Clay erupted into a shouting and foot-stomping ball of fury. Grayson remembered, 'The captain was beside himself with rage, he paced the poop deck like an angry lion, striking the palm of his left hand with his right fist and imploring the Good Lord to tell him what to do.' The short-tempered captain now had no choice but to get his illegal cargo off the boat. Distress signals were rung out from the ship and the five stowaways lined up to be visible to any potential rescuer. When a ship came near enough, Captain Clay would shout through his megaphone: 'We have five stowaways and are bound on a long journey to Chile. If you take these stowaways we will pay you for them!' Three steamers, two English and one French, signalled for the five to be sent over to them on a boat, but all three turned away under steam as the stowaways approached. Each time the unwanted five rowed back to the *Ardendee*, Captain Clay's language became increasingly obscene. Eventually a small schooner from Dublin, *Eclipse*, agreed to take the stowaways back to mainland Britain. Captain Clay ordered Grayson, the youngest of the five, to his cabin where he bundled six tins of corned beef and half a hundredweight (about 25 kilos) of ships biscuits into a sack which Grayson was to keep charge of during the journey home. 'You're responsible for them, but let the other fellows carry them!' ordered Clay.

Far from being the end of their ordeal, the *Eclipse* landed Grayson and his companions at Tenby, South Wales, and from there Victor still had to walk the 165 miles back to Liverpool. The five foul-smelling and ragged youths were rowed to the bottom of a long flight of slippery steps which led into the town. Night was beginning to fall, and a brisk sea wind blew through the group's inadequate clothing. Grayson painted a wickedly colourful portrait of his gang in his unfinished autobiography:

There was lame Mike, who wore two distinct [socks], one of which grew upwards and the other had a sorrowful downward drop. There was lanky Foden – six feet two inches high and as thin as a lath. There was little Davie Hughes of the plumed purples, Jack Sparr ... [in] whose face I have never seen anything so wickedly criminal ... and the writer, with long, white hair and a dirty Eton collar to which I clung with affectionate tenacity ... The adult inhabitants eyed us with fearful curiosity, while the children took one look at us and ran as for their lives towards their homes.

Unwillingly, Grayson was put forward by his comrades to be the group's chief envoy to beg for directions, money and food. As he recalled, 'It was evident that my youth and appearance generally were to be utilized as

begging assets and I was powerless to resist.' A fisherman came walking towards the group and Grayson summoned his courage. Despite mistakenly asking the man for directions to Coquimbo, Chile, Grayson steadied himself and asked the way to Liverpool. The fisherman took pity on him and handed him one shilling which was the cost of a night's lodging for the five at a lodging house in Saundersfoot, 5 miles walk away.

The few remaining valuable scraps of Grayson's autobiography finish at this point. However, his sister Augusta recalled that the following night was spent in a Poor House: 'The Workhouse Master took Victor aside and paid for a telegram to his parents, who sent his railway fare immediately, but he decided to share the money with the others and walk the two hundred and fifty miles to Liverpool, sleeping in barns and haystacks.' Although the distance is an exaggeration – it was nearer 150 miles – the story ties in with that put forward in a contemporary account by the Huddersfield journalist Wilfred Thompson, who knew Grayson and described his long walk home as a defining moment in the young man's life. Grayson, he said, 'thus made an early acquaintance with the misery and privations of the out-of-work, and mingling with the flotsams and jetsams of society, gained an experience of the degrading effects of soulless toil by doing odd jobs to gain food and shelter by the way.'[11] Whilst Thompson seemed to think this experience was Grayson's first real taste of poverty, he lived, as we know, in one of Britain's poorest districts. The real effect of this adventure was probably to confirm in Grayson's mind that Liverpool did not hold the monopoly of poverty and destitution; they hung around the neck of the working classes across Britain.

If it took a wild teenage adventure to truly awaken a social conscience in Grayson, he was evidently born a showman. His sister Augusta remembered him standing on a stool his father had made him, mutely gesturing to an empty room as if addressing a crowd of thousands at a religious or political rally. Victor had probably attended some of the open-air religious meetings of the Plymouth Brethren, based next door to the greengrocer's shop in which he worked weekends, and had begun to imitate the speakers. As a result, Victor's father said he would make 'a bloody parson' out of his third son. A few years later, whilst working as an apprentice, he stood on the steps of St George's Hall in Liverpool, a grand city centre landmark, and watched the busy crowds bustle past him. Victor later recalled that he felt 'an irresistible impulse to address them in some subject undefined and to make a vague ... complaint against the order of things'. Grayson paid a nearby blind man and his wife to play the harmonium and sing popular hymns. An audience started to form who joined in the singing. With a crowd assembled Grayson now began to harangue them 'in a clear voice which drew the people wandering from all directions'. It was a baptism of fire for the young man who said he left the meeting 'shaken from head to foot with nervous weeping'. Whether his intervention into world affairs that day had been a success or failure, Grayson had the consolation of having left the blind man 'with the biggest crowd he had ever had'.

We know little of Grayson's school days other than that he attended St Matthew's Church of England School in the Scotland Road area of Liverpool, described as 'a city inside a city, a place of sometimes real hardship and deprivation but also a place of enormous community spirit'.[12] It was a board school, a prototype state school set up under the Educational Act (1870) to enable the poorest children to have an education and increase national literacy levels. In staying on at St Matthew's until aged 14 – unusual for working-class boys – Grayson must have been a competent student with a desire to learn and his mother seemed to see in him the hope of a better future. But to Grayson the prospect of a lifetime in the factory was still very real and upon leaving school he immediately started a seven-year apprenticeship. It seems the thought of factory life horrified the young man so much that it had been the catalyst for his epic attempt to stow away shortly beforehand. For just a few shillings per week, Grayson worked at the Bank-Hall Engine Works of J.H. Wilson & Sons at Sandhills, Liverpool, as an engine turner. The company was located on the Liverpool docks and the now derelict building still stands near Kirkdale. The firm produced steam winches and cranes, steam crane excavators and concrete mixing machines. They had been a major supplier for the construction of the Manchester Ship Canal, which linked Manchester to the Mersey estuary, completed three years before Grayson joined the firm. The business grew to have an international reputation and the young apprentice was helping to build machines which were exported across the globe and for the new passenger vessels of P&O, Cunard and White Star.

It was during these early years as an apprentice that Grayson grew sure that he wanted to be a preacher, to save his class from the social evils amongst which they found themselves, and to build a better world. Long gone were the Penny Dreadfuls and comic pages as he started to read more about economics, politics and religion. He very quickly latched on to religion, already knowing a great deal of the New Testament from his mother who, despite being unable to write, was well versed in the scriptures. In his own words Grayson began to 'haunt all forms of open-air meetings – mainly of the extreme and crude religious type'. The young man worked up the courage to speak publicly at some of these early meetings and began to draw attention to himself with his booming voice and slender frame. After two years of studying Liverpool's various religious street-corner preachers, in 1898 Grayson began to attend services at the non-denominational Bethel Mission in Edinburgh Street. He quickly demonstrated his ability as a speaker and within 18 months the Mission elders had Grayson leading Sunday School classes and then speaking at both indoor and outdoor Christian meetings, usually in Liverpool's worst slum districts. After three years Grayson appears to have had theological disagreements with the Bethel Mission and left to join the Hamilton Road Domestic Mission in early 1902.

It was at the Hamilton Road Mission where Victor impressed the first great influence on his life, the minister of Anfield Unitarian Church, the Rev. J.L. Haigh. Although Haigh had already known Grayson for two years, it was at the Hamilton Road Mission where Haigh realised that Grayson was a truly gifted young man, though one who required some polishing. Whilst he continued to work as an apprenticed engineer during the day, Grayson spent his evenings and weekends helping to run the Mission, whilst leading Sunday School sessions and speaking at their Watchnight Service. The Hamilton Road Mission had numerous offshoots and societies including a Musical and Dramatic Society, an Evening Children's Recreation Society and a Senior Scholars' Society amongst others. But it was the Literary and Debating Society that drew Grayson from the outset. As the 1902 annual report of the Mission noted:

This is the most encouraging and delightful institution of all the Societies connected with our Mission ... Not once during the Winter have I had occasion to speak through any exhibition of roughness, or through lack of courtesy. When one remembers the places in which these young people earn their daily bread, the companions they are compelled to meet, and in a few certain cases their home surroundings, the value of this testimony will be understood and appreciated.

The annual reports of the Mission list Grayson as a regular evening speaker. In 1902 he gave a paper entitled 'Social Salvation', the following year he lectured on 'The Philosophy of Agnosticism' and in 1904 on 'The Itch of Civilization'. The lectures to the Literary and Debating Society were said to have become the main event of the week at the Mission. It is interesting to note that during this period Grayson did not speak on overtly political topics, but instead on religion and how it could be used to improve the lot of the poor and working classes. It was not that there was a ban on politics, with lectures being given on 'The Religion of Socialism', 'Socialism and Art' and 'Why I am Not a Socialist' in the years Grayson attended. His reticence is all the more surprising given that, soon after joining Hamilton Road Mission, Grayson had begun to make his first public political speeches on the streets of Liverpool and for these he gained an immediate reputation which brought a steady supply of invitations to address socialistic groups. It seems he wanted to keep his politics and his religion separate.

One offshoot of the Mission's Debating Society where Grayson honed his talent was a book club in which members gathered on Sunday afternoons to discuss literature and current affairs. Members received a card on which a penny or tuppeny stamp would be made to indicate the level of subscription and at the end of the year the member would be able to select books for purchase to the value of which they had paid into the scheme. It was through this group that Grayson began to read and discuss the works of Charles Darwin, Max Nordau and Edward Carpenter. But the book that made the most impact on him was *The Roadmender* by Michael Fairless. In fact, he carried his annotated copy with him until shortly before he disappeared nearly three decades later. Although little remembered now, *The Roadmender* became a popular classic in Edwardian England and went through more than 30 editions in the decade following its publication in

1902. Grayson would have been drawn to the Christian overtones of the book which followed a few days in the life of a roadmender in West Sussex as he reflected on living a simple and charitable existence. Mystery surrounded the identity of the author who turned out to be the female writer Margaret Barber. Though it was not a political work, some of its passages could be construed as vaguely anti-capitalist and socialist. Today it reads a little like Jack Kerouac's *On the Road*, written in Edwardian prose, set in West Sussex and without the hedonism.

With his regular lecturing and heavy reading, as well as throwing himself completely into the work of the Mission, Grayson was encouraged by Rev. Haigh to enter the Unitarian Church. Haigh was positioning Grayson to apply for the Home Missionary College in Manchester which specialised in taking young men, training them, and sending them back into their communities as preachers. Haigh later wrote a fictional account of such men coming back to the gritty working-class streets of Liverpool, many of the same ones in which Victor grew up, entitled *Sir Galahad of the Slums* (1907). The narrative paints a portrait of both the religious zeal of the young men and the conditions of deprivation they encountered on a daily basis. Though none of the characters seem to be specifically based on Haigh's young protégé, it does give us an indication of the life he was preparing for him. Grayson first applied to the Home Missionary College in November 1902 and it is worth noting some of the observations made of the young man in the statements supporting his application. When asked of his opinion of Grayson's abilities and character, Haigh responded, 'The highest. He has power and perseverance. He reads very widely and makes good use of what he reads.' On his public speaking abilities Haigh commented, 'He is good, clear and telling. His personality is attractive ... and [he] always says something worth listening to.' Haigh also considered Grayson's moral compass 'above reproach' whilst he was also 'transparent and sincere'. Another statement from a Mr John Sievers noted that Grayson possessed 'exceptional ability, and a strong unimpeachable character' with a 'large sympathy, integrity, and power of expression'. Joseph Daly felt the young man had a 'deep knowledge of the conditions of the life of the working class'. John Menzies suggested that Grayson's drive was based on a 'desire to improve the condition of his less fortunate brethren'. In his own statement Grayson demonstrated that he was only too aware of the unusual circumstances in which he found himself. He wrote:

> In my new career, should I be fortunate enough to qualify, I shall certainly do my best to justify Mr Haigh's kindly estimate of my character. The type of character usually exhibited by the average engineer in a large workshop (which for the past six years has been my daily environment) is not conducive to culture and refinements and I will, no doubt, encounter some difficulty in adapting myself to my new surroundings.

But Grayson's change of career was not without its consequences, for amongst his family there had been an expectation that the end of his apprenticeship would bring home the higher wage of a skilled engineer. This would have helped the family's financial position considerably, especially with William senior still perpetually unemployed. Grayson's younger sister, Augusta, recalled events:

> The great day arrived when all our financial trouble would cease. He had completed his apprenticeship. He discussed going to sea as an engineer, with Mr Haigh – the minister. Mother and I awaited his homecoming that night – yes, he could go to sea, but the minister wished him to be a minister, as he felt the church would have an imminent exponent if only Victor would take the chance that was offered. Of course, he would have to be self-supporting but all college fees would be found. Victor felt it was out of the question since he had just completed a seven year apprenticeship at a few shillings a week. I shall never forget that night – his eyes seemed to have a light in them which I knew. How could we do anything other than say 'be a minister'.
>
> This meant much more hardship, since the building trade was almost at a standstill and my father was unemployed. I was the only one working as my other two brothers were in London, in the Grenadier Guards, and my younger sister [Florence] was ailing. It was an anxious time; we walked miles daily to save money, in order to help him along. Victor would often walk from one extreme to the other of Liverpool, seeking second hand bookshops to procure the necessary books for his studies.

The family clearly rallied round him, but it is interesting to note that the reaction of Grayson's father is not recorded. The relationship between the two would appear to be almost non-existent as none of the young man's surviving letters to his sister Augusta make reference to their father. Yet he asked persistently after his mother, brothers and sisters. William senior may have been unhappy with his son's departure from the factory floor and the resulting loss of the steady income they desperately needed. Nevertheless, pushed by his mother and sisters, Grayson headed to Manchester for his interview at the Home Missionary College in January 1903, to start that autumn. To his disappointment, however, he was not admitted. Instead he was advised that he needed further preparation and duly attended extension courses at Liverpool University, studied hard, and eventually, in autumn 1904, was enrolled as a student and left the Hamilton Road Mission for the last time. The decision to delay Grayson's admission to the college would have a mixed effect; it robbed the Unitarian cause of one of its most gifted youngsters, but provided Britain's growing socialist movement with one of its earliest heroes.

The twelve-month period that Grayson spent studying at Liverpool University also saw him take a keener interest in accepting speaking engagements and carrying out socialist propagandising across Liverpool and further afield. He was paid little at first, but it was not long before he was able to charge a speaking fee (plus expenses if he had to leave Liverpool). After all, he was no longer an apprentice earning a few shillings per week and Rev. Haigh could only pay his extension course expenses. Victor was therefore drawn deeper into the socialist speaking circuit and the more he was, the less he saw religion as the only viable remedy for Britain's social problems. Grayson now studiously read the *Clarion* newspaper, edited by Robert Blatchford, a man who did more to further the socialist cause in late Victorian and Edwardian Britain than any other. Blatchford had started his weekly paper with Alex M. Thompson in Manchester in 1891. Both men would shortly become close intimates of Grayson's. The *Clarion* had spawned an entire culture across Britain including choirs, scouts, cycling, rambling and handicraft clubs. Clarion vans became a regular sight in towns across Britain as socialist speakers drew the crowds with the gospel of socialism and disseminated their literature. In Liverpool a

Clarion club and cafe was situated at 30 Lord Street and Grayson became a regular attendee, mingling with the likes of Jim Larkin, Fred Bower and future Irish Labour Party leader Tom Johnson, all of whom would make a varying impact on the Labour movements of Britain and Ireland. Larkin was seven years Grayson's senior but the two had experienced similar Liverpool childhoods. Like Grayson, Larkin had stayed on at school until the age of about 14 and then stowed away on a ship to New York, before returning to Liverpool to serve as an engineering apprentice. After a spell of unemployment followed by a turn as a seaman, 'Big Jim' Larkin had settled into life as a docker. Larkin and Grayson were committed teetotalers, for now, and, whilst Grayson enjoyed a cigarette, he would wait with him outside the pub whilst their colleagues took a drink before socialist meetings. Both carried out regular charitable work in some of their city's worst slums. Fred Bower was two years older than Larkin and worked as a stonemason, enjoyed his beer and, like many others, including Larkin and Grayson, had come to socialism via the *Clarion*. All three men lectured at Independent Labour Party (ILP) meetings across Liverpool and Grayson undoubtedly shared platforms with them in the period just before leaving for Manchester. The conversation at the Clarion cafe was dominated by unemployment and this was reflected in the speeches given by the men, which frequently called for the nationalisation of the means of production, distribution and exchange and argued that socialism, as a humanist religion, would unlock human potential and finally end the scourge of poverty. Yet even in these early days of the socialist movement, activists were split between two camps; the Marxist Social Democratic Federation (SDF) and the ILP. Both groups had helped found the Labour Representation Committee (LRC) in 1900 which would become the Labour Party in 1906. But the SDF broke away in 1901 for what it felt was hostility towards Marxism as the non-doctrinaire attitude of the ILP took hold. Grayson joined the ILP, but this may have had more to do with geography than ideology, as young socialists usually joined whichever group was more numerous and active in their location. He had also joined the Fabian Society, which at the time counted George Bernard Shaw, H.G. Wells and Emmeline Pankhurst among its members. All three would shortly become personal friends of Grayson.

One famous incident involving Larkin and Bower, to which Grayson was almost certainly privy, would go down in Liverpool folklore. Bower, a stonemason, was the first man to cut a stone for the foundations of Liverpool's Anglican Cathedral and he sought to leave a message for the future in the brickwork of this grand building. Larkin compressed a copy of the *Clarion* and Keir Hardie's newspaper, *Labour Leader*, into a tin with the following note penned by Bower:

To the Finders, Hail!
We, the wage slaves employed on the erection of this cathedral, to be dedicated to the worship of the unemployed Jewish carpenter, hail ye! Within a stone's throw from here, human beings are housed in slums not fit for swine. This message, written on trust-produced paper with trust-produced ink, is to tell ye how we of today are at the mercy of trusts. Building fabrics, clothing, food, fuel, transport, are all in the hands of money-mad, soul destroying trusts. We can only sell our labour power, as wage slaves, on their terms. The money trusts today own us. In your own day, you will, thanks to the efforts of past and present agitators for economic freedom, own the trusts. Yours will indeed, compared to ours of to-day, be a happier existence. See to it, therefore, that ye, too, work for the betterment of all, and so justify your existence by leaving the world the better for your having lived in it. Thus and thus only shall come about the Kingdom of 'God' or 'Good' on Earth. Hail, Comrades, and – Farewell.

Your sincerely,
'A Wage Slave'[13]

Larkin folded over another piece of tin and made the package airtight and the following day Bower placed it in the foundations. The note tells us much about the historic mission these young socialists believed themselves to be on and the certainty with which they believed their message would win through. News of the episode caused an uproar when it was publicised; but it was far beyond the point where the note could be removed. Long since had King Edward VII laid the foundation stone on top of the socialists' defiant tin; something that gave Bower immense pride.

A few months after that great gesture of defiance, Grayson headed to Manchester to begin what was hoped to be an impressive career in the Church. Though he had the support of his family and his backers in the Unitarian movement, some of Grayson's ILP colleagues remained sceptical. Fred Bower was critical of what he believed to be the 'middle-class members' who took Grayson from the workshop floor to fashion him into some sort of idealised preacher. He maintained that Grayson should have 'stayed longer at the bench or lathe till the iron of poverty had more deeply entered into his soul'. But Bower's recollections of Grayson hint at the bitterness and jealousy of a man whom history forgot, whilst his colleagues became legends in both life and death. Within a few short years the international press would christen Grayson 'Britain's greatest mob orator'.[14]

2

The Student Revolutionary

Manchester had been the hub of radical liberalism throughout the Victorian era, and now, as a new century and new era began, it became the home of socialists and women's suffrage campaigners. In Manchester, where the socialist cause seemed far more advanced than his native Liverpool, Victor Grayson was immediately confronted with the twin pulls on his time of religion and politics. The Home Missionary College would prepare him to return to his community and preach that religion would cure Britain's social ills, yet the young man had already seen too many contradictions within the religious community to accept the certainty of this assertion. In addition, his complete conversion to socialism, not only as a political creed but as the key to building a new and just society, taught him that only political power in the hands of the working class could truly alleviate their problems.

Grayson had been drawn to Unitarianism through its toleration of rational thought and undogmatic approach to the Bible. Its practitioners rejected the doctrine of original sin and believed that men and women could make their own way in life and were not constrained by destiny or predetermination. The Unitarians were also committed social reformers which further appealed to Grayson. The Unitarian Church had shaken the wider religious community by appointing England's first female minister in September 1904, just as Grayson moved to Manchester. But there is another matter that may have influenced Grayson's switch to the Unitarians, his homosexuality.

The Unitarians have traditionally been more accepting of those of differing sexuality and in the 1980s were already performing same-sex blessings in Britain at the same time that the government was promoting the notorious anti-gay legislation, Section 28. Whilst still in Liverpool, Grayson had had a relationship with a young ILP activist, Harry Dawson.

From Manchester, Grayson wrote letters to his lover brimming with faintly disguised lust and longing. Dawson worried that their relationship had ended with Grayson's move, but Grayson sought to console his lover: 'Set the thing you call your mind at rest. I love you as ever, with the same devouring passion and intensity.'

Away from his family and friends and in a new city, Grayson was freer than ever to be his own man. He made friends quickly in his two social circles, the Unitarian Church and the Independent Labour Party (ILP). Grayson joined Manchester Central branch of the ILP and became close to Emmeline Pankhurst, and her daughters, in particular Christabel and Adela. Emmeline apparently treated Grayson like a son and her family's fondness for him was later reflected in their exceptional efforts to get him elected to Parliament. Grayson was also befriended by the wealthy Agate family based in Pendleton, Salford. The Agates were strict Unitarians and Grayson was particularly friendly with the two eldest sons, James and Charles, who were of a similar age to himself. James would later become the famous theatre critic described by his biographer as a 'wit, spendthrift, homosexual, eccentric, gossip-monger, friend and acquaintance of the rich and famous, and frequenter of the opera house, theatre, club and brothel'.[1] In the final weeks of his life in 1946, James Agate would recall Grayson as a 'Genius' who had 'the ability to achieve masterpieces without trying'.[2] The family kept servants and had a live-in nurse which, whilst it was nothing out of the ordinary for a family of their social class, would have been quite a change from the poverty-stricken Liverpool streets and factory floor of Grayson's upbringing. The conversation around the dinner table was of theatre, Italian opera and music – with no mention of politics. No wonder Grayson began to acquire a taste for the finer things of life which would later raise many eyebrows in the Labour and socialist movement.

In his first term at the college, Grayson lived in a single-room top floor flat in a municipal block on Oldham Road, an area William Morris had referred to as a 'vestibule of hell'. Since Morris' aesthetic criticism, Oldham Road had become a fashionable residence for bachelors. Grayson's neighbour, Percy Redfern, was six years his senior and recorded his memories of Grayson in those days in his memoir *Journey to Understanding*.

My now experienced house-keeping he drew upon for furnishing at the open-air, second-hand dealer's below. To the grubby collection he added two rich silk cushions, worked and given by a lady admirer in his native Liverpool; and to discomfort aesthetes and the prudish he hung on his walls two florid prints picturing auburn-haired girls with proudly-swelling, fleshy bosoms. Sunday mornings, when he had gone off to platform engagements, would exhibit in his one room a unique disorder of unmade camp bed, cigarette ends, books, camp washing bowl, littered chairs, razor, soap and towel, socialist papers, clothes, slab-cake remains ... and the luxurious cushions. Vacantly, the half-nudes smiled down on it all.[3]

Throughout his life Grayson cultivated a series of female admirers, usually older and wealthier than himself, who sent him gifts and money. Redfern notes the silk cushions that had been sent to him and also that his choice of wall art was more to discomfort others than to reflect his own taste. It is also noteworthy that just as James Agate had referred to Grayson as a genius, so too did Redfern:

But my floor now held a genius. The years between us gave way to the maturity of his political judgements ... He was wise in the world; but over and above the intelligence was his infectious vitality. Whatever took his fancy in the town's motley came to life on his lips. Recitals by him, in his one room, would bring two in the morning as if it were ten at night, while the policeman on the corner outside suspiciously watched the strange tenant's late-staying guests and late-burning light.[4]

From Redfern's recollection it is hard to see how Grayson found time to study. Grayson preferred to sit in his favourite cafe, people-watching rather than attend lectures. His main preoccupation was honing his oratorical skills on the street corners of Manchester. On Tib Street, Grayson could be seen on an upturned crate delivering lectures on socialism on behalf of the ILP branch for a 5 shilling fee. On Sunday mornings he would be in Stevenson Square – Manchester's equivalent to Hyde Park corner – where he would occasionally listen, but more likely get up to give his own per-

formance. One of those who saw him speak was Bonar Thompson, a now
forgotten character of British politics who became famous as the 'Hyde
Park Orator':

> It seemed a wonderful thing to me that these men should be able to
> hold the attention of the crowds in the way they were doing. Practically
> all the arguments that were being used were beyond my comprehen-
> sion, but I felt that great affairs were under way ... The arguments
> about the unequal distribution of wealth made a strong appeal to me
> ... The workers are the people who matter ... The rich are plunder-
> ers and parasites who live upon what they have stolen from the wealth
> producers.[5]

The identities of most of these speakers have been lost in time, though
they deserve credit for their part in building Britain's socialist movement.
Grayson was a regular speaker at Stevenson Square on a crate, soap box
or the steps. He built up and harangued the crowds with his message and
helped to sell socialist pamphlets afterwards. Percy Redfern remembered
Grayson's style at these meetings:

> Here was the orator born ... However little prepared the speech, the
> stoutest chairman would not have dared to cut short my neighbour.
> He neither noted nor memorized his points. Whatever the crowd felt
> or wished to feel, he would sense and put into infectious words, always
> with a rollicking humour – as when an attack on social shams was illus-
> trated in those days of the cab-horse by his story of a rank of sausages
> on a dish. When the first sausage was taken all the others automatically
> moved up![6]

As Redfern notes, Grayson did little preparatory work on his speeches
compared to his contemporaries, yet his gift for speaking and reading the
emotion of the crowd overcame any weakness there may have been in
his argument. There was never any doubting his sincerity. Other speakers
though, as Bonar Thompson recalls, were less than convincing:

Several of the regular speakers there fascinated me to a degree which ... appears absurdly impossible ... These men were dealers in words. Few of them possessed any real knowledge of anything, but they had the jargon of revolt at their tongues' ends ... There was an abundance of revolutionary literature on sale at these meetings in Stevenson Square. It was largely penny and two penny pamphlets setting forth the socialist idea in lurid language.[7]

Grayson's popularity as a speaker began to spread from Manchester across the North of England. By the spring of 1905 he had a busy schedule of speaking engagements which involved more time aboard trains, sleeping on sofas or sharing the beds of supporters and little time for rest and study. Percy Redfern observed his growing popularity and the inevitable toll it took:

> The magnetic speaker continued to give himself to the people. Surrounding, praising and drawing upon this darling, organisers and supporters would hurry him from one overflow meeting to another. The too-willing victim would return to Manchester to fling himself on his bed, fully dressed, exhausted. For quick recoveries he began to depend on stimulants.[8]

Yet despite his rapid rise in popularity there was a brief period during his first term at the Home Missionary College when Grayson seems to have made a genuine effort to put his education before political work. When the college principal, Rev. Alexander Gordon, first interviewed him in 1903 he had been impressed by Grayson's commitment and enthusiasm. Then when Rev. Gordon interviewed the young man for the second time on 28 September 1904, he impressed even more:

> [He] impresses me very favourably, even more so than he did a year and a half ago. He applies as a probationer. He has been through the Preliminary Arts Course at University College, Liverpool, taking a first-class in Latin and in history in the terminal class results. But he failed in his Preliminary in June. I asked him particulars of the class teaching. The

Greek professor paid more attention to translation than to grounding; the Mathematics professor went on too rapidly for beginners. I then examined him in classics. His Latin, though imperfect, was fair; quite passable. His Greek was not so good, rather shaky, especially in his verbs. As he had not been able to ascertain in Liverpool the nature of his Preliminary failure, I sent him to the Registrar here, and he brought back the report that he had passed in Greek, English Literature and English History, and had failed in Latin, Geography and very badly in Mathematics. I was surprised, and so was he, for I should have thought the Greek and Latin results would have been reversed. He has been studying during the whole period since he last appeared here, with financial help from Liverpool friends, but this was insufficient, he has been lecturing on Social and Economic subjects (crammed for the occasion) at Labour Churches and that kind of thing. This had not improved his voice, for when I tried it again, I said he had a cold; he explained that it was a huskiness caused by shouting in the open air. His voice however, is naturally clear and good; He needs some tuition in voice production. He would have had another try at the Preliminary, this month, but could not raise the fee. I certainly think he is a good case for a probationary year, and have no hesitation in recommending him for this.

Rev. Gordon's note demonstrates the high entrance bar set for working-class men like Grayson who had received only an elementary schooling. There would be much hard study ahead if Grayson were to succeed. He was immediately enrolled on to a course in public finance, followed by Greek, Latin, political economy and economic history. Much to the disappointment of Rev. Gordon, Grayson failed the university's preliminary examinations in the summer of 1905. He did manage to gain second-class passes in history and Greek in the college examinations, but it was clear that his mind was elsewhere.

The Unitarian College was based in the Memorial Hall, Albert Square, in Manchester's city centre, about 20 minutes' walk from Grayson's lodgings. In 1905 the Unitarians moved the college out of the centre to Summerville, the former home of a wealthy Manchester merchant, located in Victoria Park. It stands today on Daisy Bank Road, nearly an hour's walk from

Grayson's Oldham Street lodgings. Rev. Gordon was appointed warden and Gertrude Mary Panton-Ham matron for the 26-room boarding house for student boys of the ministry. Grayson moved into Summerville and no doubt his teachers would have hoped that having the young man living on campus would tame him, but they were to be disappointed.

The matron, Miss Panton-Ham, was the single daughter of a Unitarian minister and rumours soon spread amongst students that she and Grayson were involved in an illicit relationship. Panton-Ham was 20 years Grayson's senior and, though the student would throughout his life be guilty of promoting himself as a womaniser (which helped provide cover for his relationships with men), it appears the two really did have an affair. When Grayson won his seat in Parliament in 1907, one of his former fellow students, Rev. Edgar Thackeray, wrote to his fiancée, 'I wonder if Mr Grayson MP will marry Miss Panton Ham now. That would be more sensational than the result of the election itself.'[9]

Despite his failure to pass the preliminary exams and the hopes of his teachers that his move to Summerville would concentrate his mind on his studies, Grayson continued to pile up his political commitments. In June 1905 the annual conference of the ILP was held in Manchester and the following months saw Grayson emerge as a leader of Manchester's unemployed in the guise of the Manchester Unemployed Committee (MUC). The MUC was formed after a large demonstration in November 1904 of the city's unemployed men who demanded jobs or at the very least, unemployment relief. Manchester's Lord Mayor was receptive to their demands and chaired a meeting the following month to find a solution to the growing problem of unemployment in the city. He set up a relief fund to help the Salvation Army feed 14,346 children and 10,423 adults in 1905. The problem of unemployment and underemployment was a national phenomenon, but Manchester's formation of an unemployed committee which sought to find a solution through demonstration and negotiation was pioneering. Other committees formed in cities across Britain and they established a network which empowered them to press their claim nationally, leading the Labour leader Keir Hardie to raise the issue in Parliament. Progress was slow and despite reassuring noises from Campbell-Bannerman's Liberal MPs and the Unionist Prime Minister

Arthur Balfour, the situation in Britain's cities continued to deteriorate. In Manchester there were an estimated 10,000 men out of work and whilst a scheme pioneered by the Lord Mayor found employment for 1,300 of them, private enterprise – which the government was expecting to pick up the baton – had found work for just 46. As Keir Hardie (and now Will Crooks) continued to raise the issue in Parliament, government spokesmen accused the Labour MPs of exaggerating the problem. The government felt it was merely a cyclical economic blip. The men of the MUC, who had formed initially as a non-political group and under no political banner, stating their wish to use negotiation instead of force to make their case, now lost confidence in Britain's political leadership.

It was after the breakdown of the peaceful negotiations and the loss of trust in and deference towards Britain's political establishment that Victor Grayson came to prominence in the movement. Known already in socialist circles across the North-West of England for his powerful oratory, his message of extra-parliamentary action began to stir the hearts of men who had demanded work, not charity. Henry Myers Hyndman, leader of Britain's Marxist Social Democratic Federation (SDF), first encountered Grayson at this time. 'The first I heard of him was in connection with the unemployed agitation in Manchester,' remembered Hyndman, 'where he displayed, as I heard all round at the time, remarkable vigour and courage as a leader of the men ... it was his work at this juncture and his lecturing and agitating through the country which brought Grayson to the front and deservedly gained him great popularity'.[10] Grayson became a guiding figure in the new militant direction of the MUC along with Chairman William Edward Skivington. Gone was the committee's non-political stance and so too the belief of some of its members that a future Liberal government would be better than a Conservative one. Now members marched with red flags and shouted, 'Three cheers for the Social Revolution!' whilst there was talk of marching on London. Skivington was an SDF man who denounced Britain's political system as a stitch-up to keep the working class voiceless and powerless. He distrusted ILP men such as Keir Hardie who thought they could achieve socialism by playing the parliamentary game. When Skivington and Grayson invited the SDF leader Hyndman to Manchester, he caused an uproar. The Liberals and Conservatives, he told the crowds, were enemies of the working class, and any negotiation with them was pointless. Grayson, who warmed up for Hyndman, gave such a riotous performance that Hyndman believed he must be a member of the SDF, for his views were indistinguishable from theirs.

As the national unemployment crisis deepened, the government brought forward an Unemployed Bill to tackle the worsening situation in Britain's cities. In response Manchester's Unemployed Committee stated that their new aim was to secure the passage of the Bill by whatever means necessary. They now marched daily through the streets of Manchester without requesting the permission needed from the police. On Monday, 31 July a procession set out through the city to Albert Square where speeches were to be heard and resolutions passed calling for the immediate passing of the Unemployed Bill. The demonstrators were met with a large police presence which appeared to outnumber them. By the time the marchers made it to Market Street, violence erupted when police drew their batons and charged on the unemployed men. The leaders of the Unemployed Committee came in for particular attention and Grayson suffered a minor head wound from a pair of handcuffs used as a weapon by a policeman. Nevertheless, he managed to escape the escalating brawl and likely arrest, whilst the Chairman, Skivington, was less fortunate, with witnesses suggesting that he was set upon and bludgeoned by up to four police officers. Three committee leaders were arrested, but Grayson managed to blend into the crowd and get away. Skivington was charged with obstruction, interfering with the traffic and inciting the crowd to attack a tram guard. Those on both sides knew the charges to be spurious and, after a court hearing the next day, Skivington and two colleagues, Robert McGregor and Charles Steadman, were released on remand. Upon leaving the courthouse the men were cheered by a large and noisy crowd of supporters in Market Street. From the steps of the Queen Victoria statue, Grayson harangued the mass of faces and urged them to march with him to the Town Hall where they would demand that the charges against their leaders be dropped and that they, the people, should be guaranteed their right of assembly. Grayson, Skivington, McGregor and Steadman led the crowd to the Town Hall where they demanded an audience with the Lord Mayor to make their case. Grayson and the other committee leaders were duly received by the Lord Mayor along with the Deputy Chief Constable and after predictably heated talks (the Deputy Chief Constable, one imagines, would be particularly disgruntled at having to negotiate with the men), they agreed that all future public meetings of the committee and its supporters would be held on a Sunday, therefore causing minimal disruption to Manchester commerce. In addition, Grayson and his comrades agreed that there would be no more processions through the city. In return for these concessions the committee charged that the police had deliberately attacked them and that this action had been the cause of the riot and they demanded that the charges against them be dropped. Additionally, if permission was not given for the marchers to meet in Albert Square, the men threatened that they would lead their people there anyway. On these points the Lord Mayor and Deputy Chief Constable conceded, no doubt persuaded by the baying crowd they could hear waiting outside the Town Hall. All charges were dropped, leaving Grayson and his colleagues jubilant.

As the four men left Manchester Town Hall, the crowd – which had swelled – welcomed them back with rapturous applause. As they clambered the steps of the Albert Memorial to address their supporters, a journalist shouted, asking whether, with the Manchester authorities subdued, they still intended to march on London. Yes, responded not only the men but what seemed like the whole crowd. A thunderous and near-deafening cheer erupted from the crowd when Grayson announced that a telegram had been received from Keir Hardie. With all eyes on him, silence descended as Grayson shouted its contents to his audience:

> Hearty congratulations. The spirit of the days of the Peterloo massacre is again upon the authorities, but so, too, is the spirit of revolt which then wrenched the Reform Bill from a reactionary Government also strong in the working classes, and neither bludgeons nor prisons can destroy it. As our fathers won then, we shall win now if only we have the pluck to fight on.[11]

Grayson then addressed the crowd with his own words and proposed a resolution calling on the government to deal urgently with the unemployed question and referring to the disturbances not as a riot but as a 'brutal attack' by police on peaceful protesters.[12] The motion was passed and speakers, including the editor of Hardie's *Labour Leader* newspaper, Bruce Glasier, did not shy away from threatening the use of force, if necessary, to draw the government's attention. There were no serious disturbances that day, something the local press put down to the heavy rain that began to fall over Manchester, rather than the heavy police presence.[13]

Hardie's words to Grayson and the fellow leaders of the Unemployed Committee are in stark contrast to what was to be heard from Labour leaders in the coming years. Here, Hardie applauded the mass revolt and called for the protests to continue in a bid to force the government into making concessions. Grayson and his fellow leaders had 'admitted that their object was to secure the passing of the Unemployed Bill, by force, if necessary', and the leaders of Labour, in the form of Hardie and Glasier were, in their words and presence, respectively, seemingly in agreement.[14] But within two years the Labour leadership would move sharply from supporting such action to backing almost exclusively parliamentary methods. Previous biographers of Grayson and most Labour historians have portrayed him as a hot-headed troublemaker with little grasp of policy or conception of what he was fighting for. However, when we look back at this incident we see that Grayson was then very much in step with the Labour leadership, particularly Hardie, and that it was the leadership which changed its policies and methods, whilst Grayson's faith in direct action would not waver.

The Unemployed Workmen Act (1905) established Distress Committees with government funding to provide grants to businesses and local authorities to employ out-of-work men. Its passage occupied the House of Commons throughout the summer of 1905 following the major disturbances in Manchester and elsewhere. Arthur Balfour's Unionist government was forced to act to prevent unrest spreading across the country and it became law in a matter of weeks. This success sent a message that use of the mob and violent action had worked to force the hand of government. It made a great impact on Grayson, who, as one of the leaders, believed he had succeeded in changing government policy through his oratory and leadership.

Whilst his role in the MUC and regular speaking engagements kept
him away from his studies, Grayson also began editing *The Socialist and
Labour Journal*. Little is known about this publication, though a surviving
copy indicates that Grayson was the pioneering editor and that its funding
came via one Ernest Clarke of Bootle, Liverpool. Grayson described it as
a small propaganda sheet, the idea for which he had taken from his time
in the Liverpool churches. It was cheap to produce and localised, though
its readership extended from Manchester to Liverpool, Blackburn, Bolton
and wider Lancashire. It adopted a strict tone of utopian socialism with
Grayson responding to one reader's query, 'You may be assured that we
shall endeavour to maintain the idealistic tone of the paper. Socialism is
more than a scramble for bread and butter, and aims at securing for every
man the "right to do right".' The journal also included commentary on
recent developments within the British Labour movement, with Grayson
promoting a clear policy of having an independent Labour Party in Parliament, whereas many of Labour's leaders at the time saw the movement as
merely an adjunct of the Liberal Party. 'We are sorry that you look upon
our independent attitude as a mistake,' responded Grayson to one reader,
'but the mere thought that now-a-days anyone should suggest to Labour
men that they should co-operate with Liberals, nearly takes our breath
away.' Two mottos attached to the journal summed up its political perspective under Grayson; 'Socialism is not a political catchword. It is a new
and better system of society. Socialism says the worker is entitled to the
fruits of his labour' and 'Waiting is the stumbling block of progress. Doing
is the lever that moves the world.' The journal also evidenced an important
shift in Grayson's thinking on alcohol, which later contributed to the near
destruction of his life. Back in Liverpool he had been so opposed to drink
that, whilst his socialist colleagues supped a pint before meetings, Grayson
would wait outside. Now, in an editorial entitled *The Drink Question*, he
attacked such abstentionism as a distraction from the true enemy of the
workers – capitalism:

> The habit of drunkenness unquestionably renders a poor man poorer,
> but we must remember that he is poor to begin with. Out of the total
> wealth product, which is the result of the collective labour of the workers,

they receive one-third in the form of wages, the remaining two-thirds going to glut the appetites of a number of parasites who have taken no part in its creation. The worker is compelled to submit to these conditions, owing to the fact that the land and the instruments of production are owned and controlled by the privileged monopolists. As a worker, his only possession, or capital, is his power to labour. In return for his labour he receives on average a subsistence wage ... or in Dickens' phrase – 'enough fuel to keep the engine going.'[15]

In such conditions, Grayson states, workers turn to drink because of the 'misery and monotony of industrial conditions ... The chaos of competition ... The dreary wretchedness of the worker's home.' The abstinence of the temperance reformer, claimed Grayson – demonstrating the wit that would win thousands of hearts – 'probably arises from his constitutional inability to endure a pint of beer'. It was all very well for the educated and the middle classes to forgo alcohol for they had many other pursuits and pastimes open to them. Grayson knew from first-hand experience that things were very different for the working classes. In the following example he seems to be writing from his own experience of an unemployed and drunken father and his own seven-year apprenticeship on the factory floor:

> The educated, the favoured ones, have science, art, literature, philosophy, religion to fill the mind and heart, but the great army of industrial slaves are shut out from this gorgeous banquet, marshalled in huge factories and workshops; housed in miserable hovels; and the only romance that enters their lives comes from the beer-shop.[16]

In his editorial, Grayson crudely defined a key concept from Karl Marx's *Capital* – the theory of surplus value – which denotes the value of what is produced by the workers over and above the cost of their wages to their employer. In addition, the journal reprinted in full chapter 32 of *Capital*, 'The Historical Tendency of Capitalist Accumulation'. Historians and commentators, including Lenin, have portrayed Grayson as a man without any socialist theory behind his impressive oratorial skills. Lenin painted a critical portrait of Grayson as 'A fiery Socialist, without any

principles and given to mere phrases', yet here in 1905, two years before
entering Parliament, is a clear indication that Grayson had read, and had a
working understanding of, the basic ideas of Marx, demonstrating that his
socialism consisted of more than mere Christian sympathies and spontaneous emotional rhetoric. Grayson's view of society, his attitude to capitalism
and class, and his vision of a new world went far beyond the remedies pre-
scribed by the Unitarian Church. He was preaching nothing less than a
revolution led by Britain's downtrodden workers to capture state power
and overthrow the ruling class. He felt that the Labour Representation
Committee (shortly to become the Labour Party) was the best vehicle for
this kind of social change, but that there could be no deals with the Liberal
Party as a pro-capitalist, establishment entity.

With all of his time and energies taken up by writing and speaking for
the cause of socialism, Grayson's teachers were rapidly losing patience with
him. He had approached the new Chairman of the ILP, Philip Snowden,
to write an article for a forthcoming issue of his *Socialist and Labour
Journal*. However, the college authorities had also contacted Snowden in
a desperate attempt to prise Grayson away from the socialist movement
and back to his studies. 'The Unitarian authorities approached me to use
my influence with him to attend his University work,' said Snowden, 'but
I could do nothing with him. The attractions of the Socialist Movement
were stronger than the prospects of becoming a Unitarian Minister.'[17] It
was not just his busy speaking schedule that was detracting from his university work. Grayson had thrown himself into student life at Owens College,
now the University of Manchester, as the missionary college was linked
to Owens and missionary students would attend its lectures. Throughout 1905, Grayson was active in the Arts and Science Students' Common
Room Committee and he helped facilitate regular lunchtime debates
on subjects encompassing religion, politics and science. A Sociological
Society was formed, largely of students with socialist leanings, including
law student Christabel Pankhurst, which discussed the state of the nation.
With a general election announced for January 1906, Grayson and his
socialist colleagues decided that, by holding a mock general election with
a socialist candidate, they could gauge support for socialism amongst the
students as the basis for the formation of a student socialist society, the first

of its kind in the country. The mock election was given permission to go ahead by the authorities at Owens and three candidates were nominated: Conservative, Liberal and Grayson as the Socialist candidate. The election was a pioneering one as female students were given the vote at a time when they were unable to vote in general elections. Despite having the vote, women were not allowed to enter the common room, which was strictly men only, and so Grayson made a separate address outside for the women. Each candidate had a manifesto, election agent and canvassers. News of the election and subsequent socialist activity at Owens was picked up by regional newspapers. 'Mr Grayson,' reported the *Leeds Mercury*, '... is perhaps one of the best and readiest speakers the University possesses.' But it was also noted that Grayson's campaign still had some of the hallmarks of student politics: 'Vote for Grayson,' exclaimed the posters in the university corridors, 'and no Compulsory Chinese in any Exam.'[18] A total poll of 560 votes was recorded with the following result:

Henry Bury (Liberal) 275 H. J. Tynam (Conservative) 203
Victor Grayson (Socialist) 82

One of Grayson's fellow socialist students recalled it as a 'most exciting campaign, in which Grayson easily came out best and though the Liberals won the election by a good majority, and the Conservatives came second, we had the extreme satisfaction of realising that our man received 82 votes.' It was clear that there was a considerable minority of socialists amongst the student body. To harness the momentum from the election, Grayson, together with Christabel Pankhurst, convened a meeting of like-minded students to explore the formation of a university socialist society. Amongst the 40 socialists present there was unanimous agreement on the need for such a society and Grayson was duly elected Chairman with Pankhurst as joint Vice-Chairman. The criterion for joining was a belief in 'the establishment of a co-operative commonwealth for the Socialisation of the means of production, distribution, and exchange, and, the promotion of a Socialistic party in the House of Commons'. Permission was required from the Vice-Chancellor to make the new society official. Though the latter was concerned about the negative effect on the university's reputation, he nevertheless decided to recognise the new group and, according to press reports, it was the first society of its kind at an established university. Within a month, membership had grown to a hundred students, both male and female.

Despite his active student life, time at the missionary college and in turn the university was fast running out for Grayson. However, he had not totally abandoned Summerville for Manchester street politics, for he was instrumental in the founding of the Unitarian Home Missionary College Union in October 1905. Grayson was elected treasurer of the House & Common Room Committee which collected money from the students and bought newspapers and periodicals for the common room. Grayson ensured that his favourite socialist newspaper, the *Clarion*, was regularly purchased. He was also elected treasurer for the Union at its first AGM later that month. But Grayson was not content to keep his head down and quite quickly caused a stir. He made a scathing attack on a senior student whose task it was to call the other students to prayer. It seems there was a general unhappiness amongst the students with the manner in which they were spoken to, and a resolution supporting Grayson's statement was passed. Grayson does not appear again in the minutes of the Union and he was replaced as treasurer in July 1906. Neither does he appear in the annual report of the principal, Rev. Alexander Gordon, though pointedly Gordon suggested the previous poor progress of W. Short, Grayson's replacement as treasurer, resulted 'from being a room-mate with Mr. Grayson'. His lack of dedication to his studies and growing estrangement from the author-ities at Summerville meant that by the summer of 1906, Grayson was, rather unceremoniously, expelled. Though at the time his parting from the Unitarians seemed acrimonious, he nevertheless answered one of their regular alumni circulars for funds. For the College's Jubilee appeal in 1911, he donated the considerable sum of £10 – more than £1,000 in today's money.[19] Grayson is also recorded as having later preached at the Unitarian Church in York; so he had not cut his ties with them completely.[20] But his horizons had grown considerably since his move from Liverpool; through his journalism and public speaking he could make a precarious living whilst pursuing a just fight for a better world. He believed that, whatever the hardships, it was better than the drudgery he had seen first-hand on the factory floor.

Now that he was no longer entitled to reside at Summerville, Grayson moved to the Ancoats area of Manchester. Frederick Engels, in his *Condition of the Working Class in England*, described Ancoats as one of the oldest and worst slums in Manchester.[21] The area had improved little by the time Grayson arrived and *Clarion* journalist Harry Beswick described the conditions in which Grayson was living:

> Ancoats is a district of depressing dinginess; its gloom obsesses the soul; its smells – surely, Cologne in all its appalling odiferousness cannot compete with Manchester's own particular private brick-and-mortar wen in villainous smellsomeness – confound the nose … the grease of the factory, the oil of the fried-fish shop, the reek of cheap oil lamps … Then a powerful drenching of sulphuretted hydrogen … whilst carbon particles and a choice collection of fragrant bacteria float hopefully round, looking out for cheap lodgings in the lungs of the helpless wayfarer.[22]

Grayson lodged at the humble 131 Pollard Street, amongst this noxious mix of odours and bacteria. Beswick described it thus: 'Two sparsely-furnished tiny rooms … a sitting-room and a bedroom … in the Manchester Corporation barrack dwellings constitute [Grayson's] suite. They are on top of the landing of the dwellings, and command a bird's eye view of a hideous concrete courtyard, upon which a factory chimney abuts.' Whereas the salubrious student residence of Summerville had allowed Grayson's local critics to question his authenticity as a leading voice of the unemployed and socialist movements, his Ancoats address provided no such ammunition. From the summer of 1906 his life was now entirely dedicated to socialist propaganda and, after lengthy speaking tours across the North of England followed by a three-week propaganda tour of Scotland, Grayson became a regular speaker at the many socialist demonstrations, meetings and processions held across Britain's industrial north. 'The first impression he made on his Socialist colleagues,' wrote one correspondent, 'was that of a reincarnation of one of the Hebrew prophets incongruously mixed up with a young elegant of the "nineties".'[23]

It would be wrong, however, to characterise Victor Grayson as a single-issue fighter against unemployment. Almost as soon as he moved to Manchester and joined the Manchester Central ILP branch, Grayson was brought into close contact and friendship with the emerging suffragette movement and, in particular, the Pankhurst family. The issue of women's suffrage had sown division throughout the country, and the Labour movement was no exception. Although Keir Hardie was an early supporter, the ILP's backing for women's suffrage was blunted when it joined the Labour Representation Committee (LRC). The LRC was dominated by trade unionists who resented women in the workforce because they believed their presence increased the labour pool and thus allowed employers to hold down wages. At the LRC conference of January 1905, a motion was proposed by the Amalgamated Society of Engineers and the ILP to endorse a women's suffrage bill as a step towards universal adult suffrage. Emmeline Pankhurst was present to persuade the LRC to adopt the cause of women's suffrage, but trade unionists scuppered her plan. Mrs Pankhurst's Women's Social and Political Union (WSPU) was only calling for the abolition of the gender disqualification to voting. This would give the vote to many middle-class women, like Pankhurst, but leave millions of working-class women, like their male counterparts, without the vote. Harry Quelch of the London Trades Council opposed the motion and moved an amendment stating that 'any Women's Enfranchisement Bill which seeks merely to abolish sex disqualification would increase the political power of the propertied classes ... Adult Suffrage is the only Franchise Reform which merits any support from the Labour Members of Parliament.'[24] Quelch's amendment was carried by 483 votes to 270. Grayson attacked the trade unions for their conservative attitude and narrow vision for the future, whilst the episode reinforced his growing belief that the leadership of the trade union movement would hinder the cause of socialism.

The root of the militant tactics employed by Emmeline Pankhurst and her followers is to be found in these early disappointments with the LRC. Nevertheless, many young men across the Labour and socialist movement fought for the electoral recognition of women. Most believed that more militant tactics were needed and questioned the long game of patience preached by most leaders of organised Labour. Victor Grayson was an early and enthusiastic supporter of the WSPU and Hannah Mitchell, a former maid and seamstress who joined the WSPU in May 1905, remembered that Grayson 'shared some of our worst experiences'. Together with Christabel and Adela Pankhurst, Grayson formed a revolutionary youth wing across the Manchester and Salford ILP. This called for the overthrow of the existing political order and for women's suffrage. Some believed that Emmeline Pankhurst treated Grayson as something of a son, whilst he was particularly close to her daughter, Christabel, with whom he had set up the university socialist society and now a militant ILP youth wing in Manchester.

Of all the Labour movement leaders, it was Keir Hardie who consistently spoke in favour of women's suffrage. When he came to Manchester to speak on behalf of the women's cause, a huge crowd filled Stevenson Square and two lorries were positioned as speakers' platforms. Sylvia Pankhurst demanded political equality for women and an end to violence against Suffragettes. Victor Grayson rose afterwards to move a resolution 'supporting the claim of women to the Parliamentary franchise, protesting against the imprisonment of women who were carrying on an agitation to obtain political freedom, and calling upon the Government to insert a women's enfranchisement clause in the Female Voting Bill now before Parliament'.[25] Hannah Mitchell recalled how the Suffragettes loved Grayson for 'his chivalry and the bravery with which he championed the suffrage cause', with his 'charming manners and knightly courtesy'.[26] Grayson was clearly admired by the leaders of the suffragette movement. Further afield, his charismatic performances at packed public meetings continued to convert growing numbers of young people to socialism across the North of England and beyond. Initially, his popularity was rooted in areas strong in Unitarianism: Lancashire, Yorkshire and Cheshire. But, as we have seen, from the autumn of 1905 Grayson steadily increased his national profile. He could not have known it then, in the late summer of 1906, but within twelve months he would become an international figure of the socialist movement, the poster-boy of the coming revolution.

3
The By-Election

In good-humoured, vigorous, Hyde Park style, [Grayson's] speech ... had behind it the strongest force of sincere conviction and human feeling. He seemed to realise that there is no means of saying 'Hey, presto!' and the unemployed problem is solved. His argument was, of course, that his principles, if carried into effect, would be a panacea for human unhappiness, suffering, and privation, for the starvation, want, and misery that lurk in the dirt, gloom, and bricks of modern civilization.[1]

... the Labour Party is a prisoner of its past. Myths and romantic idylls are inseparable from the onward march of British socialism ... but few individuals have more dramatically captured the Labour imagination than did Victor Grayson, the very embodiment of what the American Indians call 'the legend that walks' ...

Kenneth O. Morgan[2]

> Others have wrongly taught you,
> Lured you with words away,
> Gulled you and bribed and bought you,
> Now you will say them nay,
> Vote for yourself and neighbor,
> Vote for your children, too,
> Vote in the name of Labour –
> GRAYSON the man for you.
>
> Vote, vote for Grayson,
> And he'll vote for you!
> Give him a chance to make his promise true;
> Yellow won't help you,
> Neither will blue;
> Vote, vote for GRAYSON, and he'll vote for you.[3]

The 1906 General Election has been called 'the last great rally of nine-teenth-century Liberalism'. It was fought on traditional themes such as free trade, whilst shying away from the major schemes of social reform for which Victor Grayson and the socialist movement called.[4] Nevertheless, a majority of Liberal candidates did pledge their support for a number of socially minded policies, including pensions and poor-law reform. Liberal Party leader Sir Henry Campbell-Bannerman acknowledged the pressing social problems, particularly unemployment, that gripped the country, but put forward no real solution. In fact, he offered reduced public expend-iture, tax cuts and a policy of sending the urban unemployed back to the countryside from where their ancestors had originally come. Like Gladstone before him, Campbell-Bannerman believed lower spending would engineer an expanding economy out of which social problems could be solved. Polling lasted more than a fortnight. The first day's results were catastrophic for Arthur Balfour and his Unionist Party. Balfour lost his own seat in East Manchester whilst the Liberals made large gains and Labour won five seats. The trend continued as more results came in over the following days; it was a Liberal landslide. But after the initial shock of the scale of the Liberal victory had faded, the realisation that 29 Labour MPs were to enter Parliament sent the press into panic.

For three decades Britain's burgeoning socialist movement had been dismissed by the popular press as little more than a group of hopeless dreamers. The 1880s had seen the rise of a specifically political Labour movement, which questioned Victorian society's pursuit of Empire whilst many of its own citizens starved. The 1884 Franchise Bill added 1.76 million mainly working-class men to the electoral register, who talked of getting their colleagues into Parliament to represent their interests. Parlia-mentarians were then unpaid which made it difficult for a working-class representative, without family wealth or party sponsorship, to seriously consider election to the House of Commons. Such men preferred instead to work with the Liberal Party which was believed to be the more sym-pathetic of the two existing parties to working-class interests. But despite coveting their votes, middle-class Liberal Associations were not keen to select working-class candidates. As a result, many of Labour's early leaders, including Keir Hardie and Ramsay MacDonald, had initially been spurned by the Liberals and working-class radicals increasingly sought answers elsewhere. By the dawn of the twentieth century growing numbers were attracted to socialism, though it still appeared 'more a statement of hope and faith than a coherent system'.[5] The Labour Representation Committee (LRC) was formed in 1900 at a conference in Bradford of 130 delegates who represented 861 members of the Fabian Society, 9,000 members of the Social Democratic Federation (SDF), 13,000 members of the Independent Labour Party (ILP) and 543,316 trade unionists. Its founding resolution was a clear statement of intent:

> That this Conference is in favour of establishing a distinct Labour group in Parliament, who should have their own Whips, and agree upon their policy, which must embrace a readiness to co-operate with any party which for the time being may be engaged in promoting legislation in the direct interest of Labour, and be equally ready to associate themselves with any party in opposing measures having an opposite tendency.

Despite its clear objectives, the LRC did not encompass the whole of the wide spectrum of socialist thought in Britain. Former Labour leader and rebellious man of the left, Michael Foot, neatly summarised the breadth of British socialism in this period:

> The socialism of the 1890s and the early 1900s appealed to a whole variety of tastes and traditions: the sheer richness of it should make us pause in wonder. So much came as a direct English legacy and yet it was truly and properly woven into an international fabric. No other political creed of the age could claim such richness or command such widespread intellectual contributions: scientists who saw their socialism as the essential fulfilment of the Darwinian discoveries; artists or the prophets of the world of art, like William Morris, who believed that no civilised society could be imagined without the artists' gift; men and women of passion and compassion who could not sit quiet amid the human misery they saw all around them; bureaucratic centralisers who believed with an equal ardour that only the power of the state could alleviate such chronic ills; students of Karl Marx who thought they could foretell, and help to

shape the revolution which would bring these prizes within the grasp of those who suffered such hardships and insults; men and women of every brand and breed who inherited a peculiar English tradition of dissent, the sons and daughters of the Chartists, the Radicals, the Levellers who would always watch with a healthy scepticism any established authority. All these helped to make the Labour movement of Edwardian times, or to speak more exactly, the Labour Party, founded at the Farringdon Hall in February 1900.[6]

When Labour's electoral breakthrough came in 1906, it was met with as much expectation from this diverse group as it was with fear amongst Britain's ruling class. Some foresaw the start of a bloody revolution whilst the grins of Fleet Street editors drooped as they scrambled for articles from leading socialists on their programme and politics. But the expectations of many of the socialists were dashed by the sober reality that the Labour Party would play the game of Parliament, bow to its ancient conventions, and seek to reform capitalism, not overthrow it. In addition, Labour was dependent upon the indulgence of the Liberals – only five of the new Labour MPs had faced Liberal opposition – courtesy of a secret electoral pact.

Two-thirds of Liberal candidates at the 1906 General Election had pledged their support for social improvements – particularly pensions and poor-law reform – in their election addresses. But despite the promises, the Liberal government had no definite plan to implement such radical change. As David Dutton notes, 'The fact that Campbell-Bannerman also promised a massive reduction in public expenditure did not suggest that the new government had thought through a clear programme, let alone costed it.'[7] This lack of direction coupled with a Tory majority in the House of Lords meant that the Liberal government quickly began to tread water, despite an encouraging start with the overturning of the Taff Vale judgment,[8] a School Meals Act and a Workmen's Compensation Act. Strikingly, during 1907, the Liberals lost three by-elections – of which Colne Valley was one – and the following spring would see the resignation, because of ill health, of Campbell-Bannerman.

Outside of Parliament, the foundations of the Labour Party itself were uneasy. Relations between trade unionists and socialists seemed to be increasingly strained with the socialists' belief that they had a wider vision of a better society that lay beyond the limited horizon of the trade unionists. They distrusted union leaders who were typically unsympathetic to socialism. 'The workers, sectionalized in their trade unions, which themselves were too often embroiled in domestic squabbling,' said ILP member James Sexton, 'had not realised that their hope and strength lay in their own unity.'[9] The victory of Victor Grayson in the Colne Valley by-election of 1907 challenged not only the fragile alliance of Labour, but also the orthodoxy of Labour's leaders. Keir Hardie, Philip Snowden, Ramsay MacDonald, Bruce Glasier and others were quick to lecture their socialist supporters that their candidates could not win against the Liberals in seats with a strong Liberal presence. Victor Grayson would prove that it was in fact possible and that socialists could win on their own terms, without Liberal patronage. In doing so, he would become the rallying point for the malcontents.

*   *   *

Colne Valley folklore has it that the young, dashing and eloquent Victor Grayson appeared out of nowhere and overnight captured the hearts of the valley people. Still today, more than a century later, pictures of Grayson hang in homes, pubs and socialist clubs in this part of Yorkshire. But as with most folktales and legends the truth is a little more complicated. The Colne Valley had a tradition of radical liberalism and religious nonconformity which created a unique environment of ethical and progressive politics. John Wesley, the founder of Methodism, had been enthusiastically received by the valley folk and, later, Luddism also took hold. Wesleyan Methodist chapels outnumbered Anglican churches, whilst there was a significant minority of other noncomformist chapels throughout the constituency. The Colne Valley Liberal Party, however, was heavily influenced by the employers in a way that sapped the bottom-up radicalism and forced a conservative approach to economic and social issues amongst the local Liberal leadership. Without any significant trade union organisation in the constituency, the Colne Valley Liberal Association ignored workers' demands and the baton of radicalism was instead taken up by the growing socialist movement. The constituency had been created in 1885 and consisted of more than 20 industrialised villages – with both cotton and woollen mills – and around 600 small farms stretching across the Pennines from the edge of Oldham in Lancashire in the West, to Huddersfield in the East. With a limited franchise (which was based on property), a less than average number of men had the vote, demonstrating the working-class nature of the constituency. Trade union organisation was extremely poor, but this owed more to the series of small employers rather than a lack of political education or organisation. Almost within living memory a deputation of workers and their families had walked from Saddleworth to be present at the great Chartist rally that ended as the Peterloo Massacre.

Despite the lack of historic trade unionism, there did exist a definite thread of political labourism which culminated in some of the very earliest movements towards a political Labour Party. The Colne Valley Labour Union (CVLU) was formed on 21 July 1891 in the cellar of a cottage in Nabbs Lane, Slaithwaite, where a red flag was hoisted. The minutes of its first meeting record the CVLU's mission statement as 'securing independent Labour representation on local bodies and in Parliament'.[10] A socialist programme was yet to be adopted and, in the absence of an explicitly socialist organisation, the CVLU relied heavily on those former Liberals who no longer saw their political home being in the Liberal Party. The first Chairman of the CVLU and its early driving force was George Garside, a blacksmith. He had grown impatient with radical talk of suffrage, land reform and free education, only to see Liberal governments renege on their promises when in office. In 1892 Garside was elected to the West Riding County Council and he is thought to have been the first ILP county councillor in Britain. For the 1895 General Election, the CVLU had secured the prominent trade union leader, Coventry-born Tom Mann, as its candidate. Mann was regarded as a titan of the emerging Labour movement and by securing his candidature the CVLU showed its desire to win. The CVLU ran a strong campaign and Mann was a tireless campaigner. The result, however, was a disappointment and nationally poor results for the ILP were made worse by Keir Hardie (their only MP) losing his seat. Tom Mann came third with 1,245 votes, representing just 13.4 per cent of the total and the incumbent Liberal Sir James Kitson held the seat on a slightly reduced majority. Kitson was a well-known industrialist and close friend of Gladstone who bore a strong air of elitism and rarely took the trouble to get to know his constituents, preferring to spend his time in the capital. This only widened the gulf between the local Liberal Party and many workers who craved representation by one of their own. But just as many workers had put their trust in Kitson as in this new party of Labour. As some of Mann's campaign team later recalled:

> People crowded to hear the new gospel but were not yet ready to believe in it. The struggle was however worthwhile, the effort not wasted. He, (Tom Mann) and those who worked with him, broke ground and sowed seed which was well garnered by others in the years to follow.[11]

Though disappointed, the members of the CVLU were not disheartened and continued to expand their presence throughout the Colne Valley villages. Labour clubs, lending libraries, reading rooms and discussion groups formed across the constituency as socialist ideas took hold. Robert Blatchford's Clarion movement found many an active volunteer to help set up choirs and cycling and rambling clubs. The Colne Valley Labour Union changed its name to the Colne Valley Labour League and restructured its organisation after failing to contest the 1900 General Election. Despite this lack of an electoral contest the socialist movement grew stronger and local success soon followed. By 1906, 17 ILP councillors were serving on West Riding County Council. In addition, the *Worker* newspaper, published by the neighbouring Huddersfield ILP, had appeared in 1905. The *Worker* reported local and national political news from the perspective of the socialist sections of the Labour movement and would become a key part of Victor Grayson's future campaign. A considerable amount of groundwork had thus been laid, but the party was cautious and during the 1906 General Election chose to concentrate its efforts on securing the election of a Labour MP in Huddersfield. It was not successful, but the Labour candidate (T. Russell Williams) had beaten the Conservative candidate to finish second, just 489 votes behind the Liberal. There was a sense that if Labour could come close in Huddersfield, then Colne Valley could go red with a suitable push and not long after the general election rumours swirled in political circles that the valley's Liberal MP, Sir James Kitson, was to be elevated to the House of Lords, which would trigger a by-election.

The legend of the young Unitarian preacher capturing the hearts of the masses and converting them overnight to revolutionary socialism is romantic but, as has been seen, not true. The same legend suggests that Grayson entered the by-election contest as an unknown and stormed to victory, but in reality he was no stranger to Yorkshire or the Colne Valley. Grayson was first contacted by ILP member Wilfred Whiteley in August 1905, inviting him to the constituency to speak at the Paddock Debating Society the following February. 'I do not know how and when Victor Grayson got to Huddersfield,' recalled Whiteley, 'but I feel that he must have spoken in Huddersfield before we invited him to speak … There would have been no other means of our getting to know about him.'[12] Alderman Arthur Gardiner, former Mayor of Huddersfield and Labour Agent, believed Grayson had spoken in Colne Valley at a May Day rally in 1905. Nevertheless, though he was known to some Colne Valley socialists as an able speaker, many of the rank and file were yet to hear Grayson in person. This changed by chance on 16 December 1905 when the respected trade union leader Will Thorne[13] pulled out of a Labour campaign rally at Huddersfield Town Hall. With Labour needing a speaker at short notice, Grayson answered the telegram from Huddersfield and jumped on the train from Manchester Victoria to give the performance of his life.

The platform of the Town Hall was filled with Labour councillors and two parliamentary candidates, T. Russell Williams (Huddersfield) and Frank Rose (Stockton-on-Tees). The audience rose to sing the socialist hymn 'England Arise'.[14] The Chairman opened the meeting and apologised to the capacity crowd for the absence of Will Thorne who was in a tough electoral battle in West Ham. He had though, he told the crowd, 'secured in his place an excellent substitute in the person of Victor Grayson'.[15] It is worth quoting this speech at length as it was here that Grayson won over the Colne Valley rank and file. The *Huddersfield Chronicle* reported his speech:

The next speaker was Mr. Victor Grayson, who stated that the Radicals had a programme stocked with new wares stolen from the Socialist window. (*Laughter*). When the Liberal Party had attained to that zeal for reform they were displaying today, the Liberal Party had paid at least one honest compliment to the party they were trying to smother before its birth. They had paid the compliment that they, in their long period of political dominance and experience, had learned to get from it the idea of the people, and would grant those demands as soon and no sooner than the people dragged them from their reluctant hands.

... The Socialist and Labour movement had determined once and for all that there was something in politics if politics got lifted out of the mire and the mud. People had learned to look upon politics as a party game. Reading political history they had a right to call it a party game but it was for those who believed that politics lay at the heart of the people, that the people's future progress and happiness mostly depended upon politics ... the speaker said he did not know the local circumstances or the local papers but he knew this, and it was enough for him, that they were standing for certain principles, and he knew the kind of twaddle they would squirt from a fountain pen. (*Laughter*).

It was for the principle of humanism they stood there that night. One good sign that he noticed now was that young men were beginning to think that billiards and hotch potch suppers were not much good now for obtaining reform. They wanted workers to be collected that they might clear out these thieves that occupied Westminster. He did not wish to insult them but he regarded them as a human being regards human beings.

It has been said that workers were not fit for Parliament, their speech not being proper English, aspirates were misplaced, they talked in dialect, and sometimes said wrong words in right places. (*Laughter*). Let them keep their quantities and watch their diction, but never mind when there was a great human problem to be solved. (*Hear. Hear.*) They claimed that if there was to be a preponderance of any one class in Parliament it must be that of the labouring class.

It now remained for all to devote their lives for the accomplishment of the ideal which they had set. The time had arrived for a new political

renaissance and each in his own sphere must work hard for the return of
the Labour candidate. (*Applause*).

It was indicative of his power as a speaker that Grayson could take to the
platform as a relative unknown alongside established Labour parliamentary candidates and leave the latter forgotten by the audience and press.
'His impact was immediate and tremendous', recalled Jess Townend, then
an 18-year-old enthusiastic socialist from Colne Valley who attended the
speeches.[16] The meeting also demonstrated the growing cleavage between
the Liberal and Labour Parties, with the Liberals coming under particular attack for their radical talk on the election trail but conservative action
once in power.

Grayson was now on the radar, leaving the Colne Valley Labour League
(CVLL) to wonder why this young man was not already a Labour candidate
elsewhere. He began to receive regular speaking invitations from the CVLL,
as well as other socialist groups in the area, as his popularity quickly spread
across the sprawling constituency. Jess Townend was Secretary of Lindley
Ward Labour Committee in Colne Valley. Soon after he heard Grayson at
Huddersfield Town Hall, he arranged a debate between Grayson and the
local organiser for the Liberal Party, Arthur Withy:

> I had to meet the Junior Liberal Secretary at his club to make the debate
> arrangements. He entertained me to dinner, and that was the first time I
> ever knew there were men waiters in plaid coats. I was only a mill-hand
> and the thing was a source of great surprise and disgust to me – at that
> time.

It was a world away from the local Labour or socialist club and demonstrated the class difference between the young men of Labour and the
young Liberals. The debate between Grayson and Withy was arranged and
was later remembered as a lively affair where Grayson demonstrated his
mixture of eloquence, humour and showmanship. Jess Townend recalled:

> When Grayson came on the platform he dumped a pile of books on
> the table, and in his closing speech he referred to these. He said, 'I had

brought these to quote from as my heavy artillery, but I have been able to demolish Mr Withy with a pea shooter.' He never opened the books. Another typical quip came after Withy had said in his opening, 'I will now proceed to turn Mr Grayson upside down'. Grayson countered with, 'Upside down would be the only position in which Mr Withy could deal with me'.[17]

The meeting was another triumph for Grayson and further established his reputation locally. As invitations to speak at meetings in the constituency steadily increased, Grayson began to lodge regularly with party members and their families. 'We had a tiny cottage home at that time with two small bedrooms,' recalled Jess Townend, 'and I have always remembered with pride that Grayson stayed with us that night. He had to share with me and my younger brother.' Townend's description relays the fact that this situation was for convenience rather than comfort. However, his presence in the constituency merely led to his popularity rising more with the local socialists and Grayson took to lodging with Wilfred Whiteley at weekends in order to walk the hilly constituency and attend more meetings. It is clear that Whiteley had some sense that Grayson would be a good candidate for the area and was ensuring he was well 'bedded-in' in Colne Valley and it would be surprising if Grayson's thinking was not in line with his.

With regular speaking engagements and with Whiteley's backing, Grayson's popularity rocketed to new levels across the constituency. It would be no exaggeration to say that not since the days of John Wesley had the people of the valley greeted a travelling preacher with such enthusiasm. Grayson attracted huge crowds and it is worth noting that this was before a by-election had even been called and before he was a candidate. In the days before television and radio, his visits were a major event. Jess Townend remembered the sheer size of one of these first meetings:

At one early meeting at Golcar a crowd of thousands blocked the roadway and in the middle of Grayson's speech the driver of a horse drawn milk-float wished to get through on his round. Grayson appealed for a passage through, 'It is not my purpose to stop the wheels of Commerce!'[18]

Rumours of Kitson's early elevation to the Upper Chamber did not abate. In April the executive of the Colne Valley Labour League met to discuss the selection of a candidate to fight the expected contest. One of Grayson's young supporters in the constituency was Jack Copeland who, after finishing a morning shift at the mill, walked to Manchester to ask Grayson to put his name forward for selection. Grayson agreed and his name was submitted along with three others – T.E. Moorhouse, William Pickles and T. Russell Williams. Moorhouse was a local Labour councillor but had only recently joined the ILP from the Liberal Party and was thus disqualified from standing because of insufficient length of membership. Pickles was a Huddersfield painter and trade unionist and Russell Williams was the Labour candidate in Huddersfield on whose behalf Grayson had spoken and so wooed the audience.[19] Although he had verbally accepted the request to go forward, Grayson was not totally convinced he was ready and wrote to Keir Hardie asking for his advice:

> I am invited to allow my name to be submitted as Labour candidate for the Colne Valley Division, and am inclined to do so. I finish my University course at the end of May and feel desirous of throwing myself into the movement. As I entertain infinite respect for your judgement in such matters I should be pleased if you could favour me with your opinion.

Seeking Hardie's opinion was a respectful move on Grayson's part. The two had met in Manchester when speaking on behalf of the Suffragettes and the young man's name would doubtless have come up in conversations between Hardie and the Pankhurst family, with whom he enjoyed a close relationship. It should be noted that Grayson wanted to stand as a Labour candidate and not a 'Socialist' or 'Labour and Socialist' candidate, which, due to a series of complex and unfortunate events, he was forced to do.

The process Grayson followed in trying to be selected as the Colne Valley's Labour candidate was cumbersome and reflected the complex alliance of those organisations which formed the new Labour Party. Prospective Labour candidates had to be selected at a conference of those organisations which made up local LRCs, usually, but not always, trade unions, the ILP and the Fabian Society. Both trade unions and the ILP had lists of pre-approved candidates and it was expected that candidates selected by LRCs would come from these lists. The organisation that sponsored the candidate's application, in Grayson's case the ILP, would agree to pay the election expenses and, once the candidate was selected locally, his name would be passed to the national Labour Party for endorsement.

On 21 April Colne Valley Labour League Secretary Sam Eastwood wrote to the National Administrative Council (NAC) of the ILP for guidance on candidate selection. The NAC advised that an LRC be formed, but as had happened two years previously, there were no trade union delegates in attendance. As we know, trade unionism was weak in the valley and, though there were union members, they were almost all members of the ILP as well. Further correspondence went back and forth between Eastwood and Ramsay MacDonald, who confusingly was both Secretary of the Labour Party and Chairman of the ILP. This confusion of roles, responsibilities and procedures was natural in a new organistaion made up of autonomous parts, but the Colne Valley Labour League had tried to act properly at each step, as indeed had Grayson as their prospective candidate. However, quite unwillingly, they were to be dragged in to a national power struggle about the future of the Labour Party.

The trade unions were, contrary to the norms of today's politics, supportive of the Liberal and Conservative Parties and their leaders were very rarely socialist in outlook. But with the emergence of a credible third party and with the Liberal Party introducing only limited labour legislation, some trade unions switched their support to the ILP. A new generation of trade unionists began to believe that only an independent party of Labour could be relied upon to truly represent the workers. The ILP was committed to democratic socialism and needed the financial backing of the trade unions to contest elections properly. The alliance was strained but seemed to be producing results, especially with the breakthrough of 1906 when 29 Labour MPs were elected to Parliament. Socialist elements within the ILP were unhappy at the lack of progress made by their new MPs, whilst union leaders felt they were being taken advantage of granted that it was ILP members, not trade unionists, who dominated candidate selections, yet union money bankrolled their campaigns.

Grayson and the Colne Valley party were unaware of the complexities of this struggle within the leadership of the Labour movement. They were interested only in selecting a candidate locally (as opposed to the national leadership imposing one of their own choosing) and, in the wake of their failure to properly constitute an LRC, came up with a new strategy. A council meeting of delegates from affiliated Labour clubs would select two candidates whose names would be submitted to the membership of the Colne Valley Labour League for selection via ballot. The Labour clubs nominated four men for selection; W.C. Anderson, B. Riley, B. Turner and Victor Grayson. Grayson was the only non-trade unionist. The council meeting was held on 12 January 1907 and each delegate had three votes in the first round and two in the second.

First ballot / Second ballot
W. C. Anderson 39 / 39
V. Grayson 49 / 42
B. Riley 20 / 12
B. Turner 12 / -

The names of Anderson and Grayson were then submitted to the membership. However, Anderson pulled out before the membership had a chance to vote, telling the local press that he had 'received an organizing appointment in the South'.[20] The two other candidates were so far behind Grayson in the ballot that it seemed a waste of time and resources to re-run the original vote. The Colne Valley Labour League thus informed the NAC of their choice and requested that Grayson be endorsed as an official Labour candidate and that adequate funds be made available to employ a full-time organiser. Frustratingly, the NAC agreed to finance the organiser but gave no guarantees about Grayson's endorsement. It quickly transpired that the NAC wanted Ben Turner as the Colne Valley candidate and they sent Philip Snowden – who had already failed to persuade Grayson to stick with the Unitarians – and James Howard to meet local activists in an attempt to change their minds. The Colne Valley members would not bend and Snowden recommended that Grayson be endorsed as the membership had made it clear that no other candidate would do. Snowden's report followed:

> We found some little soreness at what the members considered the neglect on the part of the NAC to come to a definite decision on the matter ... It is perfectly evident, however, that no other name on the list of approved candidates would be acceptable, and the whole of the branches are determined upon Grayson. It is quite certain that there is no moving them from this decision.[21]

Snowden and Howard had led the Colne Valley socialists to believe that there would be no further interference in Grayson's selection. Snowden wrote to Sam Eastwood stating that the matter would be settled officially at July's NAC meeting. However, as the Colne Valley activists had astutely predicted, Sir James Kitson was elevated to the Lords, becoming Baron Airedale on 22 June, and a by-election was called. Grayson was immediately adopted as parliamentary candidate by the constituency, but still no decision was forthcoming from Labour Party headquarters. Ramsay MacDonald would write later to the Colne Valley party promising assistance in the matter, yet in other correspondence he was non-committal and even hostile to Grayson. This double-dealing allowed bitterness to ferment between the Colne Valley contingent and the national leadership of the Labour Party. Time and again MacDonald's letters show him with a foot in each camp, unable to make a firm decision either way. This behaviour, whether through calculation or indecision, set in train a series of events that threatened to rob the Labour Party of one of its most powerful voices.

With the by-election called, a Labour Party emergency sub-committee met and resolved that Grayson's candidature could not be supported as the selection procedure had not been carried out by an officially constituted LRC which included a trade union element. This was despite the Colne Valley Labour League's pleas that there were not enough active trade unionists in the area who were not already affiliated to a Huddersfield organisation (and thus ineligible in Colne Valley). The only non-Huddersfield affiliated union men belonged to the Weavers' Union based in Saddleworth. They had attended the selection meeting but were not recorded as a distinct trade union group, as they were also members of the ILP. The national Labour Party and trade union leadership did not appreciate that in Colne Valley there were men who held dual ILP and trade union membership, a rarity elsewhere.

The emergency sub-committee was chaired by the former Liberal councillor and trade unionist David Shackleton. His sympathies still lay with his old party and he was shaken that this safe Liberal seat was to be fought by a socialist with support from men whose votes the Liberals had taken for granted. The other members of the sub-committee were Walter Hudson, the Newcastle MP and railway trade unionist, Ramsay MacDonald and Edward Pease of the Fabian Society. Shackleton successfully moved a motion that no Labour Party officials should assist Grayson's campaign. Pease and Hudson agreed, whilst MacDonald, who regarded it as a 'silly step', nonetheless failed to oppose the motion. Shackleton was a consistent opponent of socialist elements within the Labour Party and fed Grayson's growing belief that trade union leaders were hindering the advance of socialism. Shackleton was also Vice-Chairman of the Parliamentary Labour Party, adding to Grayson's concern that he was being cut adrift even before the campaign had begun.[22]

The Labour Party leadership were critical of Grayson's youth and inexperience but, significantly, not his politics. Surely Grayson's popularity, confirmed by Snowden's report, and his obvious platform ability should have overcome any doubts at such a late stage? It was, after all, impossible according to the accepted dogma of the Labour leadership for their candidate to win a three-cornered fight against a sitting Liberal. The Liberals expected nothing less than to hold the seat and yet still the Labour Party prevaricated. There was no good reason, officially, for Grayson not to stand as the candidate. With hindsight it seems possible that rumours about his private life had caught the attention of the party leadership. Although he had begun to drink more, particularly whisky, during the Colne Valley campaign, it was not hindering his performance. More likely the rumours of his homosexuality had come to light and the party leadership was worried about Labour's reputation. Whatever the truth, Grayson took the withdrawal of support personally. He and the Colne Valley Labour League had made every effort to abide by the selection rules but, through no fault of their own, now found themselves pawns in a power struggle within the movement. Ramsay MacDonald's actions throughout were cowardly, whilst the whole episode confirmed what Grayson and the ILP socialists had feared: the Labour Party leadership put relations with the trade unions and the Liberal Party before the advancement of socialism. Grayson summarised his feelings in a curt letter to MacDonald on 3 July 1907:

With regard to the attitude taken up by you and the N.A.C., and the officials of the Labour Party you have consulted, I must confess myself extremely dissatisfied. You will pardon me if I say that it seems to me to manifest an amazing lack of correct information with regard to the conditions existing in this constituency, and of the negotiations that have taken place over an unduly protracted period of time. The Trade Unionists of the Colne Valley are a negligible quantity. Further, a meeting was called nearly twelve months ago with the object of forming an L.R.C. If the Labour Party were not consulted, I should be glad to know how Ald. Ben Turner came to be present as an official representative ... I feel compelled to say that the N.A.C. have for some purpose unknown to me all along adopted an apparently evasive attitude. What more could we have done than has been done? My name was, in proper form, submitted to the N.A.C. as the locally selected candidate. There was absolutely nothing of an irregular character. They hesitated to adopt me, and after much vacillation, Mr. Snowden and James Howard were appointed to meet the Exec. of the C.V.L. League to discuss the matter. The meeting took place, and both members expressed themselves agreeably surprised at the state of things, and subsequently, I understand reported favourably to the N.A.C. At the ILP Conference no reply to questions re the situation could be evoked, pending the proceedings of this joint conference. Since then, we have been led to believe that a committee has been appointed to revise the N.A.C. official list of candidates. After that we have left things entirely to the N.A.C. but were told they did not meet till July, and that the Parliamentary Committee could not meet until Mr. Hardie was better. Surely we could not be expected to let things drag thus, or instead of having made a magnificent start in advance of our opponents, we should be still negotiating about a candidate. We had no intention of 'forcing the hands' of the N.A.C. being quite assured that they were prepared to clear a way. I understand that the correct procedure is for the N.A.C. to submit the candidate to the Labour Party for its adoption. It could not have been in order for us to approach the Labour Party, while the matter was sub judice in the N.A.C.

Candidly, my dear MacDonald, if anyone has adequate ground of complaint, I think it is the present writer.

I regret not having the support of the Labour Party, but I am humbly prepared to do without it. There is splendid prospect of success, the comrades here are resolute, we can raise more than the election expenses, and the maintenance can be managed if I am returned. I am not angry at the turn of affairs, but regret the apparent pettiness that seems to control so large a part of the L.P.'s policy. I think most sincerely this cleavage has to come some time and nothing will be lost by precipitating it.

As things stand, therefore, I gather that in the event of my success at the poll, I shall be a free-lance socialist member, independent of the Labour Group. So be it. By devious ways we shall arrive.[23]

And so it was that, despite every effort to stand as an official Labour candidate, Victor Grayson was forced to stand as 'Labour and Socialist' candidate – independent of party – in the Colne Valley by-election of 1907. The whole saga pushed Grayson away from the Labour Party, when he could have been one of its greatest assets. Unwittingly, he now found himself the rallying point for every revolutionary, socialist, Marxist, feminist, suffragist or radical who had grown tired of the Labour Party's relationship with the trade unions and its timid performance in Parliament.

* * *

Throughout this selection debacle the Colne Valley party remained active and continued its relentless propaganda campaign across the constituency. Grayson's leadership team had been assembled: Edgar Whiteley managed the campaign, whilst John Iredale Swallow and fellow local mill owner,

France Littlewood, bankrolled it. By February 1907, the local press had announced Grayson as the official Labour candidate having no knowledge of the problems over his endorsement.

The Liberal and Conservative Parties had their own difficulties over candidate selection. The Liberals were confident of retaining the seat, especially after recapturing the former seat of George Garside, after twelve years, at a recent County Council by-election. On 20 June the *Leeds Mercury* announced that Sir John Barran would be the Liberal candidate despite no official word from local Liberals who remained tight-lipped.[24] Barran was a good speaker, made regular visits to the constituency and accompanied Kitson to meetings in Huddersfield.[25] But after spending weeks touring the Colne Valley, Barran appears to have gauged that the contest would not be the simple victory that local Liberals were predicting, and pulled out.[26] Speculation about a new candidate now focused on a Mr A. Rowntree of York but he also quickly disappeared from contention, leaving the local Liberals, despite their claims of being well prepared, in a state of panic.

The Liberal candidate was eventually announced as Philip Bright, son of the great Liberal statesman John Bright. Bright junior was a well-built, tall man of whom one paper commented that he looked 'the sort of man you would rather call your friend than your enemy'.[27] Born in 1863, he was also the oldest candidate and had never before stood for political office. He was very much a last-minute choice and local Liberals knew what would soon become apparent to the voters, that Bright was the weakest candidate in the contest. His only suitability stemmed from his father's name but, by constantly reminding the 11,771 electors of Colne Valley of his ancestry, he only highlighted that not all ability is inherited. Bright's political knowledge and competence as a public speaker were so deficient that, unlike the other candidates, the press were barred from hearing his speech at his adoption meeting. Still, Bright expected a comfortable victory and, in this belief, had turned down offers from Liberal Associations elsewhere.

The Conservatives also appeared less than prepared. The Colne Valley Conservative Association held a closed meeting on 4 December 1906 to discuss a candidate and settle on a campaign plan for winning the seat. They briefed the press afterwards that they expected a by-election to come within twelve months and that they were fully prepared. Yet little ground-work had been carried out by the spring of 1907 and the press reported that the Conservatives were nowhere to be seen.[28] Edgar Freeman, treasurer of the Colne Valley Conservative Association, revealed that the local party was waiting for the Central Committee in London to present a suitable candidate. 'Well, it is fairly good,' Freeman responded to questions about his party's local organisation, 'though not so good as I should like it to be.'[29] In the end the national party selected Granville Wheeler as their candidate. Wheeler was a 35-year-old West Riding County Councillor with a large majority, who sat on the local Education Committee. He lived at Ledstone Hall, Castleford, and had stood at the previous general election in the Liberal stronghold of Osgold Cross, increasing the Conservative vote by over 300.[30] Though not considered a gifted speaker, he made up for any shortcoming with his enthusiasm. He saw the primary political issue as Home Rule, which he opposed absolutely, deploring any 'Government policy in pandering to the Nationalist aspirations'.[31] Ultimately, he was concerned with the good stewardship of the Empire and building stronger economic ties with the colonies. In contrast, the Liberal, Philip Bright, was an uncompromising free trader and attacked Wheeler for his love of what he called 'the colonial preference'.[32] But free trade was the only issue on which Bright could speak with any confidence and, whilst both candi-dates' statements were typical general election fare, this was a by-election in a constituency with a politically conscious working class to whom colonial issues seemed a world away from their own struggles.

Despite their quarrel with the Labour Party, the Colne Valley Labour League had a locally well-known and popular candidate in Victor Grayson. Their hard work in the constituency had also discouraged more able Liberal candidates from standing and caught the Conservatives on the back foot. Grayson launched his official campaign on Saturday, 29 June, the same day that the Liberal and Conservative candidates were announced. Alfred Pickles, who had been appointed Labour organiser for the constituency shortly before the by-election was called, arranged a busy schedule of meetings to build on the 125 of the previous year. 'We intend to reach every nook and corner of the constituency,' Pickles was reported as saying. 'We have been holding meetings during the last four weeks in various parts of the constituency, which has come in very useful now this situation has arisen ... We are quite prepared, and are going on with our work whatever the other parties are doing.'[33] Pickles had already covered the central parts of the constituency and now worked his way outwards, whilst T. Russell Williams, the defeated candidate at Huddersfield, began addressing regular meetings in support of Grayson. As the by-election commanded increasing coverage in the national press, the valley swarmed with volunteers and political personalities from across Britain and beyond.

Upon the announcement of a by-election in Colne Valley, members of Emmeline Pankhurst's Women's Social and Political Union (WSPU) in Huddersfield unanimously agreed to postpone all branch business until after the election. Jill Liddington notes that 'Huddersfield suffragettes threw themselves with wild enthusiasm into supporting the by-election's dashing independent socialist candidate, Victor Grayson. He attracted not only Emeline Pankhurst's support but also the attention of national press photographers.'[34] The WSPU was, however, careful not to come out explicitly in favour of Grayson and continued its official tactic of non-partisanship. 'In our election work we did not support any candidate,' recalled Hannah Mitchell, 'but appealed to the all-male electorate to vote against the Liberal Government, which refused to give "Votes for Women" ... Unlike other Labour candidates Victor boldly declared himself in favour of our demands, and lost nothing by his frankness.'[35] To any mildly observant bystander, however, the WSPU's activities were clearly built around supporting Grayson's campaign. Emmeline Pankhurst came to the Colne Valley the day Grayson officially opened his campaign and addressed meetings of local Suffragists.[36] 'I think she preferred speaking in the North and liked large industrial centres, where people catch on to an idea so much more readily than they can in the South', remembered suffragette Rosamund Massey, 'she always received a loud ovation in the cotton factory districts. How quickly would those Northerners have discerned anything unreal in the interest shown had it not been genuine.'[37] It was an easy train ride for the Manchester suffragettes to get to Colne Valley and they brought piles of pamphlets with them to sell at their meetings which paid for their fares home.[38] 'I must have worked the Colne Valley from end to end, often under the auspices of the Colne Valley Labour [League],' recalled suffragette Hannah Mitchell. 'Sometimes we just went ... from door to door to ask the women to come and listen, which the Colne Valley women were usually willing to do.'[39] Grayson was the ideal candidate for Pankhurst and her followers. He was fighting a Liberal-held seat and the Pankhursts had grown tired of Liberal stalling over the vote. Grayson also found himself fighting MacDonald, elements of the Labour Party bureaucracy and the trade unions by bringing their electoral relationship with the Liberals into disrepute. He was not afraid to call for direct action just as the Pankhurst family and he himself had done as a leader of the Manchester unemployed.

As word spread in the media about his candidacy, so old friends from his Liverpool ILP days came to campaign in Colne Valley. Fred Bower, the stonemason who had buried a copy of the *Clarion* in Liverpool's new Anglican cathedral, came over to work on the campaign's crucial final week, whilst Jim Larkin caught the ferry back after organising dock workers in Ireland in order to help. Many of Manchester's leading ILP members also took part in the fight, including Richard Wallhead and his daughter Muriel, Richard Robinson, Douthwaite, Katherine Glasier, and Walter 'Casey' Hampson – known for entertaining the crowds with his fiddle. Surprisingly, help also came from high society. The Countess of Warwick, mistress to King Edward VII, had come to socialism after lengthy exchanges with Robert Blatchford, who had initially criticised her extravagant lifestyle. She had joined the Marxist Social Democratic Federation in 1904 and, like Grayson, she had been irked by Ramsay MacDonald, which would be a common bond for them. Lady Warwick had invited MacDonald to her London home, Warwick House, for a reception in honour of Labour candidates and their wives. MacDonald responded cuttingly:

> You have very suddenly come amongst us from totally different circumstances and have taken sides instantly ... Far be it from me to put any obstacles in your way if you sincerely desire the good of our cause, but at the same time I have doubts as to the permanent good which can be done to a democratic movement by the exploitation of an aristocratic convert, and I am therefore compelled to refrain from joining in the process. I am sure you are perfectly well aware that the crowds who

applaud you and the people who gather round your tables do so because you are a Countess and would neglect you if you were Mrs Smith ... That however is not in accordance with my conception of the Socialist and Labour movement nor is it consistent either with your self respect or with my own. I also regret some of the methods you have thought fit to adopt.[40]

Still incensed by MacDonald's attitude, Lady Warwick campaigned for Grayson and loaned him her car for the duration of the campaign. She also sent her secretary Mary Jane Bridges Adams – a leading campaigner for educational reform – who addressed meetings and condemned Liberal claims that child poverty did not exist in the constituency. Warwick and Bridges Adams had toured Britain in her specially painted red Argyle motor car in support of socialist candidates at the general election. Cars were then a rarity and this added a new and exciting dimension to Grayson's campaign.

This coalition of support that Grayson attracted was almost as difficult to control as the factions within the Labour Party. One example was Richard Wallhead, who had been a regular presence on socialist platforms with Grayson around Manchester and especially during the Manchester unemployment demonstrations. But Wallhead had recently left Manchester Central ILP branch because he felt it was being dominated by the WSPU and its sympathisers. He regarded Christabel Pankhurst's speeches as detrimental to furthering the socialist cause. Yet Christabel and Emmeline were now both working in support of Grayson's campaign. Wallhead was also manager of *Labour Leader*, Keir Hardie's paper, and his presence on the campaign was tacit endorsement from Hardie himself. But Hardie at this time was not in the country but on a cruise, which he called a fact-finding mission but which was designed to allow him to recuperate from what he believed was a serious illness. Despite Wallhead's presence being interpreted as Hardie's endorsement, in Hardie's absence MacDonald continued to fight against resources being allocated to the Colne Valley campaign. Up until the last moment, the ILP leaders had favoured Ben Turner as candidate (though he had been eliminated on the first round of voting at the selection contest with Grayson). Turner, knowing nothing of this, now sought to campaign for Grayson in the by-election and wrote to MacDonald for clarification. MacDonald responded:

> You are not exactly barred from going to Colne Valley. The Labour Party as such is taking no part in the contest and its officials are anxious that the party should not be identified in any way with the election. Members must use their own judgement as to whether under the circumstances they should or should not go. So far as I can hear only one member of the Party in Parliament (Philip Snowden?) has consented to address any meetings.[41]

MacDonald was right, Philip Snowden had indeed agreed to address some meetings in the constituency but it was more on behalf of the movement than Grayson personally, for whom Snowden had little regard. After all, it was only two years since Snowden had failed to persuade Grayson that his future lay with the Unitarian Church and not the socialist movement. John Iredale Swallow was a local small manufacturer and President of the Colne Valley Labour League and, since Grayson's selection, Swallow had played host to the young candidate. Swallow was at Huddersfield station to greet Philip Snowden off the train. 'You mean to persist with this candidature, John?' asked Snowden. 'I've nothing against Grayson personally ... Nothing ... except that he's so young.' Swallow responded that Grayson's age was being remedied every passing day and protested to Snowden that they had not been given one sound reason why Grayson should not be candidate.[42] None would be forthcoming. Rowland Kenney – the brother of suffragette Annie Kenney – returned to his family home in the Colne Valley to campaign for Grayson. His recollection of Snowden's visit to the constituency revealed the scale of the Labour leadership's antipathy towards Grayson:

> One evening I was asked to address a crowd on some waste ground in one of the small towns in the constituency until the speaker of the evening arrived. The speaker turned out to be Snowden, for although the party bosses had refused Grayson official support, the Independent Labour Party leaders, realizing the strength of feeling in their own section of

the movement, felt they dare not entirely ignore him. Snowden detested
Grayson, whom he regarded as a flamboyant wind-bag; so his speech
that evening consisted of a very sensible statement of the aims of the
Labour Party in Parliament, without referring to Grayson at all or suggesting that anyone should vote for Grayson.[43]

In addition, *Labour Leader* editor Bruce Glasier (who had witnessed
Grayson's moment of triumph in Manchester) made his disdain for
Grayson clear:

> Personally I feel a strong repugnance to our having much to do with the
> running of young untried men, whose sole record in the movement is
> that of platform speaking. Unless our movement can provide representa-
> tives of well-tried experience and character, we shall for certain come by
> a big disaster before long.[44]

Glasier followed this up with a letter to his sister, Elizabeth, five days later:
'I don't care for Grayson, he is a young cheap orator not at all the type
we wish to get into Parliament.'[45] But whilst Glasier's personal animosity
towards Grayson had little effect on the campaign, Ramsay MacDonald's persistent hampering of Grayson did. When Edgar Whiteley wrote
to MacDonald requesting election literature for the contest, MacDonald
refused, stating that the Labour Party executive had resolved not to supply
campaign literature to any candidates not on its approved list. 'If we are
going to have a dozen Colne Valleys we might just as well shut up shop
altogether', responded MacDonald.[46] Keir Hardie took a softer line in his
Labour Leader editorial for 19 July: 'we fail to see good reason for their
decision to restrain Labour members from individually taking part in the
contest. A complete boycott of the election is a totally different thing from
a refusal to financially endorse Mr. Grayson's candidature.' But Hardie was
still unwilling to offer Grayson his unequivocal support.

As we have seen, Grayson's campaign attracted a wide section of the
Labour and socialist movement, so much so that a carnival atmosphere was
alive in the valley. While Grayson had no lack of men and women keen
to volunteer, without the usual central party funding of the campaign,

finance had to be raised by other means. Pennies were collected amongst the workers in the mills, donations begged from the attendees of Grayson's meetings and local women pawned precious household goods. Rowland Kenney again remembers:

Funds were found, heaven knows how. Some supporters pawned half their wordly possessions, and many married women actually sold their wedding rings in order to give Grayson financial assistance. Grayson himself lived strenuously on very little. Give him cigarettes and he would carry on endlessly. He had, I remember, one suit only, and he made rather a mess of that when he sat on a cigarette butt that was still alight, but that he turned off with a joke. 'It is not that I daren't turn my back on you,' he told a band of rowdies at one of his meetings, 'it's simply that I don't want to shock your Yorkshire puritan susceptibilities by showing you too plainly what I think of you.'[47]

The key to any successful election campaign is the right candidate and Grayson was the right candidate at the right time for the Colne Valley. He walked and walked and walked across the valley, preaching his gospel of socialism until his throat literally bled. He preached the socialism of Robert Blatchford and the *Clarion*, sprinkled with Marx's economic theories. The Liberals distributed a poster *Beware of Socialist bosh*. 'It fell as flat as stale beer,' said Grayson. 'It was a very feeble bogey.'[48] Whilst the Liberal candidate reminded the electors at every opportunity that his father was John Bright, Grayson's team were quick to remind them that Bright had not quite been the great reformer his son now remembered. Grayson pointed out that John Bright had opposed the Ten Hours Bill which limited the work of young people and women in the factories to ten hours per day, five days a week. Grayson reminded them also that John Bright had opposed women's suffrage. As the latter had said:

All these risks and all this great change we are asked to make – for what? To arm the women of this country against the men of this country. To arm them, that they may defend themselves against their fathers, their husbands, their brothers, and their sons. To me the idea has something in it strange and monstrous.[49]

Liberal supporters were furious that Grayson could turn Bright's greatest asset, his father, against him. After Grayson again questioned Philip Bright's candidature, a young Liberal interrupted and asked Grayson if he knew he was talking about the son of the great John Bright? Grayson retorted, 'I always thought he was the son of the chap who invented the disease!'[50]

Ernest Lockwood, another witness to Grayson's by-election campaign, recorded his memories of Grayson's campaign and platform style in his 1936 book *Colne Valley Folk*:

> Mr. Grayson had an amazing gift of eloquence, and was a ready speaker without the aid of notes. He had a striking appearance and a powerful voice. People flocked from far and near to his meetings. No room in the Colne Valley was large enough to hold all who desired to hear him. Consequently many meetings were held in the open air, and Mr. Grayson was able to command the largest gatherings by his personality and eloquence. He could be very sarcastic with his opponents, though for the most part he was distinctly humorous, if at times unconsciously so. Once at Meltham he delighted his followers by his reply to a heckler, who had put what Mr. Grayson considered a personal question. Quick as lightning came his retort that he would answer the question if the questioner would meet him under a railway arch on a dark night![51]

To make matters worse for the Liberals, Grayson had the support of so many clergymen that his campaign gave the impression that God was indeed a socialist and that Grayson was about to usher in the new Jerusalem. Between 20 and 40 socialist clergymen are estimated to have been touring the constituency on Grayson's behalf at any one time. Many came via the Church Socialist League, formed in 1906 by Anglicans of socialist persuasion. Others were among the noncomformist clergymen for whom the valley was famous. 'For these clergymen,' notes one historian, 'socialism could appear more readily as a vehicle for God's work in history.'

There were many, like Grayson, who had thought that the work of the Church was too restrictive to win a better life and that only coupling the gospel with political action, specifically working for the success of socialism, could bring about a better world. One such man was Frederick J. Swan of the Marsden Congregational Chapel in the Colne Valley. Swan was known locally as a cultured and gifted preacher and in early 1907 he published his controversial text *The Immanence of Christ in Modern Life*. The book questioned the legitimacy of church governance and criticised the manner in which the Church, and thus God's children, had been divided and sub-divided 'as if these divisions represented totally different classes'. All social reform, according to Swan, had its basis in religion and only through the solidarity of the human race could this be achieved. Swan went further and called for the Church to take a lead in the new social movement (socialism) and finally carry out its historic mission as laid down by Christ:

> The most optimistic is compelled to admit and to deplore the presence of a vast amount of preventable misery, poverty, disease, crime and unhappiness. These are bad symptoms of the social body. They point clearly to the fact of something radically wrong in the present social and economic system. Urgent questions of housing, employment, the right to a true self-development and the fullest liberty to true self-development and the fullest liberty to live the best life, the fear of poverty, provision for old age ... are now being seriously discussed ... The good of each should be the work for all, and the good of all be the work for each.[52]

Swan seemed to embody the spirit of Martin Luther and of William Tyndale, while he saw Grayson as the modern-day John Wesley, preaching the gospel of socialism to the people of the valley. As Grayson's local activists shouted the slogan, 'Socialism – God's Gospel for Today', senior Liberal and Conservative supporters implored the Church to take punitive action against these socialist men of the cloth. Swan was one of the first to suffer. His controversial book had already won him few friends among the Church hierarchy and, under mounting pressure, he was forced to resign from Marsden Congregational Chapel in March 1907. Thereafter he threw himself fully into the socialist movement and was a key member of Grayson's by-election campaign. He wrote frequently for *The Worker* in praise of Grayson and later took up a prominent position in the Colne Valley Labour League.[53] Another marked out for special criticism by the opposition parties was the Rev. W.B. Graham, the curate at Thongsbridge near Bradford. Graham was considered the 'life and soul of the party' in Grayson's campaign and at a height of six-feet-five-inches prompted Robert Blatchford's comment that he was 'six-foot a socialist and five inches a parson'.[54] Fred Shaw, another of Grayson's helpers, recalled how big a part religion played at this time:

> There was a vast amount of effort used on the platform in those days proving that God Almighty was on the side of the lowly as in ancient times, and couldn't Grayson work this line! He knew damn all about economics, or sociology but he had the retort ready before the question was finished and in biblical phraseology.[55]

Grayson's meetings were now regularly attracting upwards of 2,000 people with little serious interruption from the audience. So hapless was the Liberal campaign in comparison that Arthur James Sherwell, Liberal MP for Huddersfield, was drafted in to address meetings and chaperone the candidate, Philip Bright. Sherwell immediately went on the offensive and made much of Grayson's lack of official endorsement by the Labour Party. He told audiences that this was due to the candidate's extreme socialist views, which of course was not the case. This prompted suspicion from the Colne Valley socialists that Sherwell was being passed information by certain members of the Parliamentary Labour Party, for as a Liberal he seemed to know more than he should. Grayson did not possess a thick skin and he responded to Sherwell's allegation in the *Huddersfield Examiner*:

> I am sick and tired of Mr Sherwell's challenges. He has been making gallery charges from the very beginning. First he says I have not the endorsement of the ILP, and when we contradict that in the most emphatic manner by producing the endorsement, he shuffles on to

the Labour group. I am standing definitely as a Socialist and Labour candidate …

In addition, Grayson's campaign team made two further assaults on the Liberal campaign. First, they published a short satirical attack on Bright:

Sherwell had a little lamb,
Its name was Philip Bright.
And every day would Sherwell cram
What Philip must recite!
To echo Sherwell everywhere
Was Philip's nightly rule,
It made electors laugh and stare
To see poor Phil at school.

Second, in response to Sherwell's attack on Grayson's lack of endorsement due to his extremism, the socialist camp published a supportive letter from Keir Hardie:

The contest in the Colne Valley will give the working-class electors in the division an opportunity of showing the strength of their convictions. Jarrow[56] has just shown what could be done when Labour is united … Let me impress upon you the importance of promoting and preserving the closest possible union among the organized forces of Labour … I am at present laid aside from active work of any kind, and so shall not be able to lend a hand in the contest.[57]

The final days before polling saw endless and exhausting activity by all three parties. The Liberals, despite a poor campaign and a poor candidate, still expected to win and *The Times* reported that 'if all promises are carried out, the result should be Mr Bright's return'. The Conservatives too feared a Liberal victory if their own candidate failed. As a result, the Conservative leader Arthur Balfour sent a supportive public letter to the Tory candidate Wheeler which attacked the Liberal government's policies for 'recklessly playing up to the forces of Socialism'.[58] By contrast, Grayson's eve of poll statement was an uncompromising rehearsal of his socialist beliefs:

TO THE ELECTORS OF THE COLNE VALLEY

I am appealing to you as one of your own class. I want emancipation from the wage-slavery of Capitalism. I do not believe that we are divinely destined to be drudges. Through the centuries we have been the serfs of an arrogant aristocracy. We have toiled in the factories and workshops to grind profits with which to glut the greedy maw of the Capitalist class. Their children have been fed upon the fat of the land. Our children have been neglected and handicapped in the struggle for existence. We have served the classes and we have remained a mob.

The time for our emancipation has come. We must break the rule of the rich and take our destinies into our own hands. Let charity begin with our children. Workers, who respect their wives, who love their children, and who long for a fuller life for all:

A VOTE FOR THE LANDOWNER OR THE CAPITALIST IS TREACHERY TO YOUR CLASS.

To give your child a better chance than you have had, think carefully ere you make your cross.
The other classes have had their day. It is our turn now!

ALBERT VICTOR GRAYSON

Polling took place on Thurday, 18 July 1907 and by all accounts it was a beautiful day. A high turnout was expected. *The Times* reported that there had been further misery for the Liberals when one of their agents attempted to set up a counter-demonstration at a Conservative meeting in Slaithwaite. The Liberal 'was turned upon by a crowd, who pinned him against a wall. A free fight ensued, and the agent escaped without injury in a railway van which happened to be passing.'[59] The socialist campaign had no such difficulties. Grayson toured the constituency in the Countess of Warwick's red motor car with supporters lining the route in some areas, whilst others followed him round as best they could. Whilst touring the polling booths, he was carried shoulder high by supporters to and from his car. Even opposition supporters were reported to have joined in the merriment. Many of the mills had closed for the day to allow their workers to vote and campaign, though few dared let the bosses know that they were voting for Grayson. Instead, they took advantage of the fleet of Tory and Liberal motor cars to take them to the polls to vote for Grayson.[60] Despite the jubilation, Grayson was still not confident. Many of his supporters were women, who did not have the vote, others were poorer male workers who were similarly disenfranchised. Standing on the pavement in Delph where twelve days before he had opened a Labour club, Grayson turned to one of his supporters, Alice Longley, and said, 'Well, we've lost. What now?' 'Go home and write your article on how you won Colne Valley', responded Mrs Longley.[61]

To reporters it seemed as if every child in the Colne Valley was wearing a red ribbon and a 'Grayson' pin badge. They crowded around Grayson wherever he stopped and sang the socialist songs taught to them at the Socialist Sunday Schools and, whilst none of them could vote, their presence was a clear indication that the momentum was with Victor Grayson.

The result was announced on the following day, Friday, 19 July at Slaithwaite Town Hall and was as follows:

Victor Grayson (Labour & Socialist) 3,648
Philip Bright (Liberal) 3,495
G. C. H. Wheeler (Conservative) 3,227
Majority 153

Thousands gathered around the Town Hall to hear the result and Grayson's supporters frequently broke out into singing 'The Red Flag'. Freelance journalist and socialist Wilfred Thompson recalled the scene:

When Mr. Grayson came to the window, pale as death, where the declaration was made, at the right hand of the Sheriff, pandemonium prevailed. The wild scene of enthusiasm which followed the announcement of the figures is indescribable. People, old and young, shouted and cheered till they could do so no longer. They then either laughed hysterically or wept for joy.[62]

With what breath they were able to catch, Grayson's supporters sang a
medley of socialist hymns and drew Grayson, in his car, down the road and
over a small bridge to the Dartmouth Arms where he held a mass public
victory meeting. As Grayson rose to speak, the cheers were deafening.
Eventually order was restored and the new Labour and Socialist MP for
Colne Valley addressed them:

> Comrades and friends, I must ask you, while I speak, which will only
> take a few minutes, to give me a quiet hearing, as I shall not be able to
> say much very loudly. This is the greatest moment that I could have
> lived for [applause] and the very first joy that comes into my mind is
> this, that this epoch-making victory has been won for pure revolutionary
> Socialism [loud applause]. We have not trimmed our sails to get a half-
> hearted vote [Hear, Hear]. We have proclaimed our Socialism on every
> platform we have spoken from. We have replied effectively to the lies
> of the Liberals and the Tories. We have cut our wisdom teeth [laughter
> and applause] and I want to say further to those who have worked and
> voted for this huge success, remember this, what I have said through the
> contest springs into my heart now that I have been returned through
> the work, the devotion, the love, the idealism of the people in the Colne
> Valley [applause] and being returned I shall feel that my duty is to be the
> old men's and women's member, the young men's and women's member,
> the starving child's member [Hear, Hear] the one who will stand above
> all things for human legislation first, and if that is not given, the mandate
> that is given me from the Colne Valley will go to other members in other
> constituencies. You have laid the first stone of the foundations of a really
> great edifice today [Hear, Hear]. You have voted, you have worked for
> Socialism; you have voted, you have worked for the means of life to be
> the property of the whole class instead of a few small classes, and I feel
> that now you have given me the courage to lay my life on the altar of
> progress in order that something may be done. I must not forget this:
> We stand for equality, human equality, sexual equality [Hear, Hear] for
> the abolition of the sex ties, and I thank the women for what they have
> done to 'keep the Liberal out' [applause]. I shall not talk longer ... Your
> duties are not yet ended until 153 becomes 2,153. The work has begun

... It is a tremendous victory, comrades [Hear, Hear]. I feel at this point I cannot do anything better than thank you all from the bottom of my heart for rallying round this splendid cause as you have done.[63]

Grayson was shaken, exhausted, but euphoric. His voice was now barely audible and his throat so swollen it bled. He retired, briefly, to the nearby Pickles household where he was given tea. 'Victor's first thought was to send a telegram to his Mother', recalled Eva Pickles – then a young girl – more than five decades later. '"I must send a telegram to my Mother" he said. He lost himself for a minute and had to put aside his first effort and write another.' The telegram was sent and, with his brief respite over, Grayson returned to the car and toured the constituency to thank his supporters.

Fred Bower, Grayson's old Liverpool ILP colleague, witnessed the announcement of the result:

I waited about noon in Slaithwaite, at the foot of the inclined street in which stood the Town Hall, from which the result was to be declared. Mrs. Pankhurst and her three daughters who, with the women suffragists, had worked like Trojans for our candidate, were in a car around the corner. A red handkerchief was waved from an upstairs window. It was the signal. We had won. I delivered the news to the wonderful woman and her daughters, and the hills resounded with the 'Red Flag'. It was a great day.[64]

So memorable was Grayson's campaign that it was recalled by those who fought it until their last days. One of Grayson's earliest contacts in the Colne Valley, who had invited him to Paddock Debating Society, was Wilfred Whiteley. In a 1969 interview Whiteley offered his memory of the campaign:

The winning of Colne Valley was largely due to his vivacity and his enthusiasm, and his youth ... I would say that it was almost entirely the platform work of Grayson that gave him his appeal, and that led people to follow him, and of course his great capacity for telling stories really attracted the listeners to a tremendous degree. In the Colne Valley by-election it was really wonderful. You could go out, say into the country between Meltham and Slaithwaite, and stand up and start speaking and somehow you'd have drawn people to you when you never expected anyone to come. I remember going up on the last Sunday morning, they hadn't advertised the meeting, they just simply said to me, go down to the quarry at Crimble and start a meeting there. You know, you gathered a couple of hundred people before you knew where you were. I remember the same at Holthead, up on the hillside – you went out and set up your stall and, quite frankly, the people seemed to come from nowhere. He was a great attraction on the platform was Victor.[65]

Twenty-five-year-old Victor Grayson had, against all the odds, overcome the long-established political machines of the Conservative and Liberal Parties, but had done so without the help of the official Labour Party. It was a victory for the grassroots and for those who dared to dream, and his victory on a clear platform of uncompromising socialism shocked the country and sent the nation's press into a panic. News of the result spread across the globe and speculation mounted that Britain and the West might be on the brink of a socialist revolution.

4

'The Boy Who Paralysed Parliament'

The Colne Valley victory was a victory for Socialism pure and simple. Mr. Grayson fought the election frankly as a Socialist with the support of the Labour organisations. It is as a Socialist that he goes to Parliament, and his mandate, given by a great industrial constituency, is nothing less than a mandate for social and economic revolution.

The *New Age*, 25 July 1907

The return of Mr. Victor Grayson to the House of Commons is an event in the history of Parliament. He is the first Socialist pure and simple who has found a constituency to elect him. His principles are clear ...

The Luton Times and Advertiser, 26 July 1907

It is said that the return of Mr. Victor Grayson ... constitutes a revolution in British politics.

Heywood Advertiser, 26 July 1907

The British press became lachrymose with visions of a red flood pouring over the constituencies.

Shaw Desmond[1]

On the morning after his victory, an exhausted and still hoarse Victor Grayson, adrenaline still rushing through him, wove between the ragged newspaper boys shouting the headlines of his election victory and caught the train back home to Manchester. He was received by friends at Victoria station as a conquering hero, then returned to his rooms in Ancoats. For a few, brief, precious days after the result, the life of Britain's newest MP barely changed and he continued to take his dinners with old student friends at Owens College. But a wave of fear and confusion ran through swathes of the British establishment and the Parliamentary Labour Party (PLP), Ramsay MacDonald, Philip Snowden and Keir Hardie were not immune. They feared the result would embolden the more revolutionary elements within their young party and threaten its very existence. Grayson had demonstrated that Labour could win on its own merits and this, they believed, endangered the Labour Party's commitment to the parliamentary road to socialism by emboldening the more radical and revolutionary elements of the movement. An added annoyance was that, although Grayson was not elected as an official Labour candidate, he was still a member of the ILP which initially paid him the same maintenance allowance as its other MPs, until his status could be ratified at the next party conference. After the bungling of his selection, this caused fresh confusion across the fragile alliance that constituted the Labour Party. The socialists called on Labour MPs to embrace Grayson into their number whilst trade unionists and former Liberals wanted him to be shunned.

Victor Grayson, whatever his growing public reputation, was an emotional and fragile soul. He had had every intention of standing as an official Labour candidate and abiding by the party's programme and procedures. But he was greatly hurt to have been spurned by Ramsay MacDonald during his selection and now the young MP found himself surrounded by impatient supporters who urged him on as the vanguard of a coming socialist society. Grayson believed, correctly, that many Labour MPs would have preferred him to lose, and now, overnight, he had become the rallying point for every revolutionary and socialist in Britain, unimpressed with what they saw as a timid Labour Party, with its internal alliance with conservative-minded trade unions and its external links with the Liberals. Whether or not Grayson wanted that crown was immaterial, it was thrust upon his head. To the leaders of the Labour Party it was as if Grayson's election had released demons. Flamboyant Christian Socialist, Conrad Noel, a leading personality of the Church Socialist League (CSL), called for a new, united and militant socialist party.[2] Robert Blatchford echoed Noel's sentiments and, much to the chagrin of sitting Labour MPs, labelled Grayson, in the *Clarion*, 'The First Socialist M.P.'. Blatchford warned the PLP that its concessions to trade unionism and the Liberal Party were killing the hopes of socialism:

There is no sword for the poor but Socialism; there is no shield for the poor but Socialism ... not Liberal-Labour Socialism, not Trade Union

Socialism. We must have *real* Socialism; Socialism without dilution, or compromise, or apology ... We decline to be respectable, and polite, and conciliatory while men are dying on doorsteps and women have no clothing to keep their babies alive.[3]

The popular radical journal the *New Age* immediately aligned itself with Grayson and saw British socialism's opportunity either to assert itself within the Labour Party or to found a new one:

Such an incident cannot fail to have deep far-reaching consequences within and without the ranks of the Labour Party. The Socialists have found their feet and proved their strength. They have shown that, standing alone, they can win ... every party will feel that in the future it has to reckon not merely with political trade unionism, but with definite Socialist conviction as a force in national politics.[4]

Some of the more radical elements in the Liberal Party saw the result as a warning that they needed to be bolder with social policy or risk further losses. 'It is time we did something that appealed straight to the people,' David Lloyd George wrote to his brother after hearing of Grayson's election. 'It will, I think, help to stop this electoral rot and that is most necessary.'[5] Another Liberal MP, Charles P. Trevelyan, wrote to his wife Molly, 'It means that you and I will have to work very hard to keep my safe seat ... the people are independent and thinking for themselves. Why shouldn't they have their own man? I dare say I should have voted for [Grayson] myself.'[6] The *Daily Chronicle* shared Lloyd George's sentiment that the Liberal Party had to adopt at least some of the socialist agenda: 'Socialism is winning ground among an intelligent, and not unprosperous, community ... The socialist theory is not accepted by Liberals, but ... the duty of Liberals is to move with the times.' Others like the *Daily News* saw Grayson's victory as an endorsement of the radical Liberal manifesto of 1906 and that what Colne Valley electors wanted was 'not less but more of the programme which the country endorsed last year'.

For the reactionaries, the *Daily Express*[7] charged that the result was another step towards the dissolution of England:

There is indeed in English politics to-day only one issue. That issue
lies between Socialism – which means confiscation and revolution, and
Unionism, which means devotion to national interests and the development of national life ... We must recognise that England is faced by
the same revolutionary forces to the combat of which all that is best
in modern France has steadfastly set its hand. Until now we have been
fighting in a half-hearted manner. Until now we have foolishly despised
our adversary. Even the General Election did not altogether make us
realise the peril, but that peril has certainly become evident in the last
few weeks in the results of the elections at Jarrow and in the Colne Valley.

Meanwhile, in the *Clarion*, Robert Blatchford gave a more cautious view
of the result. He warned the socialists that there was considerable work to
do and called for a break with the trade unions to form a new, avowedly
socialist party:

The Socialist has won, and the other gentlemen are amazed and alarmed.
But where do we, as Socialists, come in? How does this wonderful
Socialist victory affect us? Let us congratulate General Grayson and his
devoted little force, and – keep our powder dry. The campaign has not
yet begun. The real battles are all to be fought. Labour is awakening; but
it is not yet awake. There are many devoted and brave bands of Socialists in the field; but the Socialist army does not yet exist. In an advancing
working-class constituency, we have polled one hundred and fifty votes
more than the Liberals. Let us be thankful we did not poll as many less.
But do not let us be so easily and profoundly impressed as the House
[of Commons] and the Press. When we can poll two-thirds of the votes
for Socialism in a score of large towns we may begin to feel confident
and proud. When we have a Socialist Party which does not lean upon
the trade unions, but finds its own money and its own men and fights
and wins under its own flag, we may indulge ourselves with reason, and
be justified of the facts. But for the present it behoves us to keep our
mouths shut and our armour buckled tight. Victor Grayson is in. That
is well. Regarded strategically, Mr Grayson's capture of the seat can only
be placed as a victory snatched from the lap of Fortune. Mr. Grayson

and his supporters must have worked like Trojans. The result is creditable and cheering; the moral effect of the incident will be considerable; but – but we have no Socialist Party; we have no Socialist war chest; and we have only one Socialist M.P.[8]

In spite of the calls for caution from the cooler heads of Blatchford and others, Grayson's victory was rapturously received within the rank and file of the Labour movement. In his *Labour Leader* paper, Keir Hardie had warned his readers, 'This is not the revolution.' He feared that his electoral pact with the Liberals – and possibly the Labour Party itself – were threatened. Immediately after his election, Grayson had been rash and uncompromising, 'It will be for some future historian of the Socialist movement to count up the pros and cons of the past seven years of the ILP in so closely identifying itself with a political party which was inevitably non-Socialist in its political practice, if not in its economic theory.' With the reactionary press painting Hardie and Grayson as cut from the same cloth, Hardie knew he either had to bring Grayson into line or sever relations with him for good. The rest of the PLP agreed with Hardie's view, 'The Labour Party consists of members elected as representatives of labour, and it was against our rule to put forward a candidate simply as a socialist,' said Will Crooks MP. 'All that I can say is that he won without us, as the *Clarion* said he would.'[9] Bruce Glasier, who opposed Grayson's candidature from the start and had witnessed the young man's triumph in Manchester as the champion of the unemployed, rather ungraciously ascribed the Colne Valley result to a mere dip in support for the Liberal Party. Hannah Mitchell, the suffragette who had worked so hard in the Colne Valley that she suffered a nervous breakdown, recalled: '[Grayson] won the seat, much to the chagrin of the older parties, and even the Labour movement itself, many of whose members were jealous of this brilliant young orator.'[10] Grayson lamented in an interview that 'the rumour was sedulously circulated that the Labour members regarded my election with but chill enthusiasm. They certainly have dissembled their love.'[11] But the spite from the old guard of the Labour movement towards him caused a grassroots backlash, with Grayson announcing that, in view of their reaction to his election, he would not sit with the Labour MPs in Parliament. ILP activist and future Labour MP, Frank Rose, wrote to Ramsay MacDonald:

> It seems to me that the limits of endurance are just about reached. If the half-baked trade unionists are to run the show let us know and we can all assist in shoving the Labour Party into the scrap heap and starting afresh. I have seen some of the official correspondence and I declare I do not like the smell of it. The ILP is bad enough but the National Labour Party is – or seems to be – far worse. Grayson is just the man you want: he is not likely to trim or exhaust his soul in slobbering C.B. [Liberal Prime Minister Campbell-Bannerman] ... He tells me that he will not sit with you and I can hardly blame him.[12]

Four days later Rose again wrote to MacDonald:

> The SDF people up here are already using Grayson's success as an argument and indeed, claiming him as one of themselves. It is to be made the starting point of a more decided campaign of disruption between the Trade Unions and the Socialists.[13]

Parliament's newest member took his seat on 23 July 1907, five days after his success and was sponsored, however grudgingly, by Labour MPs Philip Snowden and J.R. Clynes. The three men walked calmly to the Speaker's chair, their cautious pace dictated by Snowden's limp, whilst Will Thorne shouted 'Good Old Red Flag!' from the benches.[14] Grayson entered a Commons ruled by a Liberal Party with its biggest majority in history. They had been swept to power in part on the promise of social reform but, to the disappointment of many voters, had seemed to achieve little so far in office. That sentiment had been a part of Grayson's victory, and in other by-elections the Liberals were losing ground. The hopes of the radical supporters of the Liberal government lay with David Lloyd George and Winston Churchill. Churchill, until recently a Conservative MP, was treated with suspicion by many of his new colleagues but was nevertheless embraced as a great asset, especially in the Commons. Henry Campbell-Bannerman led the Liberals but would shortly step down and pass his

Prime Ministerial office to the Chancellor, Herbert Asquith. The Conservative and Unionist opposition was led by Arthur Balfour and, despite their much reduced strength in the Commons, they retained the overwhelming support of the House of Lords. No matter the overwhelming democratic mandate for Liberal reform, the Lords were ready to reject any progressive measures that the Conservatives found unacceptable.

In light of the fears of Hardie and the PLP and with bad feeling publicly vented from both sides, Philip Snowden was dispatched to persuade Victor Grayson to join the Labour group in Parliament. Snowden assured his young colleague that this was much preferable to sitting as an Independent Member, without party backing and infrastructure. This, Snowden told Grayson, would guarantee him the opportunity to speak and ensure that he had the backing of fellow Labour MPs. In return Grayson would have to sign the constitution of the PLP, whereby members accepted the majority decision of the group and voted accordingly in the House. This was an unpalatable suggestion as far as Grayson was concerned. When the Labour Party had refused to endorse him as an official candidate, he had been elected by the Colne Valley people, independent of party. Though at the time Grayson had done his best to look like the official candidate in all but name, the immense support he had received since his victory from across the Labour and socialist movement encouraged him to retain his independence. As a result, he did not join the ranks of Labour's 30 MPs (of whom only about 50 per cent described themselves as socialists), although his party status could not in any case have been ratified until the coming party conference. Grayson would for the time being remain in a no-man's land; a member of the ILP who sat outside of the Labour Party in Parliament (the PLP). After he snubbed Snowden's offer, little kindness was shown towards the new MP. Fenner Brockway, then a young member of the ILP, recalled, 'I was distressed ... by the personal antagonisms, particularly the anger shown towards Victor Grayson.'[15]

Without the support structure of the Labour Party and the comradeship and guidance of Labour MPs, Grayson cut a lonely figure in the Commons and was thus hopelessly unprepared for the life of a Parliamentarian. In contrast to his isolation at Westminster, he jumped head-first into London's social circuit, where he was much in demand. The influential ILP member and theorist of guild socialism, Samuel Hobson, witnessed first-hand Grayson's transformation from wide-eyed new MP to avid socialite. Hobson remembered meeting Grayson on his first day at Westminster:

> I met him by sheer chance in the Outer Lobby of the House of Commons on the day he had come up to take the Oath. To my amazement he left a little group of his friends, rushed at me, threw his arms round my neck, and kissed me. After I had recovered my breath I said, 'Victor, have you any money and any place to sleep?' He told me he had a few shillings, and had not thought of the night. 'You had better stay with me until you find digs to suit you.' So he stayed with me for a few weeks. In this way I got to know him.[16]

Whilst Grayson lodged with him, Hobson noticed how the young MP was seduced by London's temptations. 'I soon realised that my quietude and abstinence irked him,' recalled Hobson. 'He came in later and later, with ever more elaborate apologies. I had had my fill of excitement; he was just beginning.'[17] As Grayson's new-found celebrity brought invitations to dinner most nights, he began to move in the circles of those he considered his heroes. One was Edward Carpenter (1844–1929) whose works Grayson had read and re-read since discovering him at the book club, at the Little Bethel Church, Liverpool. Now he was sharing evenings as well as platforms with Carpenter. 'Victor Grayson,' recalled Carpenter, 'was a most humorous creature. His fund of anecdotes was inexhaustible, and rarely could a supper party of which he was a member get to bed before three in the morning.'[18] Carpenter had had a profound effect on Grayson's politics and lifestyle. He was a founder of the Fabian Society and was the outstanding figure, before Robert Blatchford, of the early British socialist movement. Carpenter saw much of himself in the young Grayson. Both had relinquished promising careers in the Church, and both had been inspired by Christian socialists, in particular William Morris. Both were also friends of Hyndman and greatly influenced by the theory of surplus value in *England for All*, plagiarised from Marx's *Capital*. Each would campaign for, and speak at, meetings of both the ILP and the SDF. In doing so, the two men demonstrated their belief in what Carpenter termed 'the larger socialism', which stated that socialism could not be brought about by factional infighting and the proliferation of left-wing parties and groups, but would only succeed through some form of socialist unity. The other issue which united the two men was their sexuality. Carpenter had written widely on homosexuality and was an early campaigner for what we now call LGBT rights. His particular skill was to use language in such a way that he could discuss gay issues and sell a hundred thousand copies of a book without falling foul of publishers, censors or public opinion. For instance, in *The Intermediate Sex* (1908) he writes, 'That between the normal man and the normal woman there exist a great number of intermediate types – types, for instance, in which the body may be perfectly feminine, while the mind and feeling are delicately masculine, or vice versa …'[19] He lived openly with his long-term lover, George Merrill, at Millthorpe, his estate near Sheffield, which became a pilgrimage for his followers. 'He believes and practices the physical very frankly,' wrote political scientist and contemporary Goldsworthy Lowes Dickinson. 'How it is that public opinion hasn't managed to get him to prison and murdered him is a mystery.' The last years of the nineteenth century had seen the public mood whipped up against gay men thanks to two high-profile cases. First, the Cleveland Street affair of 1889 in which the police uncovered a male brothel in London frequented by well-known members of the British establishment, rumoured to include Queen Victoria's grandson and Grayson's namesake, Prince Albert. Second, the prosecution of Oscar Wilde in 1895, which featured the testimony of a string of rent boys, was luridly reported by the press. This case in particular led to the popular image of gay men as effeminate and delicate, something to which, with hindsight, we can see that Victor Grayson fell victim at the hands of jealous enemies and some, sadly, he considered his comrades.[20] 'Certainly there was a strain in early British Socialism,' wrote Michael Bloch, 'which preached sexual toleration and the rejection of bourgeois morals.'[21] Indeed, there was an air of sexual liberation for both men and women surrounding the early socialist movement. But, in contrast, 'the chapel-going, working-class trade unionists who made up its backbone tended to be one of the most homophobic elements in the political firmament, obliging those members who were "queer" ... to lead closeted lives'.[22] Grayson lived one of those closeted lives and this description of the trade union movement may help us understand the mutual dislike that existed between him and the conservative leadership of the union movement in Britain. What we do know is that the socialist intelligentsia of London showed a greater toleration for Grayson's lifestyle than either the Church or the rank and file of the Labour movement. Perhaps this is why Samuel Hobson, who allowed Grayson to lodge with him temporarily, referred to Grayson's dinner parties as a series of 'dangerous hospitalities'.

As a Parliamentarian Victor Grayson had the ability to be one of the great performers in the House of Commons. He had learnt his craft of oratory and the witty retort to the heckler on the soap-box platforms of Liverpool, Manchester and Britain's northern mill and factory towns. But Parliament is steeped in pomp, process and procedure. It is not a place where an MP can simply jump up and start to speak on any issue when the urge hits him. Parliament and the soap box are two distinct platforms and require a different approach and, as Grayson would learn, success on one is no guarantee of success on the other.

Maiden speeches in the House of Commons are by convention uncontroversial, but Grayson was not one to be bound by such tradition. On 30 July 1907 he entered a crowded chamber. He had quietly briefed a few Labour MPs and journalists that he would be making his first intervention on the government motion to give a £50,000 pension (£5 million today) to Lord Cromer and many MPs had packed into the House to see what Grayson was made of. Cromer was one of Britain's most able Empire-builders, the son of an MP and the grandson of an Admiral, born into 'one of London's most distinguished banking families'. He had effectively ruled Egypt since 1883, was supremely arrogant and, in his own eyes at least, superior to all others.[23] The Liberal government was treading water when it came to implementing a radical social policy, but here it was, set to award an extravagant pension to an official already blessed with wealth and privilege. Cromer was clearly a suitable target for the new socialist MP.

Grayson rose to speak and so too did the Foreign Secretary, Sir Edward Grey, and Labour MP Will Thorne. Both men gave way to the new Member and applauded in anticipation, as was customary. Grayson, pale, immaculately dressed with hair neatly combed, surveyed the chamber and after a sharp intake of breath began to speak:

> The condition of the House presents me with a very interesting and curious spectacle. I see the benches packed with enthusiastic politicians, and the government beaming with the consciousness of their splendid majority. When one hears speeches of a very similar character from both sides of the House one wonders at first what question is being discussed. Has someone discovered the solution of the incapacitated workman? Are they introducing a measure of old-age pensions for the incapacitated workman? Or has a rumour slipped out that the new Member is going to make his speech?

Instead of showing deference to Parliament and its history, Grayson mocked it. He questioned why parliamentary time was wasted on whether to award a pension to an already well-remunerated public servant, whilst the conditions of the poor in Britain's cities were appalling. He opposed the Liberal government's motion to award the pension and took aim at their benches:

> The Government has no mandate to vote away a large amount of public money for this purpose, whereas it does have a mandate to use every cent at its disposal to solve some of the most ghastly social problems. I remember when Liberal candidates were fighting at the last General Election it was such promises they made in regard to old-age pensions for worn out and incapacitated working men and women that gained for them so great a majority of votes. When I look around me I realise that the present Government has the most magnificent and glorious opportunity that any Government has ever had; yet enthusiasm can be evoked from these crowded benches, with the united support of the Opposition, on the question of giving a grant to an Egyptian official, while outside the walls of this House people are dying of starvation – men and women who have given good and substantial service to the State are tottering to paupers' graves.

It was a tone and language rarely heard in the House of Commons. The government, Grayson said, had reined back proposals for old-age pensions so much that what was left was derisory. Yet when a well-paid official retired he was to be rewarded with the riches made off the back of the labour of Britain's working poor. He continued the assault, telling the government that his election was a warning that their days were numbered:

> Much surprise was shown on all sides of the House when a large industrial constituency left behind it its traditions and clung to a new political doctrine. Is it any wonder to find that the Government is being discredited in the country ... The unemployed are walking the streets, men and women willing to work are denied that elementary right by the Government now in power. All our constitutional politics are a mockery and a sham while they make no serious attempt to grapple with this problem. I warn honourable Gentlemen opposite that if this policy is persisted in there will not be only one electoral change, but they can look forward to the day when all the front bench will be occupied by Socialists.

Grayson paused, unable to continue as laughter erupted from Conservative and Liberal benches.[24] When the House quietened down he continued, warning again that the Liberals were carrying out the most successful socialist propaganda in the country by back-pedalling on their pledges to the electorate. Grayson concluded:

> In this, my first speech in the House, I feel privileged to have such a night on which to deliver it, and to state the issue clearly and explicitly as it is to be presented to the country. On the one side there is organized capital and organized capitalistic interests; on the other side organized labour determined to work out its own destiny ... No man can claim to represent the real interests of the people who is already well paid, whilst the aged poor are neglected, scorned, and left to starve or die in the work-house.

With his first performance in the Commons greeted with joy by his supporters across the country, Grayson had made it clear that he would not trim his politics or speeches to suit tradition and deference. The *Westminster Gazette* reported Grayson's maiden speech:

> It was the very speech which the Socialist member in the up-to-date novel would have made ... But his language and figures of speech were not those of the dweller in such slums; they reeked of Bernard Shaw and Karl Marx, with an added touch of realism derived from personal knowledge of the lot of the poor. For there was no gainsaying the sincerity of the young man, or of his utter fearlessness as he attacked the Government for its impotency to deal with the social problem ... And yet one thought that the appearance of this strange young man, with his white face and carefully combed hair, and his bold appeal that he that hath should give to him that hath not, had a disquieting effect on the nerves of the Assembly.[25]

The question now asked by figures such as Keir Hardie, Ramsay MacDonald and the rest of the PLP was whether Grayson, after making his grand entrance, could now be wooed to settle on their benches and into the role expected of an MP. The night following Grayson's maiden speech, the ILP hired Caxton Hall in Westminster to throw a double-victory celebration for Pete Curran (who had won Jarrow) and Grayson. MacDonald chaired the meeting and introduced the two men to the crowded hall, admitting that Grayson had 'stood alone' and offering his congratulations, for which there was loud applause. Curran had come in for some criticism amongst the socialists for not displaying his politics as forthrightly during the Jarrow campaign as Grayson had in the Colne Valley, and he now used the opportunity to play up his credentials. Grayson followed and, despite what had appeared to be an olive branch in MacDonald's introduction, he went on the attack. Grayson criticised the Labour Party's incremental approach to socialism. 'We are advised,' he said, 'to advance imperceptibly – to go at a snail's pace – to take one step at a time. Surely there are some young enough to take two steps or more at a time ... the system is rotten from top to bottom, with the result that the condition of the people is pretty much the same as it was a century ago.' He opened his arms to look as if he was embracing the room: 'If you want an example of third-class intellectual mediocrity,' he said, 'you should go to the House … Let the traditional precedents of the House perish!' Whether meaning to or not, Grayson failed to add a caveat that excluded those on the Labour benches from his attacks. His words were widely reported in the newspapers the following day and it was clear that the first major struggle for the direction – and the soul – of the fledgling Labour Party had begun.[26]

The following evening Grayson spoke at an outdoor mass meeting in Crofton Park, South London. He was advertised as 'the first Socialist' elected to Parliament, which no doubt further enraged Labour MPs. *The Times* reported his speech as follows:

[Grayson] said it was gratifying to him to find that the sentiments expressed by the voters in the northern constituency which returned him were re-echoed in the cheers of a London crowd. The greatest honour and privilege that he was able to boast of was that, at all events, in that musty assembly called the House of Commons there was now fearless Socialist criticism to be brought to bear on the measures discussed. He was aware that when he was returned, Consols [consolidated stock prices] dropped. If the return of one Socialist could cause a fall in Consols, what would the return of a hundred do? Some of the sapient editors said that if any more Graysons were returned to Parliament, capital would leave the country. Capital was not a thing that descended from the skies or came spontaneously from the earth. Capital was dependent on labour. He had gone to Parliament to represent what was called 'the mob', to represent the masses of the workers and drudgers whose life he had lived and whose suffering he knew. He stood for the absorption of great undertakings by the State, and against the brutal elimination of firms or individuals by the development of the gigantic trust … The Labour Party in the House of Commons, as a constitutional Parliamentary party, had done all that constitutionally could be done to move a sluggish Government in the direction of Socialistic reform. He believed that there never was a machine more exquisitely constructed to keep back reform than the British House of Commons. They had the Prime Minister [Campbell-Bannerman] impotently saying, 'I agree with your reforms; they are very urgent indeed; but I cannot find time to consider them.' That would not happen when Socialism found its feet ... Grayson added that he was against war and that he believed the modern meaning of Imperialism was commercialism and nothing else. He was in favour of the abolition of the House of Lords, although he felt in his heart that, if left alone, the moribund old Assembly would die of inanition.[27]

Again Grayson had attacked parliamentary democracy and given his audience a classic Marxist critique of capitalism – more and more capital would accumulate in fewer and fewer hands, thereby eliminating the small businessman and sole trader. Capitalism, said Grayson, would destroy itself by crippling the workers it depended on. It was time for the disinherited millions to take back what was rightfully theirs.[28] It seemed as if Grayson was distancing himself from the PLP a little further every day, from every platform. But distancing himself from the PLP would only increase his stature in the eyes of the malcontents, and he left London for Manchester that afternoon.

Grayson called into his rooms in Ancoats before heading to the Albion Hotel, on the corner of Oldham Street and Piccadilly, a few minutes' walk away. It was in Manchester's Labour movement that he had come to prominence, and so it was fitting that the Manchester and Salford ILP had organised a rousing victory celebration for him. To loud shouts and cheers, Grayson entered the reception and rose to address the packed meeting. He told his supporters that the traditions of Parliament had to be broken up by revolutionary and unconstitutional means because only an extreme optimist could expect any serious reform from Parliament as it currently existed. Grayson insisted that he would not become another tired and indifferent Parliamentarian and that his victory had proved that the workers would support a socialist candidate against any Liberal. There had been no watering down of socialist policy to secure his victory, he told them, and only socialist action could focus the House of Commons on the real lives of those outside its comfortable confines: the jobless, the homeless and the hungry.[29]

The following morning Grayson headed back to his constituency and addressed a rally in Huddersfield. Here, he received a telegram from Jim

Larkin who invited him to address striking dock workers in Belfast. Larkin had organised across sectarian divides to bring both Catholic and Protestant workers into a new trade union, the National Union of Dock Labourers (NUDL).[30] The Belfast dockers had been on strike since April after their demand for union recognition was rejected. The strike spread to men and women workers across other trades while the press prophesised revolution. The Royal Irish Constabulary failed to quell the disorder and many had mutinied when ordered to protect and escort strike-breakers. Belfast authorities had requested support from London and the British Army intervened. Tensions rose with the presence of 6,000 troops in the city and rumours spread of British soldiers fixing bayonets when confronted by striking workers. Furthermore, some of the soldiers were being used as blackleg labour – keeping the dock railway working and unloading ships. It had been barely a fortnight since Larkin was canvassing for Grayson in the Colne Valley. Now Grayson returned the favour.

Broken Bottles

From Liverpool, Grayson took a ship to Belfast where tensions between workers and the authorities continued to mount. Just over a fifth of Ireland's industrial workers were based in Belfast. Earlier in 1907, the Labour Party had held their annual conference there, and the work and organisation of the party had been credited with quelling sectarian division. Keir Hardie 'rejoiced ... that the old order of religious bigotry was passing away from Belfast, and a new era of Labour and Fraternity had begun'.[31] Nevertheless, their candidates were defeated in the municipal elections that followed, but when prices rose significantly while wages remained stagnant, militancy permeated Belfast's industrial workers. It was in these circumstances that Larkin won the hearts of the workers as they walked through the factory gates with his stirring, emotional oratory. Descriptions of Larkin's power and presence as a speaker bear uncanny resemblance to those of Grayson and it seems possible that Grayson had learnt much from watching Larkin's performances on the street corners of Liverpool. On the platform, Larkin was hot-tempered, eyes flashing with passion, as his arms helped enunciate the drama and poetry coming from his mouth. Jack Carney, who knew both Larkin and Grayson, said of the former:

> What impressed me most about Larkin was his ability to translate the feelings of his audience in sympathetic language. One felt that through some mysterious means, he had investigated your personal position and was taking the opportunity of saying for you what you could not say yourself. His language was not the language of tears but the language of hope ... He had an uncanny insight into the worker's mind.[32]

At Larkin's request, Grayson had lobbied Ramsay MacDonald prior to leaving for Belfast. Larkin, via Grayson, asked MacDonald to summon a joint meeting of the TUC and the Labour Party executive. He warned that the deployment of troops would lead to an explosion of religious hatred.

MacDonald eventually agreed to meet Larkin in person and Grayson would make the introduction. In the meantime, Grayson was set to address a massive rally of strikers and their supporters in Custom House Square. The weather had turned for the worse, however, and the rally had to be abandoned in favour of an indoor venue. Despite the short notice, a capacity crowd packed into St Mary's Hall to hear Grayson's speech. His oratory showed a marked change from previous days. He had clearly been influenced by the fraught and violent atmosphere in Belfast. The *Irish Times* reported:

> When he saw that the forces of the Crown had been sent to Belfast to turn their guns on the strikers, he realized that the strike had assumed the importance that all such strikes should assume. The employers might get their serried battalions, might put their pickets at every street corner, but the soldiers would be useless and helpless before an enlightened majority of the citizens. The military were either going to be withdrawn from Belfast or they were going to do their duty, and if it came to warfare he was satisfied that the people who had suffered would be able to render a good account of themselves.[33]

The Belfast workers, said Grayson, were not just fighting for themselves, but for workers in France, Germany, and across the British Empire. Religious divisions did not matter. Class mattered, and all the men there were working men, denied the full fruits of their labour. When a member of the audience shouted out 'what about the soldiers?', Grayson referred to an incident which had occurred during the French Revolution, when the soldiers, ordered to fire on the people, turned their guns on the employers instead. He continued:

> If they [the soldiers] had any self-respect they could not work for their shilling a day to be treated like marionettes and officered by spurious mobs who were called the aristocracy … Let your one fixed resolution be that you are going to fight the best fight you ever made in your lives.[34]

As Grayson finished his seditious haranguing of the crowd, violent cheers echoed throughout the hall. He and Larkin hurried out the back, into the pouring rain and jumped into a waiting car. Word had reached them that, despite the change of venue, there was still a crowd waiting for them outside in the rain. Their car pulled up at 9 pm to loud cheers from the drenched men. Grayson went back into the rain to address them:

> I am on my way now to the House of Commons to demand the withdrawal of the military from the streets of Belfast … We want you to remain firm behind, and to realise that, although we have left Belfast, we are coming back with the power of the whole British Labour movement behind us to win this battle.[35]

Grayson and Larkin left Belfast on the night boat to Liverpool and, from there, headed by train to London. Grayson appeared in a Commons debate on the Belfast dispute just a few hours later. Pete Curran MP (Jarrow, Labour) asked the Secretary of State for War, Richard Haldane, whether he was

> aware that a large number of military troops were turned out yesterday morning to parade the streets of Belfast on picket duty with fixed

bayonets and that each man was supplied with twenty rounds of ball cartridge; and whether he will use his influence to put a stop to this display of militancy, which only tends to render abortive all attempts to bring the dispute to a peaceful conclusion.[36]

Haldane responded, somewhat unconvincingly, that the troops were only there because the Belfast authorities had requested them to keep the peace and that the government had had little say in the matter. Grayson had seen for himself that the city was in a state of martial law and that erstwhile peaceful protesters and strikers were being provoked by the presence of thousands of British troops, issued with bayonets and ammunition. Furthermore, troops were making it impossible for strikers to talk to workers drafted in to do their jobs. Grayson rose to speak:

> May I ask the right hon. Gentleman whether it is interpreting the spirit or the letter of the Trades Disputes Act, to make it absolutely impossible for pickets to approach men who are acting as blacklegs?[37]

Augustine Birrell, the Chief Secretary for Ireland, answered that he was not 'responsible for the civil authorities at Belfast' and asked Grayson for facts. Grayson rose to respond, asking if Birrell was aware that the presence of the troops was spoiling any chance of effective arbitration between employers and strikers. Again, Birrell claimed that the government was powerless as to whether the army remained on the streets, which was a decision for the authorities in Belfast. Then Grayson posed his most pointed question to Haldane:

> Is it proper for the soldiers to fix their bayonets when there is no sign of a riot?[38]

Haldane responded that he would only consider the question if a 'concrete case' arose. He would not have long to wait.

Although widely covered in the Irish press, Grayson's Belfast speech had not been reported in any depth in England. It is hard to comprehend now that such a controversial and high-profile politician (as Grayson had become) could make such a violent speech that did not instantly become headline news. He had always tended to get carried away on the platform and was often led by the crowd, as this speech showed, but Grayson had not realised that with his national fame would also come greater scrutiny. This naive illusion would be shattered within a few days, when, back in Huddersfield on Sunday, 11 August, Grayson was delivering his run-of-the-mill condemnation of the House of Commons and those who played the parliamentary game.[39] To a crowd of 3,000 spectators he outlined the contents of his maiden parliamentary speech and told his supporters that if they had read of Lord Cromer's actions in Egypt, they would have voted for him to receive trial by jury, not a pension. By chance, a local journalist, Frank 'Pop' Wright, was on his way to file his copy for Monday's edition when he saw the socialist meeting in the square. He recognised Grayson's booming voice and duly made his way through the crowd to listen in. Grayson began to talk about the workers' struggle he had witnessed in Belfast, the battle for trade union rights and the deployment of troops. Wright made a shorthand note of part of Grayson's speech:

> They [the soldiers] are weary of doing nothing and they would like a little blood to shed and a few bones to split. They will do that before next week. If the people have not got shrapnel they have broken bottles.[40]

Grayson would soon regret his unguarded words and fall victim to the anti-socialist sensationalism that was sweeping the establishment and press. Wright, a trusted and experienced journalist, quickly realised he had a good line for the London papers, which it seemed would publish anything if it in any way undermined the cause of socialism. What made matters worse for Grayson was that a few hours after his speech in Huddersfield, violence erupted between strikers and the army in Belfast. The following morning, the national press reported Grayson's inflammatory lines, duly varnished for effect, followed by news of the violence in Belfast in the later editions. Soldiers had charged unarmed crowds with fixed bayonets but, far from dispersing, the crowds had ripped up paving stones and, armed with bottles, charged the army. The following day, after 40 cavalry charges against the protesters, the army opened fire. Despite the warnings that Labour MPs and Grayson had delivered in the Commons that the presence of the army was a provocation, the press and Liberal and Conservative MPs now painted Grayson as the man responsible for the violence.

In the House of Commons on Tuesday, 13 August, Sir Arthur Markham (Liberal MP for Mansfield) rose to address the Chief Secretary for Ireland, Birrell, on the matter:

> May I ask whether the right hon. Gentleman is aware of a speech made in Belfast by a member of this House (loud cheers) to the effect that the people in Belfast, if they had not swords and guns, had 'broken bottles' and whether he proposes to take any action against the hon. Member for incitement to riot leading to deplorable loss of life?[41]

Birrell had sought to move on to other business, but Markham continued to press for an answer. Birrell responded, but played down Grayson's influence in what was an embarrassing incident for the government:

> The matters which are engaging my attention and also the attention of the people in Belfast have not allowed me a moment to pay attention to the wild language that has been used, and to which no importance is attached in Belfast. The hon. Member paid a hasty visit to Belfast and disappeared very soon. (Laughter and cheers) Perhaps they are not likely to take any guidance from him.[42]

Birrell was right in some respects. The 'wild' language that Grayson had used in Huddersfield on the Sunday lunchtime could never have been reported in Belfast in time to have influenced the violence that evening. However, when we recall the words Grayson had spoken (but which were not widely reported in the English press) when he was in Belfast, then some responsibility for the violence must be attributed to him.

Grayson did put up a defence, although it struggled to stand up to scrutiny. He corrected the distortion that he had delivered his speech in Belfast a few hours before the violence. However, he also stated that he had delivered his speech in the evening, which he had not, and that the words he was quoted as saying were 'a gross distortion'. Grayson called into question Frank Wright's reporting which we know was accurate. It was the London newspapers that had altered his words, albeit only slightly, to make them appear more menacing. Wright defended himself against Grayson's accusations of misreporting, but many years later told Reg Groves that he felt his report had been used out of context to unfairly attack Grayson (and the socialist cause) and attribute blame to him for the clashes in Belfast.[43] Illustrating Wright's point, Colonel Kenyon-Slaney, Conservative MP for Newport, was reported as saying:

> The greatest danger was the Socialist development, which had a most unhappy and, he thought, a most degrading illustration last week. The typical Socialist returned for a division of Yorkshire had no sooner found his tongue than he used it to encourage misguided strikers in Belfast to assault the military and the police. He wondered what the man's conscience told him today when a number of people were lying dead and others were injured through following his advice. That was typical of Socialism, a policy of the reversal of the doctrine of law and order and of inflaming the passion and cupidity of man.[44]

Kenyon-Slaney's words were used to embelish the anti-socialist narrative that so annoyed Wright. For Grayson, it was just the beginning of a press campaign that would be waged against him until the outbreak of war in 1914. The 'broken bottles' incident would follow him around for years and probably inspired one of his favourite sayings: 'Never explain: your friends don't need it and your enemies won't believe it.'[45] In fact his friends were not as easily forgiving as he presumed. Robert Blatchford was one of Grayson's highest profile supporters but even he was angry and disappointed. 'You know, Win, Victor lied', Blatchford told his daughter Winifred of Grayson's explanation of the incident. When he was absent from the Commons in the days immediately following the unrest in Belfast, he further disappointed those closest to him politically. But despite this, Blatchford defended Grayson in the *Clarion*:

Grayson may or may not be wise. He may or may not be clever. But he is young, and he is earnest. Grayson made a rash speech about bottles. Oh, Victor, a foolish speech, a blunder. But he was angry, and he loves the people. Broken bottles! Oh, mad, foolish Grayson. But Grayson loves us … He believes in us; he trusts us; and we will trust him. Let him stumble, and blunder, and get hot, and go wild; but he loves the people and will be true to them. When you see Grayson speaking to the Colne Valley men and women you understand. And *they* understand.[46]

The 'broken bottles' saga shook Grayson and, together with his always hectic speaking schedule, his health would deteriorate towards the end of 1907. The mental and physical strain on the young man must have been immense. Nevertheless, the Belfast Disputes debate in the Commons showed him actively engaging with parliamentary procedure and speaking in unison with Labour MPs. He recovered in time for the new parliamentary session beginning in January 1908. This year would see him at his most effective in Parliament and witness an incident which would make Grayson a legend, but at the same time destroy any hope of him joining the ranks of the PLP.

5

Member for the Unemployed

Dare to be a Grayson!

Cries from a Liverpool crowd towards
Philip Snowden and Katherine Glasier
Laurence Thompson[1]

I am sorry to see Grayson on the front page this week. His admission in the circle of contributors seems to mark the complete separation of the [Labour] Leader [newspaper] from its founding traditions, and makes me feel as if I never want to see you or myself in its pages again.

Bruce Glasier to his wife, Katherine, 10 September 1909[2]

Unemployment had left a deep scar on the consciousness of Victor Grayson. He grew up in a household where his father struggled to hold down a job and the children were sent out to work to make ends meet. He had grown up amongst ragged and barefoot children on the streets of Liverpool and, when in Manchester, had lived in one of its poorest and dirtiest districts. He had witnessed first-hand the lives of the wretched and vowed that the evil of worklessness should be banished from Britain. His political coming-of-age was leading the Manchester unemployed in their successful direct action in 1905 and now, three years later, he would take his fight to Parliament.

The 1908 session started well for Grayson and, despite his detractors, he seemed to be settling into the routine of parliamentary business and procedure. In February he asked two questions. He enquired of the President of the Board of Education

whether he is aware that the Willesden Education committee, the London County Council Education Committee, and other education committees forbid the use of rate-paying buildings to Socialists for the purpose of Socialist Sunday Schools; and, if so, whether he is prepared to take steps to amend the Code upon which this restriction is based.[3]

The answer came that the Board of Education had 'no jurisdiction either to authorize or to prohibit the restriction referred to'.[4] The second question came three days later and was directed to the Postmaster-General:

in view of the fact that over 20,000 sub-postmasters in shops receive as remuneration only £20 to £40 a year for a working day of twelve hours, without a meal hour, and that many of them are compelled out of this sum to pay for assistance if they desire to absent themselves for a single evening, whether he will take steps, without at present reopening the general question of postal employees' grievances, to make some improvement in the cases cited.[5]

The response was rather feeble: that the death rate among postal employees was slightly higher in Germany than in the United Kingdom. Although the questions asked may seem ineffectual, the fact that Grayson raised these issues meant they would at least be discussed and reported on, when otherwise they might not have seen the light of day.

On 13 March 1908, Grayson gave probably his most effective parliamentary performance, speaking on the Unemployed Workmen Bill. In 1905 he had been one of the leaders of the Manchester unemployed who, with their demonstrations and activism, had prompted a Conservative government into action. Now the Liberal Party was in government. Back in 1905, the future President of the Board of Trade, David Lloyd George, had called the government's measures 'a motor car without petrol'. Now, Grayson asked, in the third session of Parliament under a Liberal government, where was the petrol? He continued his attack upon the inaction of the Liberals and the system in which they lived:

[Grayson] noticed consternation when the responsibilities of the Government were pointed out to [the Liberal benches]. When they accepted office they accepted responsibility for every social problem, and he confronted them with this problem of unemployment. He had noticed an irresistible tendency on the part of hon. Members opposite to show a distaste for the hateful realism of this question of unemployment. Why upset the beautiful picture that hon. Members had built up for themselves? Why upset their castles of illusions that allowed them to go through life without bothering about these questions? Why bring into the purview of the House of Commons the haggard sight of the working man whom they were meeting every day? Not many yards from the House, hon. Members were confronted every night with a problem that made them feel ashamed, not only of having to be jointly responsible for a state of mismanagement such as that, but of the professed Christianity of their nation.[6]

In these words Grayson summed up his political outlook and the shift he had made from religion to socialism. Those in charge lived in a grand illusion in which the harsh reality of life for working people barely figured and, what made it worse, these same people professed to be upholders of the Christian faith. The report of Grayson's speech continued:

He did not believe that this Bill would solve the problem of unemployment ... Let them imagine a state of society in which every man willing to work had work to do. Let them imagine that every employer was looking for workmen, instead of hordes of workmen looking for employers. What would be the situation? If the workers were organized in strong trade unions – and that was an increasing tendency – they would demand in return for their labour what they conceived to be the product of their labour.[7]

The enemy of the unemployed was the capitalist system itself. If industry were held in public ownership and the race to the bottom of competition were no more, then all would have work. When Liberal and Tory MPs suggested that Grayson's plan would have skilled men digging holes and planting trees, Grayson retorted:

He had watched a man returning every Friday night, with his wages in his pocket, to a little slum hovel, with his wife with her apron loaded with provisions for the week. The children had been comparatively happy in their rags, and everything had been barely comfortable – an average type of working class prosperity. He had looked at him sometimes and felt that even he had got his minimum of comfort out of the life he led. But some morning the word went round that Mr. So-and-so had stopped. They could hardly realise the tragedy that charged those words. He had watched gradually all the disposable articles of furniture going to the pawnshop and to the broker; he had seen those children gradually growing more and more ragged, and the woman more and more haggard, until the thing had ended in a loathsome tragedy, when the wife had finished in the infirmary and the man gone on tramp.[8]

It was not only from the heart that Grayson was speaking but also from experience. He had seen so much of this first-hand in Liverpool and Manchester:

In the last fifty years wealth had increased by miraculous leaps and bounds, and while it was endeavoured to be shown that the increased wealth of the country was due to free trade, yet this problem remained grimly ever present through all our prosperity. It was not that they could not find work for every one; it was that they were trying an impossible task; they were trying to lift themselves up by their boot laces; they were trying to solve the unemployed problem while leaving vested interests alone; they were trying to find work for workers without interfering with the interests of those who had rents and possession of wealth. It would never be done, and he did not hope that this House would do it as at present composed. It would only be done when the means of production, distribution, and exchange, without access to which they could not live, were in the hands of the people and not in the hands of a small clique. It might seem like a dream from afar, but if the Government persisted in their present method of flouting serious social problems, if they continued their dispiriting criticism of serious measures, which might have faults but which contained vital principles, then Socialism would not be so much a dream as it seemed at the present moment, and the ineptitude and futility of the present Government would be realised.[9]

Grayson had eloquently delivered a classic argument for socialism. Furthermore, despite his struggles with the Labour Party, that body would a decade later adopt in Clause IV of its constitution something that read very much like Grayson's speech:

To secure for the workers by hand or by brain the full fruits of their industry and the most equitable distribution thereof that may be possible upon the basis of the common ownership of the means of production, distribution and exchange, and the best obtainable system of popular administration and control of each industry or service.[10]

The Unemployed Bill was defeated, but not as overwhelmingly as the Labour benches had expected. A total of 116 MPs voted for 'the most nakedly Socialistic measure ever submitted to the British Legislature' and this gave reasons for great cheering on the Labour benches.[11] Members knew their arguments were gaining ground, even in such a hostile environment as the House of Commons. Grayson had played a central role in the debate and had argued in unison with Labour and trade union MPs. The press, nevertheless, played down Grayson's contribution, with the *London Evening Standard* reporting that he had merely 'thundered generalities' in the debate.[12] On a more positive note, there was renewed hope amongst some Labour MPs that he would now settle down to life in the House.

This sense of unity would, however, not last. The very real divisions in Britain's fragmented socialist movement were never far from the surface. The ILP's 1908 conference was held in Huddersfield on 18–21 April, in the very heart of Grayson country, and many hoped that the whole Grayson saga could be put behind them. But far from healing wounds, the 1908 conference was dominated by a feeling of resentment and distrust on the part of more radical elements, and those who believed in fair play, towards the NAC and leading members of the ILP. The selection debacle of the previous year was pored over in detail. Hardie defended the party's failure to endorse Grayson's candidature:

> Mr Grayson's work in the movement, valuable as it has been, was a matter of very few years, and that there were men like Mr Joseph Burgess, to mention only one, who had given twenty years at least to the service of the movement. There was neither anger nor bias against Mr Grayson, but simply a desire that men who had grown grey in the movement should not feel that they were put aside to make room for younger men.[13]

Hardie's mention of Burgess was somewhat strange. He had, until recently, been a Glasgow City Councillor and, before that, been involved in Leicester, but had not been active in the north of England for nearly two decades. Hardie's defence betrays a naivety about electoral politics and a certain contempt for the wishes of local parties. Grayson had won against the odds due to a mixture of his striking speaking ability, his youth and his deep theological knowledge. With this combination he captured the hearts of the electorate. To rely solely on old 'men who had grown grey in the movement' would leave the party fielding some uninspiring candidates in the strange belief that age and bureaucratic political experience were as attractive to voters as were Grayson's very real qualities. Hardie's suggestion that the selection process should be treated as a sort of long-service award to veterans of the movement seemed to encapsulate the very worst aspects of the trade union influence that angered Grayson and many socialists so much. Hardie's statement also highlighted the generational gap within the Labour alliance. The old men had the committee and organisational experience, but lacked the level of education enjoyed by the younger men in the movement. The older members were more likely to urge caution and favoured a pact with the Liberals, whereas the younger men, such as Grayson, thought this would betray the movement's principles.

The Colne Valley delegate, Sam Eastwood, argued that Grayson's selection had been entirely proper. Eastwood also claimed, correctly as we now know, that the real reason for the NAC's actions had been its desire for a candidate other than Grayson. Christopher Douthwaite, another product of Manchester's ILP who had campaigned in Grayson's election, rose to launch a scathing attack on the 'big four' leaders of the ILP – Hardie, Glasier, MacDonald and Snowden – alleging that they had conspired to keep Grayson out. Hardie's speech lent credence to this view. Manchester Central ILP submitted a resolution to the NAC 'regretting both its delay in endorsing Grayson's candidature, and its failure to reply to charges of dissuading prominent party members from assisting Grayson'.[14] Jim Larkin, representing the Irish branches of the ILP, attacked the platform: 'If you are socialists, say so; but if you are only Labour people get into the Labour Party.' His words again highlighted the fragile nature of the Labour alliance and the fact that socialists of the ILP felt their ideological purity was being sacrificed in the interests of establishing a non-doctrinal Labour Party. Larkin caused uproar with his final words, 'Socialists for Grayson, the remainder for yourselves.'[15]

Despite these heated scenes, something approaching a rapprochement had been achieved by the end of the conference. Delegates voted overwhelmingly that Grayson should act as a Labour MP and take the PLP whip, but not be required to sign the constitution of the Labour Party nor be paid from its funds. It seemed as if Grayson might be coming on board. Initially, however, he rejected this olive branch as he sensed a manoeuvre to make him sign up to the constitution by the back door:

> I cannot sign the constitution of the Labour Party under any circumstances. I esteem it a pearl of great price that we should have independent socialism represented in the House of Commons, instructed by the conference. I cannot accept any other condition.[16]

Keir Hardie came to the rescue. Labour's founding father was respected as a near-saint by most party members and workers. He told Grayson that there was no attempt to deceive him and that under the proposal he would be able to attend Party meetings in the House of Commons, take the Party Whip, and continue to have his salary paid by the ILP. To the relief of all involved, Grayson accepted.

Whilst the conference was still ongoing, outside there were growing fears that the socialists were continuing to gain ground at Liberal expense and that Grayson's presence on the fringes of the PLP threatened to out-manoeuvre the more radical elements of the Liberal Party. Winston Churchill, then seen as the young star of radical liberalism, was concerned that the Labour movement, which had been in informal partnership with the Liberal Party at the time of the general election, contained a strand of extremism that did not sit comfortably with the Christian values of the early socialists. He had won the Manchester North-West division in the great Liberal landslide of 1906 but needed to fight the seat again when he was appointed President of the Board of Trade, as required by the Ministers of the Crown Act. At Cheetham, Manchester, he told a crowd:

> But there is one great difference between the Socialists of the Christian era and those of which Mr. Grayson is the apostle. The Socialism of the Christian era was based on the idea that 'all mine is yours', but the Socialism of Mr Grayson is based on the idea that 'all yours is mine'. And I go so far as to say that no movement will ever achieve any real advantage for the mass of the people that is based upon so much spite and jealousy as is the present Socialist movement in the hands of its extreme men.[17]

Churchill's attack on Grayson demonstrates the power and popularity of the young socialist MP in the popular mindset. It is also noteworthy because there was no Labour candidate standing against Churchill in the by-election and his main rival was the Conservative, William Joynson-Hicks, whom he had defeated in 1906. However, Dan Irving was standing as an SDF candidate and Grayson made several visits to the constituency in the run-up to polling day. The *Sheffield Evening Telegraph* reported that 'The advent of Victor Grayson has stimulated the Socialist faction to renewed activity and the young member for Colne Valley is drawing great crowds.'[18] Grayson's support of the SDF candidate highlighted his independence from the PLP, which would not condone his actions, but the ILP membership was overwhelmingly supportive. On the final night of the ILP conference, MacDonald and Hardie addressed a meeting where a resolution was passed sending best wishes to Ben Turner, the ILP candidate at the Dewsbury by-election. A shout came from the floor, 'and Dan

Irving!' and further cries went up about both men being socialists. Only two hands were not raised in support of Irving, and they were not those of MacDonald or Hardie, but of Philip and Ethel Snowden.[19] Some now argued that the ILP was a lost cause for socialism and that Grayson should be the standard-bearer for a new party of the left.

Suspended from the Commons – a Prelude

On 27 September 1908, the Manchester Clarion Scouts organised a demonstration in the city to inaugurate their 'Anti-Poverty Crusade'. The march concluded at the Free Trade Hall with Robert Blatchford again in the chair. Grayson was the headline speaker along with several others, including Margaret Bondfield, then organising secretary for the Women's Labour League, which she had helped to found two years previously. Bondfield was also chair of the Adult Suffrage Society and later became the country's first ever female cabinet minister in Ramsay MacDonald's 1929–31 Labour government. Back in 1908, however, Bondfield was very much in sympathy with Grayson's campaign. The programme for the event included the manifesto for the 'crusade'. Addressed to 'Citizens', the declaration called on Britons to consider the uncomfortable truth about their country:

> His is the richest nation in the whole world. Britain's trade is ever expanding. Britain's wealth surpasses anything in the way of national accumulation ever recorded. Yet one man in every alternate three or four of our population is miserably poor during life, and is property-less at death. Over 30% of our Workers admittedly abide in black, bitter poverty.

'Poverty,' the manifesto stated, 'has always existed', but the acute levels of poverty in Edwardian Britain were due to 'Industrial Capitalism', which, despite technological and scientific advances, was responsible for a 'hideous panorama of Sweating, Overcrowding, Unemployment, and Starvation'. Poverty was not cheap and the poor had to be kept, however inadequately, by someone. The manifesto warned trade unionists that it was not blackleg labour that they should fear, but the masses of unemployed labour that could be used by unscrupulous employers to lower their wages. The only solution was for all legislation considered in Parliament to deal immediately with the abolition of poverty:

> During the past twelve months, though the distress in this country has been phenomenal and many Acts of Parliament have been passed, **not one of them deals with Poverty from its standpoint as a National Question,** and a Winter of unexampled hardship is close at hand. This matter admits of no further delay.[20]

This is the crucial part of the manifesto when considering what was to come next. Grayson's actions to disrupt the Licensing Bill and attack the lack of action in Parliament to alleviate poverty were surely foreshadowed when he helped launch this campaign in September. It expressly attacks Parliament for passing Acts which had no impact on poverty in Britain. This is definitive evidence that Grayson's subsequent demonstration in Parliament was not the spontaneous action of a drunk, or a brainless youth, which is what his detractors then and since have been quick to suggest. This was the considered action of a politician trying to build a national campaign against poverty and unemployment. The final passage of the manifesto read:

> **Britons!** Let your slumbering consciences awake. You are summoned to obey the call of duty. You must join the crusade against the most hideous scourge of mankind. **WAR IS DECLARED** against Poverty.

And what better place to awaken the British people to the issue of poverty and to declare war against it, than in the very heart of British democracy, and of the British Empire, the House of Commons?

Suspended from the Commons

After the summer recess, the Commons returned for the autumn session in October 1908. In anticipation of the resumption of parliamentary activity,

Grayson had been asked by the editor of *The New Age: A Weekly Review of Politics, Literature, and Art*, to contribute an article. It was incendiary. In it, Grayson attacked Parliament as an institution and also the notion that it was a means of achieving societal change. In *The Coming Session*, Grayson outlined his current thinking:

> The pathetic reason alleged for the holding of an autumn Session is an over-crowded legislative programme. Over-crowded with what, forsooth? Is there in all the dreary catalogue of projected reforms anything to indicate that the country is in a state of tragic crisis? Does it not rather suggest an elaborate fuss to dazzle plebian eyes?

Grayson went further, identifying the coming Licensing Bill as a particular waste of parliamentary time:

> For many days a minimum of members will sit, bored to death through the weary hours, laboriously beating out obscure details of the Licensing Bill ... [with] no less than 54 pages of Amendments, each of which will elicit volumes of oratory and recrimination from the respective interests involved ... Meanwhile the country writhes and groans under its terrible incubus of poverty and unemployment. Ragged, unfed multitudes of unemployed, goaded to desperation by insistent squalor, break into futile rebellion and are bludgeoned into submission by the disciplined hirelings of the powers that be.

He then switched his fire to his fellow Members of Parliament:

> That dignified assembly is composed of 670 members – mostly capitalists ... Their good-humoured complacent apathy is hardly their fault. They have never lived near enough to the heart of humanity to feel its beat. They have never tramped the hard pavement with bad boots – unwanted by civilization ... What do they know, what can they know of the haunting spectre that tracks every step of the luckless worker?

VICTOR GRAYSON.

1. A young Victor Grayson before his election to Parliament holding a copy of the Clarion under his arm. As with many of his generation, Grayson learnt much of his socialism from Robert Blatchford's newspaper. (Author's collection)

COLNE VALLEY

PARLIAMENTARY

BYE-ELECTION, 1907.

To the ELECTORS.

▲▲▲▲▲▲▲▲

GENTLEMEN,

In consequence of the promotion of your Parliamentary Member to the House of Lords, I am enabled to offer myself as Labour and Socialist Candidate for your support. This I do at the unanimous request of the Colne Valley Labour League, which is affiliated to the National Independent Labour Party.

My attitude towards political and social problems is not unknown to you, as I have been privileged for some time to appear before you in advocacy of my views. I have had unique opportunities of studying social problems, both theoretically and practically, and as a Socialist, my life will be spent in hastening the time when the land and other means of production will be the property of the whole people, and not of a privileged class.

Far too long you have been represented in Parliament by the rich classes—such as brewers, landlords, lawyers, employers, financiers, and their numerous hangers-on. Hence the rich have become richer, and the poor poorer. Pauperism has increased, many thousands of little children have been compelled to trudge to school with hungry bellies ; old age has been neglected ; productive land has gone to waste ; the rural districts have been depopulated, unemployment has remained grimly with us, and machinery in our workshops and factories has been sped up to grind profits more quickly for the parasitic classes.

A significant change in public opinion was made manifest at the last General Election, and Labour was permitted to get its foot into the House of Commons. The result is now before your eyes. Both great parties have vied with each other to ingratiate the Labour Group, and real industrial reforms have been dragged from the reluctant grasp of the Government. Should you put your trust in me, I shall add one more emphatic voice to the cry for a fuller and freer life for all.

The Right to Work.

I deem it a stinging disgrace to a community professing to be civilised and Christian, that there is always a great number of men and women, able and willing to work, but denied this elementary human right by a cruel and unjust system. There has not hitherto been any really serious attempt to grapple in a practical manner with this problem. On the accession of the Liberal Government to power, great hopes were raised that at last something would be done to effectually abolish the curse of unemployment. But the bubble of promise has burst and we are left with the problem of unemployment as grim as ever. How long will it take us to realise that there can be no real attempt at a solution while legislation is left in the hands of interested capitalists.

Old Age Pensions.

There are in England and Wales **1,600,000** persons over 65 years of age. Some **500,000** of these are every year in such poverty that they have to receive poor-law relief—thus losing their right to vote. But this number, as was pointed out by the Royal Commission on Aged Poor (1893-95) "does not by any means represent the number who were continually destitute." Old Age Pensions, as you know, are already given by the State to those who have all their lives drawn huge salaries. At the present time, two ex-speakers, six ex-ministers and seven military men draw nearly £45,000 a year between them in pensions. Yet the present Government "cannot

2. Victor Grayson's Colne Valley by-election address. At the time its policies were deemed dangerous and revolutionary. Many were implemented in the century afterwards. (Author's collection)

Colne Valley Election. Declaration of the Poll, July 19th, 1907.

3. Just a section of the huge crowd waiting to hear the result from the by-election count. The victorious Grayson left to make his victory speech outside the Devonshire Arms, just around the corner. (Author's collection)

4. The Colne Valley Labour League after the by-election victory in 1907. Back Row, 4th from left is A. Pickles, the Colne Valley organiser. Front Row from left to right, F.C. Green, K. Brierley, Rev. F.R. Swan, Sam Eastwood, J. Swallow, Victor Grayson MP, Robert Blatchford, Edgar Whiteley (election agent), Ernest Marklew, Rev. W.B. Graham, Councillor T.E. Moorhouse.

5. Artist's impression of Grayson's protest which saw him suspended from the House of Commons. (*Daily Sketch*, 16 October 1908)

6. When he could find no audience in the House of Commons, Grayson toured the country preaching 'Socialist Unity'. Here he is speaking from a Clarion van in Newcastle in 1909. (Topical Press Agency/Stringer via Getty Images)

THE NEW KING.

PRINCE HENRY (Victor Grayson): Lo, here it sits!

7. For a brief moment it looked as if Grayson may capture the leadership of the ILP. In this cartoon, Grayson places the Labour crown on his head as MacDonald, Glasier, Snowden and Hardie exit the stage. Notice the broken bottle next to Grayson's sword. (*Manchester Evening News*, 14 April 1908)

8. Grayson with admirers in 1909. He was always well dressed, whatever the occasion. Some questioned his socialist beliefs as a result. But Grayson grew up in poverty and did not see why the working class should not enjoy the comforts of the rich. (Topical Press Agency/Stringer via Getty Images)

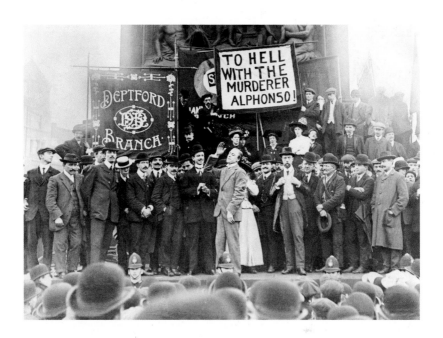

9. Grayson giving a fiery speech at the London demonstration against the execution of Spanish educationist, Ferrer. After it, he left the podium to head the march to the Spanish Embassy which ended in violence. (Mirrorpix/Contributor via Getty Images)

10. No Right to Work – No Right to Live. A rare surviving election leaflet from Grayson's January 1910 General Election campaign in Colne Valley.

11. Grayson speaking from a Clarion van at the opening of his last-minute campaign in Kennington during the freezing December 1910 General Election. (ullstein bild Dtl./Contributor via Getty Images)

12. The card which Grayson's small but dedicated band of supporters handed to voters on polling day. (Working Class Movement Library)

MR VICTOR GRAYSON.

13. The classic portrait of Victor Grayson. (Author's collection)

With fraternal greetings,
Ruth Grayson.

COPYRIGHT

14. The actress, Ruth Grayson, adopting her husband's standard salutation 'thine fraternally'. (Reg Groves archives, Modern Records Centre, University of Warwick (MSS.172/VG/20))

15. Grayson posing in his full ANZAC uniform in 1917, before the Battle of Passchendaele. (Imperial War Museum)

16. The mysterious envelope from 1930 given to Derek Forewood in the early 1960s by friends of Grayson who believed it held the answer to Grayson's disappearance. Was it just an advertising stunt or was there more to it? (Author's collection)

He ended with a call to arms for each member to act according to his conscience and not out of deference to tradition:

> An impatient public opinion is at last loudly clamouring for immediate attention to the question of unemployment ... I expect very little, I confess, in the direction of sincere attempt from the present House of Commons. Its whole procedure is permeated with an atmosphere of childish theatricality. One yearns for a strong north wind of realism to sweep through the musty Chamber, or that some god would touch their myopic visions with a sense of real perspective ... we appeal to the people in a state of crisis ... [w]e have the measure; we need the men. And given sufficient of the proper quality, we shall make rapid history in the next three months.[21]

Labour historians have tended to suggest that what Grayson did next in Parliament represented the spontaneous action of a drunken man. That is certainly what his enemies from both within and without the Labour movement argued at the time. It suited their view of Grayson as a brainless tub-thumper, an image which, unfortunately, has been shared by those writing history ever since. But his *New Age* article – launching the 'Anti-Poverty Crusade' – suggests a significant degree of premeditation and planning. Furthermore, he had shared his plan to raise the issue of unemployment in the House with others. Will Thorne, founding father of what is now the GMB trade union, remembered that Grayson 'told me that he was determined to get Parliament to deal with the urgent question of unemployment. "If they don't," he said, "I'm going to cause trouble, even if it means me getting thrown out."'[22]

On Thursday, 15 October, Grayson silently entered the Commons chamber while questions were being asked and sat on the Labour benches, with a green Tyrolean hat pulled down over his forehead, listening intently. He was thinking about his next move and whether this was the right moment to launch his crusade. As the questions session concluded, Grayson sprang to his feet: 'I rise to move that this House do immediately adjourn to consider a matter of urgent public importance. I refer to the question of the unemployed.' The Speaker advised Grayson that it was not possible to adjourn as the Licensing Bill was the next item on the order of business. 'In the circumstances I feel – the crisis of unemployment is so great, when people are starving at this moment in the streets – that we must ignore those rules.' The House, responded the Speaker, was bound by the restrictions it had placed upon itself. 'Then I must personally refuse to be bound by such rules,' insisted Grayson. 'It is all very well for you well-fed men to shout "Sit down", but I will not, and I decline to be a party to the Licensing Bill taking up the attention of the House while the people are demanding human legislation.' More toing and froing followed before the Speaker asked Grayson to withdraw from the House, which he only consented to do if the 'machinery of force' was used to move him. Grayson fired two parting shots, one at the House and one at Labour MPs:

> I am willing to leave the House, because I feel degraded in a company that will not consider the unemployed. I believe that I have the unemployed mandate behind me asking for legislation from the House at this moment. [Cries of 'Withdraw' and 'Order'.] Oh yes, you well-fed human beings can say 'Order', but the unemployed have been goaded into disorder. I refuse absolutely to be bullied into silence. [The Speaker then ordered Grayson's removal by the Sergeant-at-Arms.] I leave the House with pleasure. You are traitors to your class. You will not stand up for your class. You traitors.[23]

Grayson was escorted from Parliament by the Sergeant-at-Arms, Sir David Erskine. The latter was the epitome of the British establishment: a tall, dark, Harrow-educated, ex-Guardsmen who had fought in the Crimea. He tapped Grayson on the shoulder and the MP calmly left the chamber 'like a nephew accompanying a benevolent uncle'.[24] Later that evening, Grayson told some of his Labour colleagues that he intended to continue his crusade the following day. Despite this, none later admitted to prior knowledge that Grayson would again make a scene. As he recalled shortly afterwards, 'Not only were they forewarned of my intention – but ... Socialist Labour members indulged in elephantine wit on the possibilities of the morrow.'[25]

The following day, Grayson was true to his word and, although he had been absent from the votes earlier in the day, he quietly re-entered the chamber and took a seat. The Licensing Bill was being debated and, after the Chairman had announced the result of the division, Grayson sprang up from his seat:

> Mr Chairman, before you proceed with the next Amendment to the clause, I wish to call the attention of the House to the fact that, as I stated yesterday, there are thousands of people dying in the streets while you are trifling with this Bill [Cries of 'Order'.] I shall not keep order. I am alone in this House, but I am going to fight.

After the Chairman twice attempted to bring Grayson to order, the latter continued to insist, 'I will not keep order. I am alone in this House, but I have a large mandate behind me, and I refuse to allow the House to proceed while I am in it.' The Liberal MP Horatio Bottomley stood up, crossed the floor of the House and made his way to a still animated Grayson. Despite Bottomley's attempts to calm the situation, Grayson vigorously shook his head in response and Bottomley returned to his seat. The confrontation with the Speaker continued while MPs rounded on Grayson for disrupting the proceedings of the House. Herbert Asquith put forward a motion 'That Mr Grayson be suspended from the service of the House' which was passed by those present. Grayson responded:

> I leave the House, as I said yesterday, with pleasure, because I feel that no man – [Loud cries of 'Order'] – can stay in this House another moment. [Grayson is told that he is not entitled to address the House.] Well, then, I leave the House, as I said before, feeling that I have gained in dignity by leaving this institution, and I hope that – [Grayson's final words were drowned out by loud cries and he made his way out of the chamber before turning around to deliver one final sentence] This House is a House of murderers![26]

In that moment Grayson destroyed any hope of a reconciliation between the PLP and himself. He had burnt his bridges in the most dramatic style. It is interesting to note, however, that those Labour MPs aware that Grayson's protest was going to take place did not try to dissuade him. If anything, in fact, they almost encouraged him. Fred Jowett, who had worked to cool tensions at the ILP conference the previous April in the hope of bringing Grayson on board, wrote in the *Clarion* that members were aware that Grayson was going to create such a scene. Keir Hardie, on the other hand, wrote in the *Labour Leader* that Grayson had not even suggested the idea of such a protest. Either way, Labour MPs were later found wanting, when Grayson was accused of an act of recklessness, inspired purely by alcohol.

Though he had ended any possible future as a Labour MP, he had made himself a hero outside Parliament and some of the biggest names in the wider movement now began to coalesce around Grayson. The *Clarion* editor, Robert Blatchford, wrote of the incident:

Victor Grayson's action in the House on Thursday and Friday last ought not be mistaken for a mere personal protest.

Grayson did not speak for himself alone, nor for the unemployed, solely: he voiced the commonsense and humanity of millions of British citizens. The conduct of the government in shelving a question so urgent and tragical as the problem of Unemployment, and sitting down to discuss more than fifty pages of amendments to the Licensing Bill, constituted an insult to the intelligence and right feeling of the nation. Parliament must be taught that the misery of millions of the people cannot be treated with cynical indifference, nor evaded by contempt-ible subterfuge.

Grayson's protest, let us hope, is the first word of a much-needed lesson. If the Parliamentary machinery is too obsolete and clumsy to deal with any emergency, it is time for that machinery to be thrown on the scrap heap, and replaced by something more efficient and human.

For twenty years, to my knowledge, the unemployed poor have been with us. No real help has been given to them by the Liberals or the Tories. To-day in their despair they are asked to wait – to wait while the House discusses the Licensing Bill. Victor Grayson protests, and I, for one, thank him for protesting.[27]

The playwright and Fabian socialist, George Bernard Shaw, wrote a lengthy piece in praise of Grayson's actions, setting them in the context of other attempts to awaken the establishment, and not just in Britain, to the seemingly forgotten problems of poverty and unemployment. Shaw wrote that he thought it a pity that

the French governments of the eighteenth century would not allow their attention to be diverted from Marie Antoinette's gambling debts to the poverty of the common people by the reasonings of Turgot, Montesquieu, Condorcet, Voltaire, Rousseau, and the Encyclopaedists, they forgot them at once when the Bastille was pulled down and the country houses burnt about their ears.

Shaw was clear that the last thing he wanted to see in Britain was unruly and violent mobs taking to the streets, but he conceded that he and the Fabian Society had spent 20 years 'proposing urgently needed measures in a strictly constitutional way', but with the result that 'more attention is paid to mobs that break windows and demand Mansion House Funds than to us'. It was a damning indictment of Britain's ruling class that they ignored every opportunity to democratically enact provisions for the country's poor and unemployed and only paid attention when their own private property and wealth were threatened by extra-parliamentary rioting. 'In short,' Shaw continued,

our lords and masters (politely called the governing classes because, though they can't govern, they won't let anyone else govern) are continuously inciting the masses and their leaders to violence and disorder by constituting themselves a permanent object lesson in the uselessness of everything else ... Carlyle and Ruskin and Dickens appealed to their consciences with the pens of angels, and got nothing from them but 'sympathetic interest,' invitations to dinner, and offers of knighthoods.

In such an environment as Parliament, Shaw believed, the figures of the Conservative and Liberal establishment were hoping Grayson was 'too much of a gentleman' to make any sort of protest and that representatives

of Labour 'can be depended on to behave … as genteelly in the face of starvation as the flower of Eton and Oxford'. If Grayson's plea was not listened
to, then Shaw believed that Britain was on the brink of serious disorder
in the streets. 'One cannot but wonder gloomily whether Mr. Grayson's
action will be sufficient, or whether the unemployed problem will be
ignored until an English city is burnt, and half the inhabitants stoned and
beaten to upset order and the other half shot and sabred to restore it.' Shaw
ended his piece by asking what the point was of having Labour MPs when
they 'didn't stand by Mr Grayson, even to the point of taking part in his
suspension', just as the Conservative and Liberal MPs had.[28]

Grayson received thousands of letters and telegrams in support of his
action from across the country. Some were reported in the *Clarion*:

> Man, you are splendid. Actions like yours must awake hundreds of us
> who have been sleeping. W.S. (Wimbledon)
>
> I have the honour to take off my hat to you as the only man in the
> House of Commons who has the courage of his convictions. R.D.
> (Cheltenham)
>
> You have not exaggerated the woes and wants of the starving. I am
> a bailiff with a large practice in this city. My God, sir, the degrada-
> tion, filth, and squalor in which the poor exist in this mighty metropolis
> of the north would make any one worthy of being called a man, sick.
> Men, women, and children absolutely hungered, and then, the shame
> of it, all must be evicted from the awful hells where they live. This I do
> from sheer necessity. You need not be ashamed. Shame and brazen-faced
> effrontery is with the adventurer and professional politician. Fight on,
> the country can be aroused by a few men like yourself. God speed you.
> – Yours respectfully, W.L. (Newcastle-on-Tyne)

Many trade unions and socialist groups passed motions in support of
Grayson's staged scene in Parliament and sent congratulatory messages,
including the Amalgamated Society of Engineers, the Amalgamated
Society of Carpenters and Joiners, the National Union of Gasworkers and
General Labourers, the Postmen's Federation, the Executive Council of

the Social Democratic Party and individual branches of the ILP, Fabian Society and Clarion Clubs.

The editorial in the following week's *New Age* neatly sums up the position in which Grayson now found himself:

> The single official Socialist in the House of Commons has adopted the only course open to him. For good or for ill, he has given forcible expression to the views held by every Socialist in the country who is worth his salt ... We say without fear of contradiction and with hundreds and even thousands of proofs in our hands, that Mr. Grayson has already the support of every Socialist in the country who is a Socialist first and a politician afterwards. He is denounced and disowned, unfortunately, by nearly all the prominent members of the Labour Party, including the I.L.P. members. They have lost no time in dissociating themselves in the most bitter terms from the 'boy' who has done what they now realise, now it is too late, they should themselves have done.[29]

The Parliamentary Labour Party was denounced once and for all by the socialists and it seemed clear that a new and independent socialist party would be the only means by which true socialists could secure election to Parliament. Not only had no Labour members supported Grayson's protest, but they had also voted unanimously with the Conservative and Liberal members for him to be suspended from the Commons. Grayson was out, excluded from the House for nine weeks, but he was jubilant. He saw the whole country as his constituency and relished getting back to what he did best: spreading the gospel of socialism.

6

'England's Greatest Mob Orator'

He was turned out of the House of Commons at Westminster, but he became at once the most popular man in the country.

Henry M. Hyndman[1]

Victor Grayson could excite at one time from a Yorkshire working-class audience a reception of such burning enthusiasm ... that it reminded the old politicians of the fervour with which Gladstone used to be welcomed to Midlothian, or Parnell to Dublin.[2]

It was Victor Grayson who 'raised the devil'.

Shaw Desmond[3]

Victor Grayson [carried] the flaming torch of revolt against the official Labour Party leadership, from Land's End to John O'Groats.

H.W. Lee and E. Archibold[4]

I say with all the calm of which I am capable, if a hungry multitude wants food and the trained forces prevent them from getting it, I wish the unemployed every success if they come into collision with the authorities.

Victor Grayson, October 1908[5]

Victor Grayson [was] the Labour movement's greatest propagandist, with a voice like the Bull of Bashan, flaming meteor-like across the Red firmament, holding all in the hollow of that tremendous voice ...

Shaw Desmond[6]

Now, with Victor Grayson at the height of his power, is the moment to reflect on the nature of his appeal and on his standing and potential within the wider Labour movement. By the time he had been suspended from the

House of Commons, the impact of his election was being felt not just in day-to-day politics, but also in contemporary literary fiction. One example in particular exemplifies the genre that grew out of the fears stoked by Grayson's election. John Dawson Mayne, a barrister and failed Conservative general election candidate, put into print the fears and anxieties of the class and establishment he represented.[7] He came from a line of legal professionals and among his cousins were an Admiral, a Major-General, a newspaper owner, a Chief Justice and a Secretary of State for Canada. He was 80 years old when he published the *Triumph of Socialism and How It Succeeded* in 1908, after being inspired by what he saw and heard in the 1907 parliamentary session.

The Triumph of Socialism and How It Succeeded is an apocalyptic vision of Britain in the aftermath of an electoral landslide for a socialist party. The leader of the socialists, Mr Perkins, becomes the new socialist Prime Minister[8] and, using fictional newspaper reports, the book chronicles the resulting panic of 1912, just four years in the future. Mayne's work is a time capsule of the fears of the wealthy, as the franchise gradually expanded and socialism gained ground electorally. Despite Mayne describing the democratic victory of the socialists as 'clear, conclusive and final', his mouthpiece, a fictional journalist, when faced with a socialist government, pleads 'What can King and Lords do to prevent it?'[9] As news of the result is announced, crowds swell through the streets of London, singing socialist songs and 'knocking at the doors of the great mansions in Belgravia and Mayfair, and asking to be shown over the house, as they were coming next week to choose their rooms'.[10] The few remaining wealthy opposition MPs step down to attend to 'urgent private affairs', leaving their seats vacant for the unopposed election of further socialist MPs. Not just from Parliament, but from all across Britain, the flight of the wealthy continued:

> every train and steamer is crammed with rich men, leaving the country with all their money and personal effects, and that every great mansion swarms with carpenters, packing up in huge cases the pictures and china and costly furniture of the proprietors and that the roads are blocked with vans carrying them to the seaport.[11]

Mayne's work is crammed full, not just of the contemporary establishment's fears of socialism, but of their distrust of democracy, their subservience to monarchy, and to military and hereditary wealth and titles. Though he does not mention Grayson specifically, Mayne was articulating the panic seen in the press after Grayson's victory 'for pure revolutionary socialism'. But what Mayne and his readers failed to appreciate, at least initially, was that Grayson's power, and that of the revolutionary elements of the Labour movement, never lay in Parliament, but out on the streets. Despite press claims to the contrary, the Labour Party in Parliament was committed to the democratic road to socialism, something with which Grayson never seemed comfortable. He wanted action on poverty, unemployment and class inequality now, in the present, not at some undefined future date. Therefore, he never acclimatised to Parliament, its procedures and archaic practices, nor, except for a brief period, did he even appear to try. Well before his suspension from the Commons, at the beginning of 1908, Grayson had set out on a country-wide campaign for socialism.

The tour was something akin to a travelling revue, as Grayson was joined by an ever-changing cast of prominent ILP and SDF members, as well as by literary and media personalities. On any given night Grayson might be joined by William C. Anderson (elected ILP Chairman in 1910), Leonard Hall (a founder member of the ILP), Alfred Richard Orage (editor of the *New Age*), Robert Blatchford (editor of the *Clarion*, who usually chaired the meetings), Henry Hyndman (SDF leader) or George Bernard Shaw, among others. Another notable member of Grayson's socialist touring company was his prominent supporter and friend, Robert Bontine Cunninghame Graham. Rarely mentioned in earlier biographies, he was nonetheless a key ally and, despite being three decades older than Grayson, the two men demonstrated curious similarities of character.

Unlike Grayson, Cunninghame Graham was the son of a wealthy Scottish landowner. He was an adventurer and, by way of William Morris' Socialist League, became a prized convert to socialism. With Morris, Keir Hardie and Eleanor Marx, he had attended the Marxist Congress of the Second International in Paris in 1889 and the following year spoke at the first major May Day celebrations in London, about which Engels commented, 'The grand-children of the old Chartists are entering the line of battle.'

He had helped to found the Labour Party, supported a more militant trade unionism, fought for women's suffrage and, like Grayson, had a very close relationship with his mother. His platform ability was legendary and as a speaker he was very much in demand. Also like Grayson, he had a tendency as a young man to get carried away with his own oratory.[12] What is striking about Cunninghame Graham, and the other men who became close confidants of and mentors to Grayson in these years, is that none, with the exception of Hyndman, around whom the SDF was very much built, were party politicians, and none were familiar with political compromise or even with political power itself.

Grayson and Blatchford had met during the by-election campaign when they were introduced to one another by John D. Sutcliffe, one of the endless number of socialists who joined the ranks of Grayson's campaign. The two men got on extremely well and Blatchford had a calming, almost fatherly, influence over the young MP, who in turn said that he was merely 'a minor intellectual offspring' of Blatchford's.[13] Grayson duly became a part of Blatchford's socialist inner circle which, it was said, spent as much time telling silly jokes as the Webbs did on procedure. Unlike the images of the ever-serious and dour Hardie and Snowden, Blatchford and Grayson shared a love of the lighter side of life. One article in the *Clarion* reported how the two men had missed their train and arrived late for a meeting after becoming preoccupied in the station bar, with Grayson entertaining the other drinkers with finger-shadows on the room's blind. Quite what people thought of this socialist bogeyman, as reported in their newspapers, performing his party-piece for their enjoyment is sadly not known, but the incident reveals something of Grayson's innocent and playful spirit.[14] Blatchford said of Grayson during this period: 'I have never met a man so utterly full of the joy of life.'[15]

But there was another side to this playful spirit. Grayson had been a shy child and a teetotaler in his youth. However, by the time he reached national prominence in the socialist ranks, Grayson was, as Percy Redfern remembered, relying on 'stimulants' to help him cope with his hectic schedule. Precisely what stimulants Redfern was referring to remains unclear, but we do know that Grayson had become a social drinker in Manchester and chastised those who saw alcohol and not class as the true enemy. By the time of his election victory, his drinking was becoming more than a social endeavour, and, perhaps out of some forlorn hope to help him moderate his growing habit, Blatchford introduced the young man to whisky, with terrible consequences. Years later, Ernest Hunter, a former ILP member and *Daily Herald* journalist, told Reg Groves that the reason Blatchford refused to speak of Grayson in his later years was his 'uneasy conscience. He taught Victor to drink, and to drink double whiskies one after the other.'[16] Sam Hobson appeared to agree, stating in his memoirs that 'on the whole I blame his friends most. There is a bottomless stupidity in some kinds of cheery friendliness.'[17]

Whereas Grayson had once criticised his old Liverpool comrades for drinking before meetings, it was now he who came under their scrutiny. One such old colleague, Fred Bower, remembered meeting Grayson in a pub in Chester, where he was drinking with Robert Blatchford and Alexander Thompson (Deputy Editor of the *Clarion*). Blatchford and Thompson were trying to dissuade Grayson from consuming too much whisky. It was evident to Bower that Grayson had drunk himself into a stupor and, after seeing this, Bower wondered 'how much better it would have been for him had he come in and had a glass of homely beer, instead of waiting for me as he used to do, when we were on our way to meetings at street corners in Liverpool'.[18]

With increased media scrutiny, a nomadic lifestyle, the pressure of nightly meetings across the country, and his struggle with the Labour Party, Grayson turned ever more readily to alcohol for comfort, confidence and support. Future Cabinet Minister and Deputy Leader of the Labour Party, James Griffiths, was an 18-year-old activist in 1908 when Grayson visited the Welsh constituency of East Carmarthen. For many young socialists, the temperance movement played a significant role and Keir Hardie himself was strictly against the consumption of alcohol. Griffiths and his fellow young socialists regarded Grayson as one of the Labour movement's 'national star speakers' and the crowded audience 'were thrilled to have a visit from the hero of Colne Valley'. Although Grayson made what Griffiths remembered as 'a wonderful address', he and his comrades were shocked when the speaker came down from the platform and 'asked one of us to take him to the nearest place where he could have a whisky'.[19] Theirs was a local party with a strong commitment to temperance, but eventually a volunteer was grudgingly found to lead Grayson to the nearest pub. Even so, the strong contingent of teetotallers were clearly shaken by his behaviour, given that Griffiths recalled it so clearly six decades later. At a further meeting, temperance reformers turned up to challenge the socialist view of the cause of poverty, and began heckling Grayson. 'He responded by asking for a match. He held it up and said it represented the national income. Then he broke the match in two and said that the bit without the head went in profits, the head went in drink: so what caused the poverty?'[20]

Concerns about Grayson's drinking were still only a slight blemish on his popular image and these were amongst his greatest days. He was still basking in the glory of his election victory and his protest on behalf of the unemployed in the House of Commons. Robert Blatchford reflected the opinion of many in the socialist movement in thinking that Grayson had been badly treated by the members of the PLP, who, had they chosen to engage with and support him, could have directed the young man's energies into more positive and productive work. After all, his popularity was unrivalled and he could have become a great asset to the embryonic Labour Party. Blatchford also saw in Grayson the embodiment of the distrust and discontent that his paper, the *Clarion*, had been sowing among ILP members about the watering down of socialism that had taken place within the Labour Party. Grayson's victory had given that work a major boost, and persuaded Blatchford that Grayson should embark on a sort of victory tour of the country, which would also gauge support for a new socialist party, should the Labour Party fail to change its course.

A typical meeting would begin with Blatchford, as Chairman, introducing the speakers, which was enough in itself to bring thunderous applause and singing from the crowds, crammed into the halls. Though Blatchford did his best to settle the audience and usher the speaker on to the stage, a mere glimpse of Grayson would send the crowd wild. It was noted by those who had witnessed Grayson speak elsewhere that Blatchford was a calming influence on the young man and that, if he was chairing, Grayson was less likely to get carried away with his own words. Not that this affected Grayson's powers of attraction. Across the towns and cities of the north and midlands, huge crowds gathered, whilst a homecoming meeting in the Colne Valley gave both men the sense that Grayson's constituents had become even more enthusiastic for his socialist message than when he was first elected.[21]

The young were particularly drawn to Grayson. He was one of them. He was not like the old men of politics and was not stuck in the customs of an earlier era. One such young socialist was Sidney Ronald Campion from Coalville, Leicester. His background and story help us understand the atmosphere of those years and the enthusiasm that existed for Grayson's brand of socialism. Campion had left school aged 11, and until age 14 had scraped a meagre living handing out free newspapers in Leicester. He then progressed to working in factories and workshops around the city until Ramsay MacDonald, the local MP, spotted some promise in the young man and sponsored him through further education. It was at this point, in 1909, that Grayson visited Leicester to address a mass meeting at the Leicester Corn Exchange. On both sides of the Grayson debate, the meeting was seen as a challenge to MacDonald. Campion remembered that his sponsor had been one of Grayson's fiercest critics in the constituency, declaring him an ineffectual demagogue who 'would be here today and away tomorrow'. He 'resembles a firework which shot up into the sky, sparked in the darkness for a few seconds, and then fell back to earth as a dead stick'.[22] The younger members, however, were not put off. They flocked in their hundreds to hear their hero speak. More than 50 years later, Campion still recalled his youthful enthusiasm.

> I met Victor Grayson ... when I was most impressionable. He fascinated me because he was young and because he stood for ACTION. I held the view at that time that Socialism could arrive by the next morning's post, and that V.G. could be the postman. I admired his challenging stand in the House of Commons; I was attracted to him because of his religious fervour.[23]

Grayson enjoyed a hero's welcome, although he raised eyebrows when he arrived in a well-tailored brown tweed suit which made it seem 'as though he had just returned from a country walk'. He was his usual charming and friendly self, and his theatrical stage performance appealed to the romantic nature of many of his younger supporters. After the meeting Campion and a small group, dominated by the local SDF which was strongly anti-Mac-Donald, went for a private discussion with Grayson. Campion remembered that Grayson spoke more freely to this small group than he had from the platform: 'He was in favour of hanging certain leaders of the capitalists on the public lamp posts but with no definite plan of action.' Whether this was a case of Grayson getting carried away in the moment, as he had been accused of doing at the time of the 'Broken Bottles' speech, or of his real politics coming to the fore, we cannot be sure. In retrospect, it may reflect the influence of the more revolutionary elements of the Labour movement with which Grayson was now surrounding himself.

Whatever the meaning, Grayson had made a deep and lasting impression on the young men. Though Campion had no further contact with Grayson after the Leicester meeting, he collected reports of every one of his rallies, read the transcripts of every word Grayson spoke, and bought every pamphlet that he wrote.[24] As a young working-class man from a poor background, determined to change society, he was completely transfixed. By contrast, the Labour Party leadership was worried that Grayson could siphon off an entire generation from Labour's ranks:

young men such as I found that he expressed what we were thinking. Ramsay MacDonald was deeply disappointed in me, and also took the view that if I could be so easily influenced by V.G. then my contemporaries would go over to the Colne Valley MP and provide him with the necessary mass following.[25]

Despite what Campion suggests, it was not only the young who were drawn to Grayson. He would twice be invited to attend and address the Durham Miners Gala, demonstrating his support amongst the more militant and radical of the trade unions, such as the Miners Federation of Great Britain. Furthermore, despite his general antipathy towards conservative union leaders, he continued to support trade unionism in principle and its use as an instrument of working-class power. The example of Grayson's appearance at the annual opening of the Birmingham Labour

Church also demonstrates his considerable increase in popularity within another section of the Labour and socialist movement.

In December 1906, the then relatively unknown Victor Grayson had given a Sunday lecture to the Birmingham Labour Church. Records show that he attracted an audience of 83, compared to 117 for the translator and biographer of Tolstoy, Aylmer Maude, and 84 for a general session of Bible readings and hymns. The biggest annual event of the church calendar came every autumn when the new session was opened with a meeting in the city's Town Hall. In 1907, Pete Curran was invited to speak and, though Grayson's name was proposed as chairman for the meeting, the motion was narrowly defeated in favour of a local speaker. Curran was a respected platform performer, but he was not at his best and, although the Town Hall was crowded, the event left a hefty £6 deficit in local party funds.

For the 1908 annual meeting, the parishoners' preferred list for a main speaker consisted of Ramsay MacDonald, Arthur Henderson and Victor Grayson. MacDonald turned down the invitation, stating that he was already booked for a meeting in Birmingham that year, whilst Henderson refused because he never accepted speaking engagements on a Sunday. Grayson was much more in demand than in 1906 and proved hard to track down. Two letters were sent without response and only a wire to the House of Commons finally proved successful. Grayson agreed to speak on condition that Robert Blatchford acted as the meeting's chairman. It shows the closeness of the two men, and how much Grayson depended upon the guidance of Blatchford, that he would not speak without him.

Grayson's star was near its zenith, as indicated by the fact that the Birmingham Labour Party sought to move the meeting from the Town Hall (which they could use free of charge) to the much larger Hippodrome, at a cost of £12.[26] The Hippodrome event proved to be one of the largest the local party ever hosted. The Clarion Scouts were employed as stewards, two local socialist choirs (Aston and West Bromwich) were brought in, 100 large posters, 10,000 handbills and 4,000 hymn sheets were printed, and advertisements were placed in *Labour Leader, Clarion, Justice, Woman Worker* and even the *Daily Mail.* A capacity 3,500 tickets were sold and the true attendance was even higher due to 200 of these tickets being designated to 'admit bearer and friend'. With Grayson's growing reputation in the press for militancy and his recent suspension from the Commons, Birmingham Conservative and Unionists wondered publicly whether there would be violent clashes at the Hippodrome meeting. But despite such anxieties, reports of the meeting show that it was a great success:

> It was crowded in all parts and almost as many were turned away. In spite of fears to the contrary, the meeting was entirely peaceful, thanks no doubt to 200 stewards … When the Secretary of the Hippodrome found that Grayson and Blatchford were to be the speakers he expressed his indignation that the Hall should be used by two such firebrands and stated that if he had known he doubted whether the Directors would have let the hall.[27]

A second appraisal of the Hippodrome event was reported to the quarterly meeting of the Birmingham Labour Church in January 1909:

> There was widespread interest in Grayson due to his suspension from the Commons on unemployment, but there was some criticism of the chairmanship of Blatchford. An agenda was prepared for him but he did not adhere to it, committing the second hymn and omitting to announce the collection in the gallery. There had been disquieting rumours of violence, but the meeting was entirely orderly … There was valuable co-operation from the Clarion Scouts with stewarding and the sale of literature.[28]

The financial success of the meeting was in stark contrast to Pete Curran's event the previous year. Despite the greatly increased costs of holding the event, profits stood at a striking £32 2s 9d. Nor was this a one-off success. Grayson's appeal was felt by the Labour churches across the country. The 1909 annual report to the Labour Church Union Conference ended by admitting that 'but for Victor Grayson many of these Labour Churches would be penniless'. It is a point glossed over by Grayson's detractors, that his popularity and self-destructive speaking schedule were keeping large swathes of the movement financially afloat. Also, no doubt as an additional sign of Grayson's impact, the Birmingham contingent moved to change the name from Labour Church to Socialist Church.[29]

This name change of the church from Labour to Socialist may seem a minor point, but it was symptomatic of a significant chasm between labourism and socialism across the country, which had grown ever wider since Grayson's election. His unemployment protest in the House and the silence of Labour MPs led to him being courted as a popular champion by Britain's more militant left-wing factions. The SDP now wished to align themselves with Grayson's protest. Their Executive Council passed the following, rather breathless, resolution:

> The Executive Council of the Social-Democratic Federation warmly thanks Comrade Victor Grayson, M.P., for his manly protest against the contemptuous attitude of the Liberal Government and the House of Commons as a whole towards the hundreds of thousands of unemployed workers deprived of the means of earning a livelihood for themselves and their families by the action of the Capitalist class, and strongly condemns the cowardice of the great majority of the Labour Party in Parliament who, bound by their arrangements with the Capitalist Liberals, are much more anxious to keep their seats at the next General Election than to champion the cause of the people ... The Executive of the S.D.P. calls also upon all Socialists to demonstrate throughout the country in favour of the organization of useful work for the unemployed upon co-operative principles under national control.[30]

The SDP and Hyndman had thought about re-affiliating to the Labour Party to strengthen the 'Labour Alliance', but after Grayson's election the mood amongst many on the left was moving towards the formation of a new, independent and united socialist party which would bring together Britain's splintered Marxist and socialist groups. It would be independent of the Labour Party and its alliance with the Liberals and, most important of all, be explicitly opposed to capitalism. The 'socialist unity' movement was built on the notion that the Labour Party leadership had neutered the socialism and anti-capitalist potential of the PLP in exchange for electoral support from the Liberals. The lack of militancy displayed by the PLP, especially in contrast to Grayson's words and deeds, had made it almost impossible to defend Labour's parliamentary record to a sizeable number of Britain's socialists.

John Maclean, the future revolutionary Red Clydesider, wrote to *Forward*, the paper of the Glasgow ILP, in defence of Grayson's position against

> the Labour MPs who, whilst claiming political independence, silently listen to a wearisome discussion of the Licensing Bill during a period of almost unparalleled unemployment and starvation for the workers, and who strut about on Liberal Temperance platforms, exhorting the starving to end their drunken habits ... The Labour MPs have fawned upon Asquith and his crew whilst at the same time using the vilest language against Grayson, Blatchford, Hyndman and others.[31]

With the columns of left-wing newspapers proclaiming the need for revolutionary tactics, Grayson was soon calling for an uprising of the unemployed on the streets of Britain. In the *New Age* he was reported as saying:

> I am concerned to tell the class to which I belong ... that if they are to be saved, they must save themselves by destroying with their naked hands the barbed-wire entanglement of an unrighteous covenant with vested interest and privileges that circumscribe them. It is not enough for them to luxuriate in the knowledge that they are a peaceably-disposed and law abiding people. It was not enough in the days when Wat Tyler used his hammer upon the head of a King's tax-gatherer and rode forth at the head of his tatterdemalion rabble to meet his death – and achieve immortality – at the hands of another mercenary of the King. It is not enough now. You may bow the head and snuffle supplications, you may do your genuflections and say your prayers to a deaf and blind Deity until your soul sickens within you and the fires of your manhood are become cold ashes. It is not enough. You must put the fear of Man into the hearts of your oppressors ... as they have put the fear of man-created gods into you. You – the Dispossessed and Unemployed – must

possess yourselves of the means of life even at a cost of lives. You must no longer be the Unemployed, but employ yourselves in wrestling from the robbers who have plundered you the fruits of your labour.[32]

The editor followed up the report of the speech with a simple statement of support: 'And so say I.' In *Justice*, the paper of the SDF, one contributor wrote the following words after hearing a Grayson speech:

You cannot get Grayson in a report. Felicities of language, shafts of sarcasm, burning jokes, can be transferred from the lips to print. But not the impassioned zeal of the man; his almost awful sincerity; his pure, fierce revolutionary ardour – these are for his hearers only, and these are what make converts, and confirm the old believers in their faith.[33]

It was this 'fierce revolutionary ardour' that would result in one of the biggest demonstrations on Britain's streets of this period, and Grayson was at its head.

If there was one significant event that united Europe's socialist movement in the years before the outbreak of the Great War, it was the killing of the Spanish educationalist Francisco Ferrer on 13 October 1909. Ferrer was born in Barcelona and started his political life as an anarchist, developing into a radical free-thinker who wanted to build a new education system that was 'anti-militarist, anti-clerical, rationalistic and humanitarian'.[34] He had been transformed from revolutionary to educationalist during a period spent living in Paris, where he lost faith in the Spanish revolutionaries and concluded that, as long as the mass of his fellow countrymen remained illiterate, any political revolution would have no lasting effect. For Ferrer, the building of a better society had to begin with a sound education. To this end, he opened his Escuela Moderna (Modern School) in 1902, which gained international fame whilst exciting horror in clerical and conservative minds. The teaching was anti-religious, rebelled against the established class structure and, whilst it has been said that Ferrer's school turned out good Europeans, it turned out bad Spaniards.[35] When Spanish troops were sent to Morocco, demonstrations against Spanish militarism began, and a week later a general strike was called. This developed into a rising, with churches and religious institutions attacked as symbols of Spanish authority. After three days of street fighting in Barcelona, the uprising was finally suppressed and martial law declared. There followed two months of terror from the military and, although Francisco Ferrer had no direct involvement with the uprising, he was denounced, arrested, framed, tried and shot in quick succession.[36] Ferrer's execution sent a chill through the spines of socialists and radicals across Europe, who held that his murder revealed the obstacles confronting those who wanted a just and democratic society. They were in a struggle against the combined power of Church, state, and military: in other words, the ruling class.

As news of Ferrer's execution spread throughout Europe, demonstrations and protests erupted. In Britain, his murder particularly affected those whom he had met during visits to England. He had developed a network of contacts and sympathisers amongst radicals, socialists and educationalists throughout the country. In Sheffield, 12,000 people marched in protest at his execution and burnt effigies of a priest and a soldier. It was reported that much of the chanting from the crowds was anti-Catholic, the Church being seen as intrinsic to the Spanish establishment.

Before Ferrer's execution, and possibly under Grayson's direction, the *New Age* sent a telegram to the British Foreign Secretary, Sir Edward Grey, urging him 'to make friendly representations to the Spanish government with a view to the commutation of the death sentence upon Ferrer'. After his execution a second was sent, which read, '*New Age* holds you responsible as accessory to Ferrer's murder.' On the Sunday after his execution, 17 October, 10,000 people gathered to demonstrate in Trafalgar Square. J.F. Green, National Treasurer of the SDF, presided over the meeting whilst Grayson mounted the platform to attack King Edward VII for his supposed lack of action to save Ferrer's life.[37] The King, said Grayson, was complicit in Ferrer's murder through his own inactivity. The crowd was whipped into a frenzy and Grayson then implored it to march with him, to the Spanish Embassy. Shaw Desmond, who was with Grayson on the platform, was startled. As he later recalled, 'Grayson shouting, the crowd cheering, and the writer wondering what devil possessed him to suggest from the plinth an assault upon the Spanish Embassy and what was going to happen next' when they clashed with mounted police. Not for the first time, Grayson played to his audience and was led by his emotions, a dangerous situation in the context of such a large, angry crowd.[38] Victor Serge recalled that during the corresponding Paris demonstration, 'The revolutionary groups followed rather than guided these masses' and that thousands of ordinary Parisians had flocked to the centre of Paris, much as they did in London.[39]

Two days later, Grayson followed up these scenes with an intervention in Parliament. Continuing with the stance adopted in the *New Age*, Labour MPs questioned whether the Foreign Secretary had made any intervention in the Ferrer case. Grey protested that it was not the place of the government to interfere in the internal affairs of other states. Given that response, Arthur Henderson asked Grey if he had done anything since receiving representations from Ferrer's British supporters. Grey refused to add anything to his previous answer. Pete Curran asked whether there were not precedents for British interference in the business of foreign governments. Grayson then rose:

In consequence of the unsatisfactory answer received from the right hon. Gentleman, I beg to move, 'That this House do now adjourn in order to discuss a definite matter of urgent public importance.' I refer, of course, to the matter which has been the subject of the questions to the right hon. Gentleman.[40]

The Speaker replied that the trial and execution of Ferrer were 'hardly urgent'. Grayson protested that there were others under arrest and victims of torture, who were 'accused of complicity in exactly the same business' as Ferrer. But the Speaker was still insistent: 'I can hardly recognize that as a matter of urgent public importance.' Throughout this exchange, Hilaire Belloc, Liberal MP for Salford South, goaded Grayson in defence of the Ferrer judgement. Grayson, becoming extremely animated and passionate, retorted:

If the hon. Member for South Salford has anything to add, I hope he will do it later. What I wish to point out is that prisoners are now in gaol in Spain, and practically under sentence, who will be shot as Ferrer was shot unless the matter is recognized by the House today as one of urgent public importance.[41]

The Speaker now relented, and put forward Grayson's motion for an adjournment:

> The hon. Member for Colne Valley seeks to move the adjournment of the House in order to call attention to a definite matter of urgent public importance, namely, the non-intervention by the Foreign Secretary on behalf of prisoners now in gaol in Spain, and shortly coming up for trial before courts-martial.

Grayson made one minor addition: 'Owing to the action of the Foreign Secretary in not endeavouring to induce the Spanish Government to give a fair trial in the civil courts to those now in gaol on charges similar to those against Senor Ferrer.'[42] He needed 40 MPs to support his call for the adjournment, but just 18 did so, and Grayson's motion fell. Upon leaving the chamber, he told the assembled press in the lobby that he was satisfied with the protest he had made over Ferrer's execution. He was surprised, however, that only 18 fellow Parliamentarians had supported his motion for the adjournment. Grayson added that he would 'probably to-morrow ask for an answer to the question put by Mr Curran this afternoon as to whether there were not precedents for the interference of Great Britain in the internal affairs of a country'.[43]

Two points about Grayson's actions in the Ferrer case merit further comment. The first is that, despite the conventional historical narrative that Grayson had little organisational ability, his actions in this case (as with his unemployment protest) do show a degree of planning. Along with the *New Age* he had called on the Foreign Secretary to act to save Ferrer. After the execution, he had addressed a huge demonstration, and led the protestors into violent clashes outside the Spanish Embassy. Then he came to Parliament to follow up his attack on Grey, branding him as responsible for the murder. The second point is that, if Grayson had enjoyed a better relationship with the PLP, he might have received greater backing for his motion, though it remains unlikely that he would have gained the support of as many as 40 Members. His powerful, emotional oratory and clever turn of phrase were his biggest assets, but these were near-useless in the Commons without solid party support.

When we try to analyse Grayson's abilities as a speaker, we see that his oratory was as effective as it was precisely because it was based on emotion. He had come to socialism, as he had come to Christianity, looking for a solution to the poverty he had seen as a child and which he still witnessed around him. Edward Carpenter, a hero of Grayson's who shared a platform with him on several occasions, argued that 'On the platform for detailed or constructive argument he was no good, but for criticism of the enemy he was inimitable – the shafts of his wit played like lightning round him, and with the big mouth and flexible upper lip he seemed to be simply browsing off his opponents and eating them up.'[44] Even hecklers were dealt with in the best way – with humour. In 1926 a newspaper reader offered his recollection of a Grayson meeting. He remembered that a man had shouted from the audience that Grayson should be shot and buried. This caused an outcry and some pushing within the crowd. But Grayson calmed and settled his supporters, 'Don't mind him. I quite understand. He's an undertaker.'[45]

Yet, to set against his evident platform skills, Grayson also showed a curious propensity for bizarre behaviour at key moments.

At the 1909 Labour Party conference in Portsmouth, Grayson was expected to defend his actions in Parliament whilst also formulating and proposing an alternative, more definitively socialist, policy for the ILP. The first day's discussions were set to be dominated by the unemployment issue, so the moment seemed ideal for Grayson to state his case and use the platform to formulate policy. His nationwide campaign of speaking engagements had built up to this moment and the conference was highly expectant. Both the Countess of Warwick and Henry Hyndman were attending in support of Grayson. But things did not go to plan. Hyndman recalled:

Everybody therefore expected [Grayson] would rise to the level of the occasion. There was a crowd of reporters – English, American, and foreign – present, and ready to flash his utterances to London and thence to all parts of the earth … It was, in fact, a most dramatic situation, which appealed to the imagination of every man and woman among us.

We waited on tiptoe in a very agony of expectation for the great man of the day.[46]

But there was no sign of Grayson.

Time passed. Where was Grayson? Time passed still. Where was Grayson? Luncheon arrived. Still no Grayson. The day came to an end. No Grayson. It was all over. A very promising young leader had lost the chance of his life.[47]

This was not the end of the episode. Grayson, confronted with the opportunity to make a real change, threw it away in the most whimsical manner possible. Hyndman recalled another chance squandered, even though he and Lady Warwick attempted to save the situation:

On the second or third day the missing man turned up – cool, cheery, unflustered, quite himself. Did he understand? I have never been able to say. But if he did not it was not for the want of our telling him. We put the thing to him as plain as plain could be. He had sacrificed the great hearing he must have obtained, but yet there was time. The conference would listen to him, the press would report him, the people would rush to acclaim him. He listened. An hour later he lounged elegantly against one of the pillars of the hall, and – carefully – held his peace. At last more than one of us told him in so many words that if he left the Conference without making himself felt, Socialists as well as Labour men would have no further use for him: he was not only making a fool of himself but us.[48]

But Grayson did not intervene. Instead, he watched on as his chance of leadership within the ILP slipped through his fingers, unmoved by the encouragement of his supporters around him, which was beginning to turn to anger. These were strange actions on the part of a man who had spent his political life building up to this moment. Hyndman never forgot it, either, and towards the end of his life, wrote: 'It was a very bad business, and to this day I cannot understand it ... I can never forget that terrible Portsmouth fiasco.'[49]

7

Revolution Delayed

I went [to Parliament] to stand for the helpless and outcast, for the starving child. I went with that pledge on my soul. The Liberals combined with the Tories, and I was thrown out of the House. I am going back again.

Victor Grayson launching his general election campaign,
Marsden, Colne Valley, 30 December 1909

Socialism must be Parliamentary or it is nothing.

Ramsay MacDonald[1]

Victor Grayson's quest for re-election as the Colne Valley's socialist MP would be markedly different from his by-election campaign just two-and-a-half years earlier. Grayson was unable to attract the nationwide support he had previously enjoyed, as many of his supporters from outside the constituency were now fighting elections elsewhere. At best, he could only expect their divided attention this time around. There would be no active support from Labour MPs or even tacit backing from Keir Hardie. Grayson's most dedicated supporters also fell victim to what some Marxist historians have seen as the first witch hunt in the Labour Party's history. When Keir Hardie addressed moderate Labour members, he declared, 'In almost every branch there is this snarling disruptive element. You have got to fight it down and fight it out.'[2] That he had Grayson in mind would have been evident to his listeners. Another problem was the damage that Grayson, and others, had done to his own reputation. Rumours about his personal life dogged him, and he had certainly lost support amongst what should have been his core vote, especially its more religious elements. Some had seen first-hand the firebrand's descent into alcoholism, which increasingly caused him to miss meetings at which he should have been the star speaker. When he did appear, some of his performances were erratic and blundering, where they had once been spellbinding. Despite his loathing for the temperance movement, many of its members still backed Grayson for his wider programme. But now he lost much of their support. There was also a more dangerous rumour, hinted at but never made explicit, surrounding Grayson's sexuality. The image of a young man in the public eye, prone to excess, living a secret double-life and lacking wise counsel was a destructive combination.

Yet this is not to deny that Grayson was still regarded as a near-messiah by a great many people in Britain. The first biography of him was published as the election campaign began, and in the foreword to Yorkshire socialist and journalist Wilfred Thompson's *A. Victor Grayson M.P., England's Most Illustrious Socialist Orator*, a Mrs M. Moorhouse from Blackpool revealed some of the passion that still gripped Grayson's more ardent followers:

He arrests, rouses, and inspires the people with noble purpose. He stirs to high endeavour the poor, cramped, and self-contented slaves who gather to his presence. He is of the New Order: Herald of the Coming Race, who shall claim as their rightful heritage beauty and plenty, and whose ideal of goodness shall not consist in observing rules formulated in past ages, but in the full development of their faculties and powers which clamour for expression.[3]

Thompson felt confident enough to state that 'Victor Grayson is at present the most popular M.P. in England. He is also well known and revered among Continental Socialists; and his constituents almost worship him.'[4] The book sold its entire print run and, such was the demand, an expensive new edition was printed a few months later, complete with a foreword from Grayson himself and several photographs. Few British political figures enjoyed this kind of adulation. But such enthusiasm counted for little in the practical world of winning elections, which required compromise and the ability to build coalitions of support. It was a truth Grayson struggled to learn.

Grayson suffered a severe blow when France Littlewood, an avid supporter since 1906, now refused to back him. Grayson's attitude towards

Keir Hardie and his behaviour in and out of the Commons had angered Littlewood who, with Grayson proposing to stand again as an independent, chose to resign as President of the Colne Valley Socialist League and refused Grayson's invitation to chair his election committee. Littlewood had been a key figure during the successful by-election campaign and enjoyed the respect of political friends and foes alike. Without him, Grayson's campaign was bound to struggle. Just two days after the MP's campaign launch, a damning letter from Littlewood was published in the *Huddersfield Examiner*:

> The [Colne Valley Socialist League] having decided to run an independent Socialist candidate at the forthcoming General Election, the time has now arrived when those who believe in the continued action of the Socialist and Labour parties must make a determined stand. The policy of the ILP has been to unite the workers in one party. Those who agree with that are inside the Labour Party today and the existence of that party is proof positive that the ILP policy is sound.
>
> The member for Colne Valley has had abundant opportunity to put himself in line with the organised Labour movement. Having failed to utilise that opportunity, he now proposes to fight the decision on independent lines regardless of the fact that the Colne Valley League is in membership with the ILP and therefore under the discipline of ILP conferences which have definitely decided that all ILP candidates at the general election must be prepared to sign the Labour Party constitution.
>
> As one who believes in the ILP, I have forthwith to end my official connection with the CVSL and have this day tendered my resignation of the position of president as I cannot allow myself to be identified with a candidature which is not in accordance with the regulations of the ILP and which in my opinion can only do harm to the great movement which my comrades in Colne Valley have so carefully and zealously built up during the past twenty years.[5]

What was not made public were the rumblings against Grayson from within the Colne Valley party. There was justifiable concern that Grayson was spending too much time on platforms across the country instead of in the House of Commons. His response, that parliamentary democracy was a sham, was hardly a reassuring answer for those who had fought so long to have a representative of their own at Westminster. Furthermore, at the beginning of December 1909, Grayson had informed some in the local party that he intended to retire at the forthcoming election on grounds of ill health and because of his disillusionment with Parliament. Both were good reasons to retire, but Grayson had left it too late. There was no hope of finding a suitable replacement and getting him embedded in the constituency in time. So Grayson was persuaded to stand again, his price being that he would stand as an independent socialist.

In contrast to the disorganisation in the socialist ranks, the Colne Valley Liberals had learnt from their shock defeat in 1907 and had spent a great deal of time in finding the right candidate to wrest the constituency back from Grayson. They selected the Reverend Dr Charles Leach, a man whose pedigree was almost uniquely suited to breaking up the local coalition of religious, socialist and progressive elements that had sent Grayson victorious to Parliament. Leach was a former ILP member, sympathetic to the cause of the working class, but with little time for socialist doctrine. He was also an ex-Methodist preacher who had held successful ministries across some of Britain's major cities – London, Birmingham and Manchester – where he attracted large congregations of working people (reportedly up to 3,000 at a time in Birmingham). His sermons have been described as 'highly orthodox and conservative but sensationally publicised'.[6] Leach told his audiences how he had joined the ILP at its creation in 1893, after Keir Hardie had converted him to social reform during a heated debate the previous year. He also advocated the public ownership of utilities and the nationalisation of the railways as a means to better social conditions.[7] He was a radical, religious man, who promised social reform, but without the wild theatrics and blood-curdling language that Grayson so often deployed in the heat of the moment. What is more, Leach came without the personal baggage and rumours of private misdeeds that beset Grayson.

With the local newspapers in the hands of unsympathetic Liberals, without the fanfare of insurgency of 1907 and with division in his own ranks, Grayson was never likely to hold the seat. His campaign was significantly better financed than it had been in 1907, but its execution was poor. Another factor was the winter weather. Gone were the great outdoor evening meetings in which he excelled. In Dr Leach, he also faced a far more politically attractive and astute opponent than he had before. The result was declared at Slaithwaite Town Hall on 21 January 1910:

Dr Charles Leach (Liberal) 4,741
A. Boyd Carpenter (Conservative) 3,750
Victor Grayson (Socialist) 3,149

His supporters still sang 'The Red Flag' and carried him to the front of the Dartmouth Arms pub, as they had in 1907, where Grayson made a concessionary speech. It brought to an end his brief but tumultuous parliamentary career.

Most observers now regarded Grayson as a spent force. Historians have seldom looked beyond this defeat and have thus ignored his third and final parliamentary contest at Kennington, South London, in the second general election of 1910. Yet the Kennington campaign involved some of the great political characters of the age and merits more attention than it has previously been given. More importantly, it may be argued that Grayson's riotous but beleaguered socialist campaign laid the groundwork for the Labour Party's subsequent domination of the Kennington and Lambeth constituencies.

The second general election of 1910 was called by the Liberal government to secure a mandate to reform the House of Lords after inter-party talks in the summer had ended in deadlock. Up until the last minute, the Kennington contest looked like being a straight fight between the incumbent Liberal candidate, Stephen Collins, and the Conservative Colonel Francis Alfred Lucas. The pair had faced each other the previous January, with Lucas slashing Collins' majority from 1,585 to a slender 381. The infant branch of the Kennington ILP had chosen the local Lambeth Borough Councillor, C. Iremonger, to contest the seat. However, for reasons now lost, Iremonger pulled out and the ILP branch debated who might stand at this late stage. With no local candidate forthcoming, some of the younger members had an idea. Charles Gibson, a future Labour MP but then a young member of Kennington ILP, later recalled: 'We were only a small branch of the ILP but, greatly daring, invited Grayson to be our candidate which, to our surprise, he accepted.'[8] Though Colne Valley Socialist League activists had pressed Grayson to accept the nomination to stand for a third time, Grayson wrote to the local party explaining his decision to stand instead in Kennington, where he lived, on the grounds that his health could not withstand the physical demands of a sprawling, hilly Yorkshire constituency in the grip of a harsh winter.

Polling day in Kennington was set for Tuesday, 6 December, but as late as 24 November, with just twelve days to go, local newspapers still carried no mention of Grayson, whose candidature had yet to be finalised. The election was still being referred to as a two-horse race. It was not until the following day that news broke of Grayson's candidature, described by the *Brixton Free Press* as 'one of the startling developments during the past few days', leaving just 11 days to campaign. If the limited time period put him firmly on the back-foot, the difference in the resources available to the candidates delivered Grayson an additional blow.

The Conservative Colonel Lucas was backed by a military-style organisation, and had been promised a fleet of motor cars to be at his disposal on polling day to ferry his supporters to and from the polls. The Liberal candidate Collins similarly had the use of several offices and committee rooms with pledges of motor cars for use on polling day. Grayson's organisation, on the other hand, was at best spartan. Nor did the bitterly cold winter weather help his cause. Unlike the plush surroundings enjoyed by the Liberals and Conservatives, the socialist candidate's single committee room was warmed by a solitary stove, over which Grayson and his shivering campaigners crowded to warm their hands. One of his supporters had to lend the candidate an over-sized heavy coat to keep him warm whilst speaking from a travelling Clarion van.

Despite the odds stacked against him, Grayson called in favours from his political and literary contacts, which at least enlivened the campaign and turned a spotlight on to Kennington. George Bernard Shaw promised Grayson use of his motor car for polling day, whilst the writers G.K. Chesterton and Hilaire Belloc visited the constituency and spoke in his support at public meetings. Belloc had been elected Liberal MP for Salford South at the Liberal landslide of 1906 and had won re-election in January 1910.

He had befriended Grayson in Parliament and called for leniency when
the young socialist member was thrown out of the Commons for bringing
it into disrepute. But Belloc had become disillusioned with the workings
of British politics and stood down when the December 1910 election was
called. Instead, he engaged in writing *The Party System* (1911), along with
G.K. Chesterton's cousin, Cecil. Belloc and Chesterton wanted to 'expose
and ridicule ... to destroy and supplant the system under which Parliament, the governing institution of this country, has been rendered null'.[9]
The party system was corrupting politics with policies and positions of
power cynically traded to bolster election funds:

> The ordinary method of replenishing the Party Funds is by the sale of
> peerages, baronetcies, knighthoods, and other honours in return for sub-
> scriptions. This traffic is notorious. Everyone acquainted in the smallest
> degree with the inside of politics knows that there is a market for
> peerages in Downing Street ... Yet the ordinary man is either ignorant
> of the truth or only darkly suspects it. And most of those who know
> about it are afraid to bring the facts to light ...[10]

Belloc held his former Liberal colleagues in just as much contempt as he
did the Conservatives and he was attracted to Grayson's rejection of the
party machine in refusing to compromise his socialism in order to ingratiate himself with the Labour Party leadership and the PLP. In fact, there
is no record of a single Labour MP coming to speak in this election on
behalf of Grayson who, despite his ILP backing, was standing as a 'socialist'
candidate without reference to Labour.

However, despite his celebrity endorsement, the simple lack of socialist
organisation in Kennington compared with the Colne Valley soon brought
home to Grayson the reality that he had no chance of victory. If the young
members of Kennington ILP had hoped that their famous candidate
would manage to organise an effective campaign and professional polling-
day machine, they were to be sadly disappointed. Grayson had never had
the time or patience for the sort of mundane party work of canvassing,
leafleting and organising members and supporters that this would have
entailed. He did, however, secure some large donations. Two local women

each gave the then very considerable sum of £50 (equivalent to around £5,000 today) to Grayson's campaign. Smaller donations of £1 or less came in from individuals across the United Kingdom, demonstrating Grayson's still powerful appeal, whilst his old comrades in the Colne Valley also sent donations by way of their branches.

News of Grayson's presence as a candidate caused a stir across London and socialists, as well as the merely curious, travelled from afar to hear him speak in packed-out halls. Kennington ILP members took the opportunity to shake buckets to gather campaign donations. As Charles Gibson, then working on Grayson's campaign team, remembered: 'We held public meetings almost every evening which were always filled to overflow ... we had enormous meetings and great oratory, and collected enough money to pay all the election expenses with a considerable sum left over.'[11] In comparison, neither of Grayson's opponents attracted much attention outside their own supporters and the Kennington electors. But press attention and the popular enthusiasm which Grayson's meetings aroused created the illusion that the socialist candidate enjoyed far more support than he did. Yet, in a pre-television age, Grayson could still maintain a degree of anonymity among his electorate. As the *Brixton Free Press* reported, on polling day itself he 'was about the constituency all day [yet] he often passed unrecognised'. Even so, it seems probable that some of this lack of recognition was the result of Grayson's failure to engage sufficiently in traditional canvassing – knocking on doors and meeting his prospective constituents on a one-to-one basis.

Though Grayson knew that the prospects of victory were remote, he was determined to use the election as a platform for his ideas. Consequently, the socialist candidate's election address held nothing back. He declared that both the Conservative and Liberal candidates 'stand to buttress the present rotten system of private enterprise and cut-throat competition' and was explicit about his own mission:

I am in Kennington to fight them both. I am here to fight them as a Socialist. I want to do more than limit the Veto of the Lords – I would abolish them altogether. If we cannot govern ourselves without the aid of the deteriorate offspring of dissolute kings and Norman buccaneers we had better shut up the shop of democracy. I am out for protection, but it is protection for the disinherited worker against the mean and greedy aggression of the capitalist at home.[12]

The bustle of activity in the socialist camp, the press coverage, celebrity endorsements and crowded meetings began to unsettle Grayson's rivals. Both the Liberal Collins and Conservative Lucas had initially rejected the notion that the entry of the famed socialist would have any impact on the poll. The Liberals claimed that the local ILP had put up Grayson as 'revenge' for losing to the Liberal candidate at the previous County Council election. Somewhat spuriously, they also suggested that local socialists would in any case never vote for a Liberal, so it would be impossible to lose votes to Grayson. Indeed, Collins was quoted as saying that 'the Socialist's entry will make no difference whatsoever'. The Conservatives seemed nearer the mark on this issue. They believed that there was a small but growing core of socialist support in the constituency, which had shown up in their detailed canvass returns from the previous January. These socialists, claimed the Conservatives (rightly as it turned out), had voted in January and had voted Liberal. In contrast, 'it is to tax beyond credibility to think for one moment that a Socialist voted for a Tory'.[13] Despite their outward calmness, the Liberals were in fact beginning to panic that Grayson's entry into the contest threatened to gift the seat to the Conservative Colonel Lucas. Their fears were not without foundation. As the Conservatives understood, those with Labour and socialist sympathies had previously voted Liberal but were now tempted to vote for Grayson, despite the resulting danger of the seat falling to the Tory candidate.

The Liberal Prime Minister Herbert Asquith sent a letter of support to his candidate, Stephen Collins:

My heartiest wishes for your success. I feel sure that if the electors of Kennington exercise a sound judgement they will choose as their representative one who is prepared to support a policy of ordered progress and to resist that policy of revolution which must necessarily produce great evils to the whole nation. Let Kennington do its duty at a moment so critical to every section of the community.

It is clear that Asquith's letter was sent not to entice waverers or Conservative supporters to switch to the Liberals, but to discourage Liberal voters tempted by Grayson's message of revolution. It is interesting that Asquith seemed to see Grayson as the main threat to the Liberal candidate. The Chancellor of the Exchequer, David Lloyd George, was also moved to send a message of support to Collins: 'You stand by the only practicable line of democratic advance ... if the electors wish for a decisive triumph over monopoly and privilege they must vote for you.' Again, the message was clearly aimed at those tempted to vote for Grayson's uncompromising and extremist vision rather than to entice Conservative voters to switch.

Despite these messages of goodwill, the press sensed a growing pessimism amongst Liberal supporters. Winston Churchill, then Home Secretary, was dispatched by Asquith to the constituency to hold a major campaign rally at Lambeth Baths on Monday, 28 November. But Churchill had been warned to expect trouble.

The day after Grayson announced his candidature, his old friend Christabel Pankhurst descended on Kennington with a team of WSPU suffragettes. Grayson and Pankhurst knew each other from the Manchester Central ILP branch and Manchester University Socialist Society.[14] Although the Suffragettes had played a key role in Grayson's 1907 by-election victory, he appears thereafter to have drifted away from his friendship with the Pankhurst family. Nevertheless, the suffragettes of the WSPU were keen to damage Liberal election chances wherever possible as revenge for the lack of progress since 1906 on the issue of votes for women. With Grayson now standing in a Liberal marginal seat, Christabel could help defeat the Liberal candidate by encouraging Liberal voters to look to other parties on polling day.

Christabel Pankhurst opened a committee room in Kennington and set teams of canvassers to work, whilst suffragettes harangued voters from street corners to 'keep the Liberal out!'. Collins' record as a Liberal MP had enraged the suffragettes. When the WSPU asked him to sign a petition to Asquith, Collins replied that, as other London Liberal MPs had not signed it, neither could he. In fact, he intimated that he would sign if others did so first, but that 'he did not feel inclined to do so on his own responsibility'.[15]

The visit of Churchill, long a target of the WSPU, was bound to entail a certain amount of disturbance. Suffragettes lined the road to Lambeth Baths with placards calling for votes for women and attacking the Liberal government. Stephen Collins chaired the meeting at which Churchill was the chief speaker. The minister was accompanied by a uniformed police inspector and a squad of plainclothes police and had insisted that, apart from his own wife, the meeting be open to men only, because of persistent suffragette disruption of his meetings. The press reported that 'Great care was taken to exclude the ladies and a strong effort, ineffectual as it subsequently turned out, was made to keep out those who differed politically from Mr. Churchill.' Despite the organisers going to great trouble to keep the meeting free of supporters of votes for women, a man stood up and shouted at Churchill, 'What about the women?' At this point the meeting descended into chaos and a 'prolonged struggle followed for at least ten minutes'. The Home Secretary was left with little time to speak after the disturbance died down as he had another speaking engagement to attend. Nonetheless, he made some general comments about protesters denying free speech by not allowing others the opportunity to speak.

Though it is not clear whether it was because of Grayson's presence in the contest, Collins pulled off something of a coup by securing Harry Gosling to speak on his behalf. Gosling was a committed trade unionist who sat on the parliamentary committee of the TUC.[16] Though he had previously stood as a Labour council candidate, Gosling was now standing as a Labour parliamentary candidate (with Liberal support under the terms of the ongoing electoral pact) in the neighbouring constituency of Lambeth North. This had caused considerable consternation among some ILP members and socialists. As far as Grayson's supporters were concerned, the fact that Gosling should appear on the same platform as Churchill was a demonstration of the essentially conservative nature of the trade unions. Whether Gosling's appearance made much impact on Grayson's vote is now hard to tell, but it can hardly have helped his cause to have a trade unionist and supposed Labour candidate standing on a public platform and asking the electorate to back the Liberal nominee.[17]

Though the Conservative campaign seemed to have little to fear from Victor Grayson, a minority of their supporters were alarmed at the crowded meetings and the extensive press coverage that the socialist candidate was receiving. The Anti-Socialist Union of Great Britain, closely linked to the Conservative Party, sent four speakers and a group of young female leafleteers to campaign specifically against Grayson. They were well organised and well funded and press reports detail a considerable amount of antisocialist literature and posters being distributed across the constituency, with Grayson as the sole target of attack.

The Anti-Socialist Union (ASU) had been formed in 1908 by Ralph D. Blumenfeld, the American-born editor of the *Daily Express*. Blumenfeld was particularly concerned about the social reforms of the Liberal Party which were usually the main focus of his group's activities, and it demonstrates the fear that Grayson generated that on this occasion he was the sole focus of its campaign. Given the resources deployed in the constituency, we can expect that the ASU held anti-Grayson meetings in the days before polling and it is probable, given that ASU meetings elsewhere are reported to have ended in violence, that there could have been some minor disturbances.[18] In fact, of all the Labour and socialist candidates standing in December 1910 only Keir Hardie had a similarly heavy ASU campaign waged against him, some indication of how much of a threat the British establishment still considered Grayson to pose, despite their best efforts to dismiss him as a drunk and an extremist.

Grayson could not shake off his reputation for heavy drinking. Alcohol had cost him the support of some key Colne Valley colleagues during his re-election campaign and now, in the ranks of the Kennington ILP, there was disquiet about Grayson's taste for whisky, which had gone far beyond the realm of social drinking. As Charles Gibson recalled, 'Grayson was, at that time, obviously taking much alcoholic stimulant and disgusted some of the local comrades who could not square this with his idealistic oratory.'[19]

Whilst Grayson forfeited some local socialist support through his drinking, criticism also arrived from another wing of the socialist movement. The *Brixton and Lambeth Gazette* received a letter from Harry Martin,[20] a member of the Socialist Party of Great Britain (SPGB), who announced:

Dear Sir, – The following resolution was passed at our meeting on Monday last, and I was instructed to forward same for publication, trusting you may find it space in your next issue:-

'To the Electors of Kennington
December 1910

The above branch desires to place on record the fact that it disassociates itself entirely from the candidature of the "so-called socialist", Mr. Victor Grayson; and just as strongly opposes the idea that either of the other capitalist nominees are doing anything other than working in the interests of the master class and, consequently, in direct opposition to the workers; and, further, declares that the only thing remaining for working-class electors to do, pending the time the candidate of the Socialist party is put before them, is to go to the polling booth and write "Socialism" across their ballot paper, and thus express themselves in the only way that is open to them at present. The Socialist party calls upon all workers to enroll themselves in its ranks, to speed the day when the emancipated working class will for ever have settled the business of political fakirs of all kinds, – I am, on behalf of the branch,
Yours faithfully
H. Martin'[21]

To this day, the SPGB's statement of revolutionary intent remains unchanged from 1904. Its Declaration of Principles states that the party is

> determined to wage war against all other political parties, whether alleged labour or avowedly capitalist, and calls upon the members of the working class of this country to muster under its banner to the end that a speedy termination may be wrought to the system which deprives them of the fruits of their labour, and that poverty may give place to comfort, privilege to equality, and slavery to freedom.[22]

That it felt unable to support Grayson's candidacy in Kennington smacks of an unrealistic doctrinal policy. Though the SPGB could hardly claim, even in 1910, to have a mass following or influence, its explicit attack on

Grayson's candidature would undoubtedly have caused some soul-searching amongst his potential voters. Harry Martin was a well-known local campaigner, familiar to many Kennington electors, though few would have voted for him given the option. The real impact of his attack was probably to sow even more doubt in the minds of those considering supporting Grayson, who had already heard reports of his drinking and who understood the possibility of aiding a Conservative victory.

As polling day approached, Grayson's brief honeymoon with the local press abruptly ended. The *Brixton and Lambeth Gazette* ran a small feature in which it said that the socialist candidate 'cuts a very solitary figure in the election. He won't attach himself to the Labour Party, and the Socialist Party won't own him, so he is, one may say, a party on his own.' The paper, now openly hostile to Grayson, informed its readers that the term 'comrade' was 'enforced as much as possible' when addressing a fellow socialist. They likened this to the Terror in revolutionary France, when it was possible to lose a hand for failing to use the correct address of 'citizen'. Despite its general antipathy, the newspaper did at least concede that 'Comrade Grayson is a clever speaker, and is quite amusing at times. That is probably why his meetings have been so well attended.' The *Gazette* also commented on Grayson's election address: 'Comrade Victor Grayson ... states that everybody is entitled to the privilege to work. M'yes! but the pity is that everybody doesn't seem to appreciate the privilege.'[23]

While the press turned firmly against Grayson, his Liberal opponents were also urgently reassessing their campaign. Despite publicly writing him off for the previous ten days, the Liberal camp was in a state of panic on the eve of the poll, with speculation growing about the extent of socialist support in the constituency and its potential to impact the result. The Conservative team revealed that their canvassers had found at least 200 Liberal voters who had switched to Grayson. Considering the Liberals' slim 381 majority, this revelation coupled with the superior quality of Tory literature and their greater resources, brought on a mood of depression at the Liberal campaign centre. With less than 24 hours to go until the polls opened, the Liberals desperately changed tack. Their new strategy focused on retaining Liberal support by warning that a vote for Grayson would facilitate a Conservative victory and possibly contribute to the rolling back of Liberal reforms achieved since 1906. Meanwhile, the ASU went on a final offensive against the socialist candidate and warned voters of the danger that Grayson's socialism would put too much power into the hands of ordinary people and alienate the business community.

More drama unfolded in the final hours of the campaign. The WSPU held a raucous thousand-strong meeting at the Priory Institute on the night before polling. Christabel Pankhurst, who had led the WSPU campaign in Kennington, was the main speaker. She rose to loud male interruptions, but insisted that the men involved should not be removed from the meeting. Instead she asked them, and other men in the audience, how they would feel if they had to pay the salaries of MPs without being able to vote for them. At that time MPs received no set salary, although Asquith had promised to introduce a Bill to rectify this. The WSPU was hostile to such a measure, unless a Bill proposing the enfranchisement of women also went forward. Asquith refused to be drawn on the subject. Pankhurst told the crowd, 'This payment of Members of Parliament is the last straw. And if the Prime Minister doesn't give votes to women we shall send a deputation not of 300 or 400, but of 1,000 women to Westminster, to protest against this wrong.'[24]

Pankhurst closed the meeting by imploring the crowd not to vote Liberal, though she remained non-committal as to whom the men should support and nowhere was it reported that she actually urged a vote for Grayson. She criticised the men for being more concerned about limiting the power of House of Lords than they were about achieving votes for women on equal terms with men. Grayson had made the power of the Peers the central theme of his election address, and with the WSPU backing neither parties nor individuals, it had few ways in which to offer him its express support.

Despite the political attacks made on Victor Grayson from all sides, the *Brixton Free Press* had polled its readers and estimated that there were 1,200 avowed socialists in the constituency. It told its readers that if only half of these individuals spoilt their ballots (as the SPGB advised) or voted for Grayson, then the Conservative Colonel Lucas would win. The latter had spent the previous twelve months cultivating the constituency and on polling day gangs of his confident supporters sang:

The Liberals they must pack,
The Socialists they must fly,
Tie their Budget upon their backs and
Say good-bye
To push our Lucas in we'll work with might and main,
We'll keep the Liberals out of it; they shan't go back again.

Polling day saw suffragettes posted outside polling stations with placards calling for the all-male electorate to boycott the Liberal candidate. Liberal and Conservative motor cars, still a novelty out of the reach of most, whizzed back and forth carrying supporters to and from the polls. The previous week's canvass returns were used to knock on the doors of supporters to make sure they got to the polls and voted on time. Grayson toured the constituency in George Bernard Shaw's car, the single vehicle available to his campaign, speaking to voters and ferrying his supporters to the polls.. But his lack of organisational skill, coupled with the absence of the sort of socialist campaign experience that had been present in the Colne Valley, resulted in a lacklustre polling-day performance. The *Brixton Free Press* reported that Grayson and his team 'had no organization, and were relying upon catching chance votes by distributing cards outside the polling stations'.

The count took place at Kennington Road School and the press reported that Liberal supporters were 'emphatic in their expressions of indignation' towards Grayson. It was clear why. As the votes were counted it became evident that Grayson was well behind the other two candidates, but that the final result would be even tighter than in January. Though no recount was called, Liberal faces showed relief that their candidate had narrowly prevailed.[25] The result was as follows:

Collins (Liberal) 3565, Lucas (Conservative) 3510, Grayson (Socialist) 408, Liberal majority – 55

A huge crowd awaited the result as Collins' re-election was announced. The news 'was received with tremendous cheering, mingled with a few groans ... At the committee rooms the demonstrations in favour of the respective candidates were renewed, though the Socialists made no attempt to conceal their chagrin at the scantiness of the support accorded them.'[26] Although his agent, E.O. Joyce, had estimated that Grayson would poll around 500 votes, younger members, particularly those who hero-worshipped Grayson, found the result difficult to accept.

In an editorial in the *Clarion*, Robert Blatchford suggested that Grayson was 'not prepared for such a complete and overwhelming defeat'.[27] Grayson, however, was not one to appear downhearted in public and in an article for a souvenir programme of the campaign he wrote:

We have been beaten in Kennington, we never of course expected to win. With a rock-bottom Socialist vote of 408, the Liberal still reigns with a majority vote of 55. Needless to say, the result has not effaced our smile, nor dampened our enthusiasm. Indeed, when I consider all the peculiar circumstances of this very peculiar election, I feel an inordinate pride in my gallant 408. They must be sturdy fellows, a splendid nucleus for future fights, for there will be fights in Kennington until the obstinate ignorance has been overcome by the Gospel of Socialism. Viewed from the point of view of propaganda and the welfare of the London Socialist Movement, the contest was grand. The seed has been sown, and in due time a rich harvest will be reaped.[28]

How prophetic were the words that Grayson had written! The Kennington ILP had been blooded in its first general election campaign and the money collected at Grayson's packed meetings set the local party up for future contests. Charles Gibson, a young Kennington ILP member in 1910, looked back half a century later and wrote of his experience of the campaign:

It taught me that we needed good ward organisation to get our supporters out to vote, as well as great oratory and packed meetings ... This is certainly true, that he inspired us to go on in spite of Tory and Liberal opposition and the heartbreak of lost elections, until we finally won Kennington for Socialism and have held it ever since.[29]

Kennington finally turned red with a Labour victory in 1929, though this triumph was short-lived. Leonard Matters lost the seat at the subsequent 1931 election. Kennington would have to wait until a 1939 by-election for its next Labour MP, the future government minister John Wilmott. However, when Wilmott switched constituencies for the 1945 contest it was Charles Gibson, the same young ILP member who had proposed and campaigned for Grayson in 1910, who won with a landslide 70.2 per cent of the poll. Gibson held the Kennington seat until it was abolished in 1950.

And what of Grayson? As Gibson recalled:

Immediately after the election he disappeared and we never saw him again. It was a great tragedy because we felt that he could have become a first rate leader of the Socialist movement, but, like some others, he wore himself out and could not control his desire for alcohol.

The Kennington election was Grayson's final campaign for a parliamentary seat. At the time, however, the loss appeared to be a blip and not the end. The election may have shown that Grayson could not work miracles where there was no history of socialist organisation, but it also revealed how much the Liberal Party feared his socialist message. The Liberals recognised that, in a close contest, he and his rhetoric represented as much of a threat as might be posed by the mainstream Labour Party. In this light, Grayson now continued his public speaking across the country as part of a 'socialist unity' campaign.

8

The Battle for a Socialist Party

When any part of Socialism presents itself in the raw reality of a concrete proposal, capable of being adopted by a real government, and carried out by a real Executive, the professed Socialists are the last people in the country who can be depended on to support it.

George Bernard Shaw, 1897[1]

The business of a Socialist Party in the House and in the constituencies can be defined in one word. Fight.

Victor Grayson, 1909[2]

I am an English Socialist. My creed did not come, scimitar in hand, out of the East, it came from what I learned in an English nonconformist chapel.

Robert Blatchford[3]

It needed all the tact and patient persuasion of the leaders to convince the Socialists that their ideals and projects were not to be sacrificed ... [to] the political necessity of supporting the Liberal Party. Bills relating to the budget and the House of Lords ... were not readily comprehended by the average workman ... it is, we think, now admitted that it was a misfortune that the Parliamentary Labour Party ... never managed to put before the country the large outlines of an alternative programme based on the Party's conception of a new social order ... The failure of the Parliamentary Labour Party between 1910 and 1914 to strike the imagination ... led to a certain reaction against political action as such and to a growing doubt among the active spirits as to the value of a Labour Party which did not succeed in taking vigorous independent action, either in Parliament or on the platform and in the press, along the lines of changing the existing order of society.

Sidney and Beatrice Webb[4]

[A]s one who has been on the executive of a trade union he was convinced that there was no possibility of the trade unions striking for socialism. The Socialist Party was not out for the pettifogging reforms which the trade unions were striving for.

Delegate to the Socialist Unity Conference, 1911[5]

It seemed to all those present a preposterous thing that in Great Britain, economically the most advanced country in the world, there should still be no thoroughly organised and disciplined Socialist Party embracing all sections of Socialist thought and consolidating all sorts of Socialist bodies.

Henry Hyndman's Chairman address at the
1912 British Socialist Party Conference[6]

Ever since Grayson's suspension from the House of Commons in 1908, the campaign for a new and explicitly socialist party had gained momentum. The *New Age* and *Clarion* had consistently trumpeted the need for a socialist breakaway from Labour, with Grayson becoming the focal point of this new movement. The Socialist Representation Committee (SRC) – whose name echoed that of the old Labour Representation Committee (LRC) – was gaining ground in Britain's cities and large towns. The SRC's mission was to promote the election of explicitly socialist candidates to public office, whilst building the foundations of what would become a new – and national – socialist party.

Despite the steady growth of the SRC in cities such as Manchester and Birmingham, there were areas where the traditions of the ILP were hard to break. After all, most ILP members regarded themselves as socialists, just as did most Labour MPs. The older pioneers of the Labour movement were angered by what they saw as newcomers, revolutionaries, or simply the politically naive, telling them that they did not believe in the right kind of socialism. But there was genuine and growing discontent within the ranks of the ILP, reflected in a drop in both membership and the number of active branches across the country. Between 1909 and 1911, 46 branches collapsed as a result of inactivity, with a £200 drop in subscriptions. The sale of ILP pamphlets had also fallen by a staggering 50 per cent.[7] This institutional decline was matched by a fall in the number of Labour MPs from 45 to 40 at the January 1910 election.

Although this discontent did not necessarily indicate the desire for a new party, it certainly demonstrated a significant drop in support for the concept of business as usual within the Labour movement. It was only a matter of time before a schism came about, and the only question then would be how many of the discontented would abandon the Labour Party altogether. An informal alliance between the Clarion group, the SDF and other unaffiliated socialists now sought the formation of a united socialist party in order to gain a foothold in Parliament and the country. The malcontents inside the ILP also made their move.

Christopher Douthwaite, a Grayson ally since their days together in the Manchester ILP, had been a steady and unswerving critic of Ramsay MacDonald and the current political trajectory of the Labour Party. Despite his hostility to the leadership – or perhaps because of it – Douthwaite was elected to the National Administrative Council of the ILP, the equivalent of today's National Executive Committee of the Labour Party. From that position, he and three other NAC members authored an incendiary document, published in July 1910, entitled *Let Us Reform the Labour Party*. Due to the colour of its cover, the document became better known as the Green Manifesto. It contained strong criticism of the Parliamentary Labour Party's relationship with the Liberals and the overly cautious electoral strategy pursued in January 1910. Instead, the manifesto called for the Labour Party to vote on issues on their merits, and not according to what would best prolong the Liberal government's hold on power. It was an argument even echoed within the PLP, Fred Jowett MP (and ILP President since January 1910) having called for the same approach. Douthwaite put the case forcefully:

Branches throughout the country are losing members who feel it worse than useless to continue supporting a party which in the eyes of the average man is indistinguishable from the Capitalist Party in the House and country ... Having learned the lessons taught by the failure of the Chartist movement when it became absorbed in the Radical Party and the weakening of the Irish Party in Alliance and its strength in independence, I have faith that when the danger at hand is resolved, the rank and file of the ILP to whom we appeal will not hesitate to reaffirm their belief in the alternative policy of strict independence, supporting or opposing each measure or matter before the House governed, not by the convenience of Governments, or even the importance of retaining a few Labour Seats, but acting in strict accord with that vital principle of independence which alone is the justification for a new political party ...[8]

Douthwaite and his fellow oppositionists were, however, outmanoeuvred. They were condemned at the Birmingham conference of 1911 and lost their seats on the NAC. The ILP dissidents now had few options left other than to look to Grayson to form a new party.

The inclusion of the SDF, Britain's Marxist party and the core of the original left-wing defection from the LRC, was not an unmixed blessing. It tended to believe that it had a monopoly on British socialism. Grayson insisted that the SDF and its leader, Henry Hyndman, would have to be convinced that a new party, bigger and more inclusive than itself, was needed. And, just as he had argued in relation to the ILP, a small number of men should not be able to control everything about the putative new party:

If the same men are chairmen at the conferences, officers of the executive, directors and editors of the official paper and wire-pullers of the political policy, all at the same time, why not turn the whole thing into an absolute monarchy, or ... a composite Popedom inside a latter-day Vatican.[9]

An illustration of the difficulties of united action emerged in September 1910, when the Executive Committee of the SDF prohibited Hyndman from speaking at a meeting of the Manchester SRC. Grayson mocked this decision and challenged the SDF to help build a united socialist party, a British Socialist Party:

The time is ripe for the drawing together into a national scheme, all the tentative and sporadic efforts towards unity that have been going on for

the last few years ... We are on the eve of a great industrial storm. We
socialists should be ready with our compass and chart.[10]

After the loss of his Colne Valley seat and his heavy defeat at Kennington,
Grayson pinned all his hopes on and devoted his energy to the formation
and success of the British Socialist Party. This party is not now much
remembered, save that it was a key element in the birth of the Communist
Party of Great Britain in 1920. But for a brief moment, it looked as if
it might eclipse the ILP and become the new force on the left of British
politics. And it could not have been formed without Victor Grayson.

In August 1911, Grayson finally resigned his membership of the ILP.
Although he had never stood against a Labour candidate, he had twice in
1910 put himself forward as an independent candidate and had spoken
freely in favour of a split in the ILP and the creation of a new party. On
reflection, it is surprising that his membership had not been revoked,
though this was probably a political calculation on the part of ILP officials
that Grayson would pose more of a danger outside the party than within
it. In the *Clarion* on 4 August, he announced:

> The psychological moment has at last arrived. There can be no shadow
> of a doubt about it this time. In the last few years, several moments have
> seemed to be the psychological moment; but this is the real authentic
> one. The time for the formation of the BRITISH SOCIALIST PARTY
> has definitely come!! This is the supreme moment for action. If we miss
> this moment, we have missed the opportunity of a century.[11]

It was a powerful and emotional call to arms from a man whose vision
of this new party was not of a comprehensively mapped out alternative,
but something that came purely from the heart. Nevertheless, more SRCs
began springing up across the country and there was a determined effort
from disparate socialist organisations to pull together and, in the first
instance, ensure that no two socialist candidates would run against one
another. Harry McShane, then a 19-year-old Scottish ILP member, recalled
Grayson's announcement in the *Clarion*, proclaiming the formation of the
British Socialist Party (BSP):

I had no hesitation in joining and I went to my branch of the ILP and moved: 'that we sever all connections with the Independent Labour Party and form the Kingston Branch of the British Socialist Party.' I got three votes with fourteen against. The three of us joined the BSP.[12]

McShane's recollections confirm two points: that Grayson was seen as the main figure in the formation of the BSP, and that dissidents such as McShane were usually in the minority. However, around 40 branches of the ILP did vote to break away and join the BSP. Smaller socialist groups, previously non-aligned socialists, and many who retained dual affiliation with the ILP, made up most of the initial membership. It is also clear, as McShane put it, that those early formative weeks of the BSP felt like 'a fresh beginning for the whole socialist movement in Britain'.[13]

Two weeks after his first article announcing the new party, Grayson wrote a lengthy piece for the *Clarion* entitled *Still They Come*:

Comrades, the deed is done! The British Socialist Party is practically launched! The rally to our call has been magnificent and has heartened us for the task before us. It will not be an easy task, but nothing that was ever worth accomplishing has been easy. It will mean hard and dogged work, sacrifice, and not a little persecution ... from those of our own household of faith ... In the applications already received we have material for one of the finest fighting parties that ever entered battle ... Twelve months of patient and persistent endeavour will see the British Socialist Party, powerful and pugnacious, in the fore-front of the fray. And I sincerely trust it will be so organized and constituted as to render impossible any further compromise with the enemy. We are building up this party not to provide parliamentary careers and lucrative posts for superior working men, but for the purpose of fighting; not merely for the amelioration of the wage-slave's lot, but for the total abolition of the system of wage slavery.[14]

As with previous articles, a form was attached at the bottom which could be filled in, detached and returned to the *Clarion* offices. Thousands expressed an interest in the new party by this means. But some were under

the misapprehension that the BSP would be merely an umbrella organisation, under which existing socialist groups would continue under their
own steam. Grayson rejected any such notion:

> Before signing this declaration form, the question you must ask yourself
> is not whether you are a member of the SDP, ILP, Fabian Society, etc,
> etc. What we want to know is whether, quite regardless of your present
> membership of any organization, you *desire to see established a British
> Socialist Party*. I do not mean a fusion of existing organisations, each of
> which retains its own name and identity in a joint federation. I mean
> an Independent British Socialist Party, and no one should sign this form
> who is not desirous of seeing such a party formed and of joining it ... I
> want these difficulties removed at the outset, so that the work of organi-
> zation may not be impeded.[15]

During the following month, Grayson set out on a short programme of
mass meetings, building up to a Unity Conference, the aim of which was
the creation of the new party. The first of the meetings was held, symboli-
cally, in Bradford where, in 1893, the Independent Labour Party had held
its foundation conference. The Unity Conference took place a few days
later on 30 September and 1 October in the Caxton Hall in Manchester,
the city which had nurtured Grayson's meteoric rise. It was a great success
with socialist groups represented from across Britain:

> Two hundred and nineteen delegates representing some thirty-five
> thousand members were present. Of these 41 came from the ILP, repre-
> senting some 36 branches; 32 were from Clarion Clubs and Fellowships,
> representing 30 organisations; 12 delegates from the 8 freshly estab-
> lished branches of the nascent BSP; 86 more were sent by 77 sections
> of the SDP; 48 more came from miscellaneous groups ranging from
> the Southport Fabian Society through the Hyde Socialist Church to
> the Aberdeen Marxist Socialist Society and the Colne Valley Socialist
> League; 43 organisations sent messages of support but were unable to
> appoint delegates.[16]

Hyndman later summarised the success of the 1911 Unity Conference:

> The Conference was in itself very successful ... the delegates were
> numerous, the discussions were vigorous, the resolutions passed were
> sound and thoroughgoing, the congratulations received from the
> Socialist Parties all over the world were greatly encouraging ... We thus
> proclaimed at one and the same time our solidarity with foreign Social-
> ists in their struggle to obtain political freedom, and established the
> historic continuity of our own efforts to achieve complete economic
> emancipation for the workers of the world.[17]

During the conference itself, Harry Quelch of the SDP put forward a
resolution on the new party's aims and objectives, which were uncom-
promisingly militant and revolutionary. He added that if those present
'did not mean what the terms of the resolution expressed they had no
business there at all'. Only a minor amendment to delete an inoffensive
line was carried, while another to delete reference to 'class war' was soundly
defeated. The amended resolution, as now passed, read:

> The Socialist Party is the political expression of the Working Class
> Movement, acting in the closest co-operation with the industrial organ-
> isations for the socialization of the means of production and distribution
> – that is to say, the transformation of capitalist society into a collec-
> tivist or communist society. Alike in its objects, its details, and in the
> means employed, the Socialist Party, is not a reformist but a revolution-
> ary party, which recognizes that social freedom and equality can only be
> won by fighting the class war through to the finish, and thus abolishing
> forever all class distinctions.[18]

With the carrying of the motion the attendees stood to applaud, sing 'The
Red Flag' and give three cheers for 'the Social Revolution'.[19] Delegates were
immersed in an atmosphere of hope and anticipation that, finally, a party
was being built which would usher in the socialist society.

Disparate groups really did seem to be coming together in the manner
Grayson had envisaged and written of in his *Clarion* article. Among the

delegates in Manchester were two former members of Labour's NAC who had signed the Green Manifesto, Leonard Hall and Russell Smart, and even the arch-sectarians of the SDF seemed to come on board. On the second day a ten-man provisional executive committee was elected, under the supervision of Henry Hyndman as honorary chairman, to prepare a constitution for adoption at a founding conference to be held the following year. Grayson was elected to the committee, along with four members of the SDF, Hall and Smart from the ILP, two members of the Clarion Cyclists and George Simpson, a Marxist and syndicalist.[20] The committee met in London to approve the following aims and objectives for the new party:

OBJECT. – The object of the British Socialist Party is the establishment of the Co-operative Commonwealth – that is to say, the transformation of capitalist competitive society into a Socialist or Communist Society.

IMMEDIATE ACTION. – The British Socialist Party supports all measures that tend to protect the life and health of the workers, and to strengthen them in their struggle against the capitalist class.

METHODS. – The education of the people in the principles of Socialism.

- The closest possible co-operation with industrial organisations tending towards the socialization of production, and the advocacy of the industrial unity of the workers as essential for effective organisation to that end.
- The establishment of a Socialist Party in Parliament and on local bodies completely independent of all parties which support the capitalist system.[21]

Briefly, the British socialist movement seemed to be on the cusp of a great leap forward. And it was Grayson, no matter what his critics said of his lack of organisational ability, who had brought this moment about. For the younger generation of socialists, he was their leader and their inspiration. Harry McShane, one of the earliest active members, recalled:

We began to get in between the two [SDF and ILP] and to preach class struggle, revolution, and extra-parliamentary activity without being anti-parliamentarian. At all our meetings we advocated the Grayson line, that every MP should feel he was in the camp of the enemy and sitting on pins and needles. We weren't big but we were very active.[22]

Many BSP policies that McShane and his comrades were urging the British left to adopt seem curiously mild by today's norms. They included the introduction of Child Maintenance, a Minimum Wage, the Eight Hour working-day, Proportional Representation, universal adult suffrage, Home Rule for Ireland and the abolition of the House of Lords. Some socialists, however, including the SDF's Harry Quelch, who called for the abolition of the military and the formation of a citizen army, wanted a much more militant programme. Neither were those Marxists, who had flocked to the new party, in agreement with a programme of moderation. Younger men such as McShane, the syndicalists and the ILP contingents saw the workers themselves as the harbingers of the new dawn, and were suspicious that the older men of the SDF, especially Hyndman, viewed matters differently. In his influential *England for All*, which plagiarised large sections of Marx's *Capital*, Hyndman had stated that the idea that

the emancipation of the workers must be brought about by the workers themselves is true in the sense that we cannot have Socialism without Socialists ... But a slave cannot be freed by the slaves themselves. The leadership, the initiative, the teaching, the organization must come from those who are born into a different position and are trained to use their faculties in early life.[23]

Some feared that this was a warning that the high-born Hyndman believed the working class to be incapable of bringing about a socialist society in Britain without the leadership of upper-class, well-educated men such as himself. But Hyndman, the self-professed Marxist, had strayed far from Marx. In *An Open Letter to the Social Democratic Party*, Engels had written:

The emancipation of the working classes must be brought about by the working classes themselves. We cannot therefore associate ourselves with

people who openly state that the workers are too uneducated to eman-
cipate themselves and must be freed from above by philanthropic big
bourgeois and petty bourgeois ... for which purpose the working class
must place itself under the leadership of the 'educated and propertied
bourgeoisie' who alone possess the time and opportunity to acquaint
themselves with what is good for the workers.[24]

There were also those who believed that the whole enterprise of binding
disparate groups within the unitary organisation of the BSP was doomed
from the start. John Maclean, then a member of the SDF and outspoken
supporter of Grayson, pointed to fundamental differences in political
outlook and methods between the two main groups, the ILP and the SDF:

> The ILP are loving brothers when they wish SDP members to aid in
> open-air summer propaganda. They work separately when the indoor
> season begins, and when the selection of constituencies and candidates
> arrives, they carefully avoid taking the SDP into consideration until
> the candidate has been put in the field, and then again they become
> anxious for socialist unity to return their man ... Those who dream
> of the accomplishment of a single socialist party by a kindly feeling
> being fostered between the leaders, etc, are Utopians ignorant of history,
> ignorant of men, and ignorant of the material forces that compel unity
> for any purpose.[25]

Unfortunately for Grayson, Maclean's instincts were correct. Any lingering
jubilation or sense of brotherhood deriving from the Unity Conference
was lost once the provisional executive committee got to work. It quickly
became apparent that the SDF contingent had no intention of liquidat-
ing their own party to form the new BSP, but instead intended to use the
whole process to strengthen themselves. First, the secretary of the SDF,
H.W. Lee, was appointed as the BSP secretary, rather than David Reid,
who had been processing membership applications made to the *Clarion*
offices. Then the committee voted to close down the small, temporary
office being used by Reid and to move instead to the SDF offices. Finally,
the executive committee declared that the BSP was formed, without the

SDF having first dissolved its internal structure and branches. Grayson suddenly realised that he had been outmanoeuvred, and that the SDF had secured full organisational control of the new party. But it was too late. Nor did the non-SDF committee members come to the rescue. Leonard Hall from the ILP suspected that Grayson wanted to set up 'a Grayson Party', whilst the SDF men probably saw Grayson as being of no more use to them; he had built the foundations of a party with 40,000 members and now they were ready to snatch it from him. So Grayson left the second meeting of the provisional executive committee and did not attend another. He played down rumours that he had left the BSP altogether and made one last attempt, via the *Clarion*, to persuade the SDF that 'the new Party must make a fresh start or it is doomed to failure'.[26] But he himself had failed.

When the BSP's first annual conference was held at the Manchester Free Trade Hall on 25–27 May 1912, Grayson was absent. The delegates were told that he had attended only two out of seven provisional executive committee meetings. In his chairman's address, Hyndman told the conference: 'I should not be telling you the truth if I were to say that my post has been wholly a sinecure. There have been difficulties to surmount, and there are still some divergences of opinion to be bridged over.'[27] It was a classic example of British understatement. McShane and his younger comrades were asking 'where is Grayson?' and it took time for the full story to emerge.[28] With the SDF's domination confirmed, McShane realised that the project was not working out as he had hoped: 'We had all joined the BSP because we wanted a different kind of party, a party that was more lively, with less of the old phrases, more active and able to lead struggles.'[29] But in the event, the BSP was led by 'the same sort of reformers as the leaders of the ILP, only they used Marxist phrases'.[30]

With hindsight, it was a wasted opportunity for the British left. The timing of the launch of a fighting revolutionary party could not have been better. The summer of 1911 had seen a wave of industrial unrest, the like of which Britain had never before witnessed. The transport workers' strikes of 1911 saw the seamen, the dockers, and finally the railwaymen all go out on strike. New socialist clubs were opening across the country and Grayson returned to the Colne Valley to lay the foundation stone of the

Marsden Socialist Club. The Church Socialist League, whose Conrad Noel had demanded an independent socialist party after Grayson's by-election victory, was now calling publicly for such a party. Grayson was again invited to attend the Durham Miners Gala on 22 July, this time not as an MP but as the leading light of a new party. The appetite was there, so was a ready membership. But the concept was flawed from the beginning.

It is difficult to believe that Grayson would have felt anything other than betrayed on the part of Hyndman and the others. At the peak of his powers, they had lauded him, and he had shared platforms with them to raise their own profiles. But now Grayson would not even get the chance to join the party he had done more than anyone else to create. He had imagined that these old hands would give up their existing parties and positions of power within them, to start a new party in which they risked having little real influence. The SDF never had any intention of dissolving itself into the BSP, though some of its members played along for a short while. Grayson lacked the battle scars from long hours spent in committee meetings that these men had, and was thus ill-prepared to negotiate with them on equal terms.

The British Socialist Party limped on and many key figures of the British socialist movement passed through its ranks. But it was predictably riven by sectarianism, as became only too apparent at the outbreak of the First World War.

9

More Than Just a 'Cheap Orator'

I don't care for Grayson, he is a young, cheap orator, not at all the type
we wish to get into Parliament

John Bruce Glasier[1]

The Journalist

Historians have largely overlooked Victor Grayson's career as a prolific
and accomplished journalist. His writing appeared in popular progressive
papers and magazines, particularly the *Clarion* and the *New Age*, which
enjoyed a respectable level of circulation and readership. In general, his
written output was not up to the standard of his oratory, but on occasion
it was no less influential. Later socialists and trade unionists recalled some
of his parables word-for-word several decades later, such was their power.
The inconsistent quality of his writing was no doubt affected by the scale
of his speaking commitments. The message, however, was always consistent: the need for socialism.

Back in 1907, two northern socialists, with a love of Nietzsche and the
arts, purchased an ailing but radical Christian socialist weekly called the
New Age. With financial assistance from George Bernard Shaw, Alfred
Richard Orage and Holbrook Jackson worked as co-editors to turn around
the magazine's fortunes. Orage declared that the paper should now act
as 'a free platform for socialist discussion' and that such discussion 'must
be kept open at all costs' as socialists could agree on little apart from a
dislike of private property.[2] Although it continued to encounter financial
problems, the *New Age* was one of the most important political papers
of the era, rising to a peak circulation of 23,500 in 1908, at a time when
Victor Grayson was closely associated with the title.

The political commentary of the *New Age* was fine-tuned by Orage
throughout 1907 and 1908, to keep up an unstinting criticism of those

Labour leaders who he felt had 'easily succumbed to the charms of parliamentary membership, and insensibly adopted the ambitions of their
fellow-members in the House of Commons'.[3] Rank and file trade unionists
and socialists were increasingly impatient with their leaders, and the *New
Age* 'fomented their discontent, often leading their clamour for a militant
and uncompromising policy in Parliament'.[4] Its readers were bombarded
with calls for Labour MPs to violate the ancient customs of the House of
Commons and adopt the revolutionary tactics necessary to secure genuine
socialism.

Orage was never one to miss the chance of publicity and, just six days
after Grayson was suspended from the Commons for his unemployment
protest, Orage offered him the role of political editor. Orage needed a big
name to turn around the fortunes of the ailing paper, and it turned out to
be an astute appointment. Grayson's name sold papers and *New Age* acted
as a national vehicle for his political call to arms. Almost immediately, the
Labour establishment turned its fire on the paper, with Keir Hardie stating
that the 'handful of irresponsibles who control the political policy of the
New Age, most of them disciples of Nietzsche – the neurotic apostle of
modern Anarchism – who assail the Labour Party, are thereby assailing the
canons of classical Socialist doctrine'. Orage responded that it was 'a mere
trifle that not a single member of our staff is a disciple of Nietzsche; it is
even a less trifle that Nietzsche is not an apostle of modern Anarchism'.[5]

Grayson's tenure was short: he only served as political editor from
October 1908 until February 1909. But he was one of the few contributors to get paid for his efforts and it undoubtedly helped him to reach a
wider audience. Politically, the *New Age* could not have done more to side
with Grayson. Its columns were loyal to his views and regularly attacked
the lethargy of the Parliamentary Labour Party. One edition even lauded
Grayson as 'the most significant force in British politics'.[6] It would become
a major advocate of the formation of the British Socialist Party.

Initially, however, Orage had seen things differently. He had written to
H.G. Wells in the summer of 1907 to say that 'the *New Age* will work for the
Socialist Movement, and not for a socialist party' and agreed with Wells's
opinion that 'the idea of a doctrinaire socialist political party should be
rejected'.[7] However, by 1908 Orage had changed his mind. With disquiet

in the ranks of the Labour Party showing no signs of abating, the *New Age* proposed the formation of a new socialist party. Shortly after Grayson's appointment in October 1908, Orage wrote again to Wells, hoping that the latter would appreciate 'the significance' of this development.[8] The significance was that there were those who believed Grayson would shortly capture the leadership of the ILP, and with it the Labour Party. Orage was one of them.

Grayson's fellow contributors to the *New Age* were major figures in the British literary circles. H.G. Wells, G.B. Shaw, Cecil Chesterton, Sam Hobson and G.R.S. Taylor all wrote political pieces during Grayson's editorship. Chesterton, Taylor and Hobson all used the columns of the *New Age* to advocate a new socialist party. Wells, however, was not in agreement with them. In a letter to the *Christian Commonwealth* he wrote:

> For my own part, I have no hesitation in saying that my confidence is wholly with Keir Hardie, Snowden, and Ramsay MacDonald. There are no men fit to replace them in the party. They and their associates stand for all that is sane and practicable and hopeful in Socialist politics. I don't believe in Grayson. I think he has all the levity of youth added to an instability that will last his lifetime. He may do all sorts of things in the world, but politically he will never be anything but a nuisance to his own side. I wouldn't lend him a horse. If I found myself commanding a besieged fort short of food, water, and ammunition, and hard pressed, and Grayson was in the fort, I should put him outside … I think I speak for almost all commonplace, sensible men when I declare that the alternative in Socialist politics to loyalty to the old I.L.P. group is simply no Socialist politics at all. To build on these others would be like building on a hill of soapsuds and sodawater.
>
> Very truly yours,
H.G. Wells[9]

Wells was, however, in a minority at the *New Age*. The paper had given significant coverage to Grayson's suspension from Parliament and during his tenure as political editor, it became his personal propaganda organ. Contributors called for the formation of Socialist Representation Committees and built up Grayson as the de facto leader of a new party. As Grayson's star shone brightly, Orage did his best to appear the power behind him. The editor had made such a strong impression on Beatrice Webb that she said that she 'gained the impression that Orage himself would soon be at Grayson's right hand leading a socialist Labour Party'.[10]

But there were more casualties than just Wells when the *New Age* swung definitively behind Grayson. Holbrook Jackson, Orage's business partner, parted ways with the paper, supposedly over attitudes to advertisements, though this was a flimsy excuse. When Sam Hobson called on the Fabian Society to cut its ties with Labour and throw in its lot to form a new socialist party, the Fabians, who had initially supported Orage's editorship, also withdrew support. Only the lone Fabian voice of a Mr E. Nesbit remained and, as a dedicated follower of Grayson, he contributed glowing poems in praise of his hero. The *New Age* continued to build up Grayson as the coming socialist successor to the Labour leadership of MacDonald, but after the former's bizarre behaviour at the 1909 Portsmouth conference, where he failed to take the platform and challenge the leadership, Orage dropped him like a stone. The following month Grayson and the *New Age* parted company. The paper moved away from party politics whilst Orage himself was increasingly drawn to spiritualism.

After Grayson's departure from the *New Age*, the *Clarion* carried two of his fictional short stories in 1909, 'A Dead Man's Story' and 'The Myopians' Muddle'. In the first, Grayson's fictional persona recounts a dream in which he has a conversation with a ghost who represents suicide. The ghost of suicide sets out his case for the narrator, choosing death over life: an end to unemployment, an end to starvation, and an end to living in the prison of an economic and legal system over which the narrator has no control. Grayson ends the story with the political statement, 'Life must be made worth keeping. It must be as free as the sun and as dignified as the stars.'[11]

In 'The Myopians' Muddle' Grayson launches into a bitter attack upon the Labour Party and its supporters. He introduces two groups – the Myopians and the Panopians. The Myopians represent the workers and voters, who see politics in terms of short-term gains and opportunities, whilst the Panopians are the politicians and employers, who see the big picture and hold on to power by enslaving the Myopians. Then we are introduced to the Fakir who represents the role of religion in society. The Fakir's work consists of peddling stories of a distant paradise to the Myopians, with the aim of cooling any feelings of disquiet they may have about the system in which they find themselves. The party political system – and Parliament itself – is represented by a circular railway on which the Myopians travel, convinced they are moving forwards and progressing. The train driver wears a blue uniform (Conservative) and the conductor a red uniform (Labour). There is no yellow uniform (Liberal Party) as Grayson seems to be suggesting that they are already encompassed in the red uniform – an attack on the Labour Party's relationship with the Liberals – and that they are one and the same. The fact that the driver and conductor both work together on the same train speaks to Grayson's accusation that the Labour Party in Parliament is just as culpable as the Conservative Party in fooling the workers into believing that real change was achievable through the ballot box. When the conductor (Labour) shouts 'All change here!' he is in fact signalling the return to the start. His call is as illusory as the journey itself. The hero of the story is a young man, clearly Grayson, who attempts to show the Myopians the reality of the world in which they live. He tries to open the eyes of the British worker to the conservative nature of Britain's political system and suggests that only he, Grayson, and his socialist message can save them. The fictional Grayson is unsuccessful and is thrown from the train whilst it continues its circular journey of no progress. The whole railway system is a trick because the Myopian traveller always ends up where he began. It all confirms the lack of faith Grayson had in Britain's parliamentary system.

'The Myopians' Muddle' remains one of Grayson's more imaginative and memorable works. It is particularly poignant in that he appears accurately to predict his own political future. He was, at the time of writing, still an MP. He must, thus, have suspected quite early on that he himself – and his vision of socialism – would have no long-term place in the British political establishment. The struggle would have to be fought from the outside. The fable is a call to arms directed at the workers, telling them that the change they are offered at election time is an illusion, and that Parliament is a veil masking the truth, that voting has no effect on the actions of employers and politicians, who run the country for their own ends.

The story demonstrates not only Grayson's hostility to the Labour Party but also his total break from organised religion. Only four or five years earlier, he had seen religion as the best vehicle by which to change society; now religion is presented as a mere sponge, owned by the establishment and the capitalist class and designed merely to soak up the discontent of the working class, to maintain the status quo and enhance their grip on power.

By 1912 Grayson was writing in *Justice*, the newspaper of the SDF. By this time, he had been manoeuvred out of the British Socialist Party, which he had striven so hard to create. It was the SDF that had hoodwinked Grayson, and the other socialists, by not dissolving itself, so it was surprising that he was still prepared to write for its paper. This was undoubtedly a Faustian pact: Grayson needed the money, desperately, and the SDF knew that his name still sold papers. One of the major pieces Grayson wrote for *Justice* was 'The Lost Vision: A Spring Fantasy'. It was another autobiographical story featuring a young man, but this time the emphasis was on lost hope and youth. In retrospect it has the feel of a political obituary. The young man finds himself standing in a 'green-budding wood' in early spring, as the earth has pulled itself from the darkness of winter. With an eye perhaps to his own early successes Grayson wrote:

> A song was singing in the young man's soul. His eyes beamed with the light of joyous vision. He was sharing Nature's dream of coming glory; in his heart fresh shoots of hope were springing; he bathed his spirit in the gladness of the world's new birth. From sheer joy of existence he shouted aloud, and a thousand birds responded with an anthem of confident and forward-looking faith.[12]

The story continues with a bitter description of the lives of the working class. The young man sees

> rows and rows of putrid hovels where starved and hopeless slaves breathe out tired and paltry lives ... dens at sunrise spawning forth their semi-

human contents into the congested reek of mean streets ... children
– sweet little flowers of humanity soiled and bruised in the bud ... their
little skeletal arms and hands grasping at the disease-fouled air ...

Grayson develops this dystopian nightmare to include mothers bending
over infant graves and daughters selling their bodies for food, whilst the
remainder are 'cooped for long hours in sultry factories, and being done to
death in accursed sweat dens'.[13] The acute desperation of the worst conditions of the industrial working class are laid bare, whilst the hero, Grayson,
sees the idle rich living in 'mansions whose bricks are compounded of the
wage-slaves' flesh, and whose mortar was their blood'.

The familiar theme of politicians and establishment figures colluding
to maintain the status quo, recurrent in Grayson's writings, returns here:

He saw crafty lawyers – out for gold – and ambitious politicians – out
for place – sitting together in the seats of the mighty – protecting the
Constitution. He saw the whole tangled mess of lies, cunning, cant,
chicane and fraud which buttresses and sustains the vast structure of
privileged tyranny.[14]

The young man returns to the wood only to find that what was previously paradise is slowly being destroyed by its own inhabitants. Revealed
to him is the 'universal horror' that '[h]ere in the wood, as in the world,
were paupers and criminals and idle rich'. But in his pit of despair, the
sun suddenly shines upon him through the trees and he finds again the
'Vision', straightens his back, lifts his head up, clenches his fists and strides
confidently back to 'the human battle-field'. The story then ends abruptly
with the young man, now considerably older, physically weaker but also
wealthier, trying once again to find the 'Vision'. But he has lost what he
once had and now only remembers 'the first few battles with greed; the
glamour of power, the cunning deals, the attainment of riches – and now'
he realises, 'though he can *buy* anything, he can truly own nothing'.

The story is clearly autobiographical, but written by someone in the
depths of depression. Grayson had once been the young man – the hero
whom thousands followed – but he had then seen power from the inside.

He had seen how politicians and the rich colluded in luxury, whilst the workers toiled in unbearable conditions and suffered constant privation. Grayson had returned to the wood – possibly signifying the Labour Party – only to find it infected with the same diseases of greed and power. Then he sees a vision which reignites his faith – the launch of the British Socialist Party in which he had placed his hope for the future of socialism and the working class. But the vision is lost and Grayson, now a physically older and weaker hero, can no longer discern a brighter future.

Perhaps the test of any journalist is the longevity of their writing and, shortly before his death in 1965, Willie Gallagher, the former ILP and SDF member and Communist MP, could still remember with clarity one of Grayson's socialist fables:

> He published a pamphlet entitled *The Fly Fly, and Other Stories*, the opening story of which was a sort of parable illustrating the method used by trade union leaders to get a rise out of the working class. A group of flies got stuck in a jam pot. One of them pulled a leg out, licked it clean, then – stuck it back into the jam as it pulled out another. After doing this several times, it saw that it was never going to get free. Then it had a great idea! It licked a leg clean, and put it on the back of another fly; this it did until all its legs were clean and free and so, on the backs of its fellows, secured its freedom. The moral we were intended to draw was that the trade union leaders got out of the struggle by standing on the backs of the rank and file, or, as it was popularly put by the cynical: 'They believe in the emancipation of the working class, one at a time!'[15]

Although a copy of the pamphlet cannot now be found (not unusual given that they were cheaply produced and often restricted to short print-runs), it chimes with the essence of Grayson's other stories and highlights his antipathy towards trade union leaders.

A forgotten piece of Grayson's canon which merits resurrection is the preface he was invited to pen by George Simpson, for his pamphlet, *Infantile Mortality and the Birth Rate*. While those in power called for a higher birth rate to sustain the development of the Empire, Grayson railed against the blindness of the British class system:

Someone has foolishly declared that England's battles were won on 'The playing grounds of Eton'. We can dismiss the arrant snobbery of the remark and still recognise the germ of implied truth which it contains. It would be infinitely more pertinent and true to say that, if the British Empire ever smashes up, its fall has been prepared in the foetid atmosphere of our town and city slums.

He considered appeals for a higher birth rate 'futile' as

thoughtful persons are beginning to ask if they are morally entitled to bring more children into a world which butchers its infants with an indifference and a callousness which out Herod's Herod ... The circumstances into which the great mass of British Children are born, preclude them from being efficient, either as warriors or workers ... Socialism is the only remedy for all these evils.

This latter point had been pitifully apparent at the time of the Boer War (1899–1902), when a disproportionate number of working-class men were turned away from the recruitment offices due to ill-health and physical disability. But it was only when the country needed these men to put on a uniform and fight that those in charge appeared at all concerned.

The Problem of Parliament

Written in conjunction with fellow *New Age* contributor G.R.S. Taylor, *The Problem of Parliament* (1909) was Victor Grayson's only attempt at a serious theoretical work. In brief, it called for unity amongst Britain's various left-wing and socialist factions as the starting point from which to seize power. The introductory message on the fly-leaf read:

We dedicate this little book to H.M. Hyndman, Robert Blatchford, and Keir Hardie, who can give this country a Socialist Party tomorrow, if they care to lead the way. If our leaders will not lead, then to the rank and file, who are getting ready to go forward without them.

Despite many rank and file socialists across the country identifying him as a leader – if not the leader – of the socialist movement, Grayson did not see himself in this light. This perhaps explains his refusal to take the stage at the Portsmouth ILP conference in 1909, where he was expected to challenge for the leadership of the party. Grayson had no wish to be the leader of the new movement but felt that the mantle was continually being thrust upon him. Throughout the work, Grayson's presentation of socialism shows how far he had fallen under the influence of Hyndman and the SDF. Unlike his earlier and later years when he put the emphasis on the unemployed and workers themselves to take power, *The Problem of Parliament* calls for established leaders and intellectuals to show the way, intimating that the workers themselves were not suitably ready for such a task. It was the responsibility of the intellectuals, he said, to 'fire the people with a desire for reform'. Grayson's views at this time show some similarity to what Lenin had called for in *What Is to be Done* (1902), published seven years earlier, and to what Hyndman had been proposing for the last three decades. The major difference between Leninism and Graysonism was that the former called for a vanguard of professional revolutionaries to lead the masses, whereas Grayson suggested that state power should be 'put in the hands of the most experienced and highly trained men of business who can be discovered … Control by expert officials … that is the ideal before Socialists.' It is interesting to note that Grayson's notion, which was very much the SDF line, bears striking similarities to the concept of the corporate state (or Corporatism) espoused later by Mussolini, and, in Britain, by Oswald Mosley.

Whatever the retrospective criticism, *The Problem of Parliament* was embraced by the activists who would make up the newly formed British Socialist Party. After all, it had been written specifically for them, but it encountered considerable criticism from elsewhere on the left. The Socialist Party of Great Britain attacked Grayson's insistence on the need for leaders because the alternative

is the one thing dreaded by the ruling class; an intelligent working class without leaders. The latter, too, object to any scheme in which they do not figure conspicuously. Leaders, therefore, become identified with the ruling class – their interests are identical and in opposition to the working class, which can never be free, even in thought, while it submits to leaders.[16]

Marriage

Grayson certainly attracted women of all classes and ages, married or not. There are stories of women moving to the Colne Valley to be represented by him, and of others who moved to London (one even to the same building) when he went there. Some pawned wedding rings to fund his elections, whilst wealthy widows frequently gave him large sums. The love from these women rarely seems to have been reciprocated, at least in the long term. The cynical may question whether Grayson, well aware of the effect he had on women, used his appeal to elicit money to support his lifestyle, and even as cover for his homosexual life.

Although there had been frequent rumours of Grayson marrying, after Miss Panton-Ham at the Unitarian College, there had been no serious prospect of this happening until Robert Blatchford's daughter, Winifred, came onto the scene. She was an attractive young woman who wrote for her father's paper, the *Clarion*, and also the *Woman Worker*, to both of which Grayson also contributed. They spent so much time together that they were regarded as being as good as engaged. But despite his own close association with Grayson, Robert Blatchford put an end to the budding relationship between his daughter and his political protégé. Several letters from Blatchford to his daughter survive and reveal interesting insights into Grayson's character:

> Once or twice when I have thought you seemed interested in Mr God I have bumped myself. I like Victor; but that would be a calamity. You and he would not hit it off even if all the conditions were good. I don't think Victor will ever marry and I hope he won't.

'Mr God' was the Blatchford family's pet-name for Grayson, but his most striking observation was his hope and expectation that Grayson would never marry. The point is developed in a further letter:

I have never seen him show nor heard him express any regard for any woman. His general attitude towards the whole sex is one of suspicion. I have never known a young man so cold towards women. I don't think he ever loved anybody. There is always something odd about him. I don't think he will ever marry and I don't think he or his wife would be at all happy if he did ... And then there is the other thing. No, I would not trust him. He may alter; and he may get worse; but he is not safe.

We cannot be sure as to what exactly Blatchford was referring. It could be Grayson's epilepsy, but this seems rather unlikely, or it could be his growing dependency on drink. Epilepsy would hardly have been a matter of 'trust' and there should have been no difficulty in openly criticising Grayson's excessive drinking. This leaves the probability that Blatchford was obliquely referring to Grayson's liaisons with men, which were illegal and, in that sense, 'not safe'. It was also a topic which a father at that time would have found it difficult to discuss with his daughter. At all events, his intervention had the desired outcome, Grayson and Winifred ended their relationship and Grayson quickly met someone else.

Although his political career had taken several blows, Grayson's London social life was hectic. He was particularly drawn to spending his time with figures from the world of acting and he formed a close bond with Arthur Rose, a socialist and impresario. It is likely that Rose and Grayson had an illicit affair as Rose admitted years later that the two enjoyed 'a love deeper, perhaps, than the love between man and woman'.[17] It is probably no coincidence, then, that the surviving letters between Harry Dawson and Grayson documenting their love of each other appear to end in 1911, when Rose and Grayson seem to have been at their closest. But the two grew apart when, through Rose, Grayson met Ruth Nightingale, who performed under the stage name, Ruth Norreys. She was the 25-year-old only child of a Bolton bank manager. She had appeared at several British Socialist Party meetings to recite Elizabeth Browning's 1843 poem, *The Cry of the Children*, a moving attack on the lot of child labourers, forced to spend most of their short lives working underground or in factories. Norreys was understudying at the Comedy Theatre when she unexpect-edly married Grayson at Chelsea Registry Office on 8 November 1912. To the knowledge of her colleagues, Grayson had not attended any of her performances, nor had she given them any indication that the two were in a serious relationship.

Ruth had in her something of the same wayward streak that Grayson also possessed. She had attended an exclusive boarding school in Heaton Chapel, Greater Manchester, to which girls were sent from around Britain and the Empire. She had a love of the arts and performing and had joined the Esmonde Bramley Shakespearean Company, described as 'probably now the finest Shakespearean Company touring' by the *Lancashire Evening Post* in April 1906. By 1911, according to the census, she was living in a large shared house in Edgbaston, Birmingham, describing her occupation as 'Elocutionist, Teacher and Reciter'. By this point she had spent at least three years living in the city and it was here, in the suburb of Moseley, that she was baptised in October 1908, aged 21. Adult baptism was unusual, granted the religious convention of the time, but later, whilst married to Grayson, she converted to Catholicism. Some called her 'flighty', whilst Rose, who knew her well, found her amoral. Few of their friends thought the couple a good match and even fewer thought the marriage would last. But for a brief period, Grayson and his new wife were certainly happy and, despite his political setbacks in 1912, it was hoped that marriage might stabilise his private life sufficiently to build the foundation of a political comeback.

On the evening of their wedding, Mr and Mrs Grayson travelled to Walthamstow for Grayson to fulfil a speaking engagement. The *Daily Herald* reported:

> Victor Grayson and his wife had an enthusiastic reception from several thousand socialists ... with that great, gruff voice and humorous manner of his, he gave the audience incident after incident, witticism after witticism, making the great Walthamstow Baths vibrate to each note of pathos or indignation or humour.[18]

But as the newspaper reports of their surprise marriage receded, any illusions Ruth may have had about her new husband were quickly shattered. The Graysons had no steady income and Victor's increasing reliance on whisky was to hinder any prospect of an imminent return to politics.

10

A Taste of War

The telegram telling of the capitulation of the German Social Democrats shocked me even more than the declaration of war.

Leon Trotsky[1]

The world war has changed the conditions of our struggle, and has changed us most of all.

Rosa Luxemburg, The Funius pamphlet, 1915

In abstract terms, all prominent socialist leaders opposed war and denounced imperialism, and it was believed that the great majority of the rank and file, party members and trade unionists, were also committed to peace and 'internationalism'. In the event, however, the area mass of the people supported enthusiastically their respective states in the war effort, and the 'betrayal' of internationalism by social democratic leaders only reflected mass feeling.

R.N. Berki[2]

In the opening weeks of 1913, Victor Grayson was in poor mental and physical health. Only a few weeks after his marriage to Ruth, he suffered a breakdown and, after a brief recovery, suffered a more serious nervous collapse in February. What speaking engagements he had left were cancelled on the advice of his doctor and, with them, Grayson's primary source of income disappeared. Leading up to his collapse, he was drinking at least a bottle of whisky a day which caused him to miss meetings and forego his pay. Grayson was also obliged to give up his rooms in Stockwell Park Road and move to a poorer area. The young Fenner Brockway visited Grayson at this time and later recalled:

After a time [Grayson] became impossible, failing to appear at meeting after meeting. I remember waiting for him at Victoria Station, Manchester, whilst thousands crowded the Free Trade Hall expecting him. He never arrived. The last time I saw him he was down and out, occupying with his actress wife a room in a side street off Theobalds Road in London – the room furnished only with a bed, one chair, a sugar box for a table.[3]

Without the income from his meetings, it seems that Grayson had taken to pawning what few possessions the couple had. His political and social life had collapsed almost as quickly as his health and, with a wife who had expected much more from married life, he seemed to be in an impossible slump. But there were still those who believed in him, amongst them many of the men and women of the Colne Valley, on whom he had made such an impression. On 14 February 1913, a letter penned by Arthur Rose and Fred Gorle was published in the *Clarion* announcing that Grayson was in poor health and in need of a long period of rest. A national appeal for donations was launched and a committee was set up to administer the funds. In three months the appeal raised £106 16s 10d (around £9,000 in today's value). Fenner Brockway and Margaret Bondfield were amongst those who donated, alongside socialists and well-wishers from across Britain.

With the funds raised, the Graysons set sail for the warmer climes of Italy, though his health again faltered when the Sirocco winds from North Africa brought with them the sandy 'blood rain'. They set sail again, this time leaving Naples for New York on 3 April 1913, a journey lasting a fortnight. Once docked, they were greeted by a wave of industrial unrest across New York and New Jersey, with an ongoing strike led by Industrial Workers of the World (IWW). Within 48 hours of his arrival, Grayson gave an interview to the *New York Times*, whose publication, despite the interviewer saying the couple looked 'harmless', caused a stir. Under the headline 'Says He'd Justify Murder in Strikes – Grayson, Expelled Socialist MP Thinks It's Warranted to Gain Victory', he was quoted as saying:

I am in full sympathy with the Industrial Workers of the World. Although I would not entirely abandon the political instrument, I would use it only as a means of obstruction. Yes, I believe in sabotage, too. I believe any action would be justified which would prove effective … I certainly shouldn't encourage or propagate the idea of wholesale murder to win a strike. But, should murder occur, I should be prepared to justify it on ethical grounds. Anything is defensible ethically which is necessary to win the cause.[4]

This was an example of the wilder side of Grayson that had not been seen since the 'broken bottles' saga of 1907, and his subsequent comments would justify the headline and remind his audience of his antipathy towards the moderation of Britain's Labour Party. It also hinted at a change of political direction on Grayson's part as he increasingly embraced syndicalism as the best hope for the workers. After his disappointments with the Labour Party and the British Socialist Party, syndicalism would place the trade unions – not a socialist political party – as the basis for a new, post-capitalist society. The economy would be organised federally and controlled by the workers themselves, with each industry having one union. The general strike would be used to bring about a fundamental change in society.

Political action by unions as a weapon has been a dismal failure up to now. Our chief hope lies with a well-knit industrial organization and connected direct action in the industrial field. The Labour movement in England has been rather disappointing on the official side. I believe that the organized Labour Party has permitted itself to be taken in tow by the Liberals and that, in the words of one of its greatest leaders, Keir Hardie, it has ceased to count as a force in Labour struggles in England.[5]

Ruth Grayson was asked whether she shared her husband's political ideas. She showed that she was no mere passive wife, telling the journalist that she was a militant suffragette and that

I believe the women of England are justified in burning houses … Sixty years of quiet agitation did nothing until militancy made women's suffrage a matter of serious political consequences. I believe that anything is justifiable. It would do the movement a frightful amount of good if the State murdered Mrs Pankhurst by starvation, but I am afraid that the Government is much too clever for that.[6]

So much then for the rest and recovery that Grayson was supposed to be enjoying. Instead, he was raising the ante, unshackled from any party or organisation and with a new audience, like a wandering revolutionary. None of this aided his health. Whisky had become the main focus for the little money that Grayson still had. Sam Hobson, who had written for the *New Age* and with whom Grayson had lodged during his first parliamentary session, recounted meeting Grayson in New York. Hobson, who was having lunch with William Walling, a leading American socialist and author, was asked whether Grayson was in a position to write, granted his financial predicament. Walling gave Hobson Grayson's address in an 'obsolete type of flat' in Manhattan.

From the hall a speaking-tube went to each apartment. You blew the whistle, and if you were to be admitted the tenant pulled a wire and unlatched the hall door. So I blew. In a moment I heard his voice, 'Who's there?' I told him. In a maudlin tone he kept on repeating my name. Apparently he was trying to collect his faculties.

'Don't stand there gibbering like an idiot,' I shouted impatiently, 'open the door.'

There was a click, the latch was drawn, and I went up. To describe the appointments of the flat as austere would be to pay it a compliment. At the corner of the fireplace sat a young woman, looking unhappy and frightened. At the table, on which were a bottle of whisky, a syphon of soda-water and glasses, sat Grayson.

'What are you doing in these joyous surroundings?' I asked.

'Oh' he said, 'I'm on my honeymoon. Allow me to introduce you to my wife.'

She inclined her head without speaking. To have offered my congratulations would, I believe, have brought tears.

'Yes', he went on, 'they collected a wedding fund and gave me half. I've cabled for the other half.'[7]

Grayson was masking the truth: the fund was in fact meant to aid his recovery. What was more, he seemed to be drinking his way through it at some speed. He also sent a begging telegram to American businessman Joseph Fels, to whom Grayson was evidently already in debt:

> Sent letter meet ship missed you am recalled England family trouble and business must sail Saturday with wife cannot get funds in time will you help by advancing further forty pounds by telegraph direct to 220 West 107th Street urgent and desperate posting letter with IOU for sixty send today if possible to get passage.[8]

Fels was a philanthropist who made his fortune manufacturing soap. He funded left-wing organisations in Russia, Britain and elsewhere and was an advocate of the single tax. He was particularly close to George Lansbury and had contributed financially to the founding of his *Daily Herald* newspaper, at the launch of which Grayson had been invited to speak. Fels had seen Grayson as the great hope of socialism in Britain, but he would not fund the drinking habits of an alcoholic. Despite the desperate tone of the telegram, Fels scrawled across it: 'decline advancing money'. He then forwarded it to Lansbury, who was also on a visit to New York, with the note, 'I suspect G[rayson] is drinking ... Perhaps you will want to look G up & see what you can do to get him straight.' The note went on to give details of a friend who had witnessed Grayson clearly the worse for drink.

Despite their deprivations, the Graysons travelled extensively, with Victor addressing socialist meetings in Pittsburgh, Iowa, Seattle and Boston. The tone of his speeches and public statements varied from the violence of his first interview with the *New York Times* to more measured words. However, for his final American meeting he used the familiar language of his 'broken bottles' saga:

> If the occasion is necessary, as when the soldiers shoot down their brothers and sisters, they shoot in return ... when the workers are winning, the capitalists send in the militia and police to try and suppress the workers. Then should the strikers be in a position to defend themselves.[9]

On the whole, however, their American adventure had been a disappointment. Grayson found the country – and its people – so obsessed with
'the hunt for the almighty dollar' that they had few other ideals and aspirations, and were almost cultureless. Their buildings were shoddy and lacked
architectural merit and only the American education system was superior
to Britain's. Ruth, interviewed later by an Australian newspaper, concurred
with her husband:

> We did not like America. We think it is a hard and heartless Country.
> Unless you have money no one has any time for you there … Don't try
> and copy the Americans here. You are all quite as nice as you are.[10]

As 1914 dawned, Grayson returned to Britain and went straight to
the Colne Valley, where he assured an audience at Saddleworth that he
intended to fight once more to represent them in Parliament. 'I want to
go back to Parliament feeling that I have the big battalions of enlightened
workers behind me, and not crying as one lost in the wilderness.'[11] But
whilst he was contemplating a political comeback, the newspapers also
carried the news that the Graysons had not left their financial difficulties
in America. Victor had attended meetings of his creditors at the London
Bankruptcy Court. The receiving order was made on the petition of Baron
Wolfe, a moneylender from Manchester, to whom Grayson owed £101.
The Receiver stated that 'the debtor had surrendered to the proceedings,
and had filed accounts showing debts of £451, and no available assets'. The
meeting heard how Grayson's health had seriously broken down in 1912
and, apart from occasional appearances on the public platform, he 'had
done little or no work'. Grayson's earnings were assessed as £250 per year
whereas his outgoings were estimated at £275 and he had only £30 owed
to him, and even this was 'unrealisable'. The court heard that Grayson was
currently of no fixed abode, had sold his furniture the previous year and
was going from friend to friend, staying with each as long as possible. It
was a graphic description of how Grayson's life had fallen apart and how
the young hero of 1907 had, by 1914, become a broken-down alcoholic
on the brink of bankruptcy which would have made him ineligible to
stand for Parliament. Fortunately, this situation never arose, thanks to

one creditor writing off a £150 debt and Grayson finding enough cash to set up a repayment plan. John Nightingale, Ruth's banker father, is the likeliest candidate to have been Grayson's financial saviour, not least because, amongst all of this chaos, Ruth was heavily pregnant, and on 13 April 1914 gave birth to Elaine.

The couple moved to a new home in Clapham, also no doubt financed by Nightingale. Grayson now appears to have been too ill to work. His nerves were shattered. In the past two years he had gained a reputation, thanks to his drinking, as a speaker with an unreliable attendance record. The British Socialist Party leadership had even written to its branches, warning them not to book him. None of this helped either Grayson's sense of self-worth or the family's financial situation. But across Europe, the international clouds were darkening, and the outbreak of hostilities would give Grayson a platform from which to rebuild his life.

The First Experience of War

Grayson had never made any secret of his loathing for the Kaiser and had for years warned of the growing danger of German militarism. The Labour Party leaders, Hardie, MacDonald and Snowden, were all declared pacifists, whereas Grayson, the pro-war socialist, suddenly found himself in step with the majority of the public and the British establishment. Given the stance of Labour's leaders, he would also be a valuable asset to those tasked with keeping up the supply of men and munitions for the war effort.

By September 1914 Grayson was speaking at recruitment drives, his central message being that it would be much harder to build a socialist society under the jackboot of the Kaiser. Offers were once again coming in for his journalism and he accepted a role as a war correspondent in France. His editor gave him a free hand, as well as a blank cheque, as long as the articles entertained. These were the opening weeks of the war, with the sense of excitement, adventure and bravado that it would all be over by Christmas. At first, Grayson made the most of his editor's patronage by staying in top hotels and enjoying some good living, but the reality of the

war and its consequences soon hit him as he made daily visits to wounded
men to hear their stories and keep up their spirits.

I left my anchored security and forged forth into the area of carnage.
I had several reasons for venturing forth into the realm of bloodshed,
and perhaps the greatest of these was that my speeches and articles on
the way had sent numberless recruits to their possible, and in some
cases, certain graves. Some of the lads whose names were signed in my
presence, as fighters, were already reported as dead.[12]

In Paris, he and Ruth found a city and a people devastated by war:

Instead of dainty women sweetly garbed, we met widows with sad,
drawn faces. All the old vivacity and sparkle had gone out of their eyes,
and instead, there remained the dull, dead remembrance of their lovers
who lay under the clod of their Fatherland not many miles away. After
them came soldiers with their arms amputated, hundreds and hundreds
in a single stroll, who had lost an arm or an eye or had been otherwise
wounded.[13]

Grayson's mission was to report back from the front, and to get close to the
real action by any means possible. This he did by hiring a plane to fly him
over German lines. It was a rudimentary two-seater, open-topped, biplane,
about which Grayson soon had second-thoughts after sitting behind the
pilot. Nevertheless, they took off and made their way to the frontline.
Quickly, a German plane came out from the clouds and began firing at
them. The pilot shouted at Grayson to draw his pistol and fire back. The
German plane withdrew after Grayson seemingly damaged its wing. He was
now free to fly low over the frontline, a view he described for his readers:

There, below, in long slits of trenches, crawled the warrior moles of both
the enemy and the Allied armies. Every now and then one could hear
dull explosions, and the little moles scurry to and fro in the clearing
smoke. It looked funny to me. I felt as a god, watching from above the
flurried antics of his little creatures.[14]

Upon landing, Grayson found the French authorities waiting for him. He appeared not to have the correct paperwork to be anywhere near the frontline in a plane. He was duly charged with being a German spy, though after hours of questioning in German – which Grayson could not speak – the interrogating officer gave up. The case was eventually dropped, as also was the pilot's court martial. Grayson had somehow persuaded the French that it was all a misunderstanding. Far from taking this as a warning to keep his enthusiasm in check, he continued to hunt out good stories and regularly put himself in harm's way to do so. He was wounded in an air raid on Dunkirk and, on another occasion, found himself lost in the country-side, where he was nearly run through by a wounded German soldier, who fortuitously collapsed and died during a stand-off with Grayson. Perhaps surprisingly, given the anti-German rhetoric for which he had become well known since the outbreak of war, Grayson was fully respectful towards the German dead. He buried the young German as well as he could and then set off to find his guide, Pierre. He stumbled across a German graveyard and was so moved that he picked some flowers from a nearby garden:

> With an uneasy thrill I had placed my chrysanthemums on the grave of a nameless German soldier. I may have been wrong – and patriot-ism is a grand thing. But I thought of this soldier's mother, and perhaps children – and I heard the baby sobbing or the lacerated boy soldier in the broken shed.

None of this shook his conviction that the war was just, but he realised early on that it would change everything and that the world would never be the same again.

> I no longer call myself a socialist. I am merely Victor Grayson, waiting. This tremendous conflict is going to bring about a complete readjust-ment of all our political faiths and beliefs, and that is what I mean when I say I am waiting for the new spirit that is going to come over our nation … I believe that this war is very much more than a matter of carnage; it is the crucible to which all our old ideas and parties have been cast, and I feel confident that, as a result, a new civilization will emerge.[15]

But his health failed him again. Grayson experienced another breakdown, brought on by what he had seen of the war. Days after the armistice, Grayson would tell an audience in Hull that he returned with two other young war journalists and that what they had seen had shaken their mental health and that only he had recovered: 'one went into a lunatic asylum, and another shot himself in a London hotel'.[16] As he said, he did eventually recover, but when he returned to England with Ruth, he was without an income and found himself at odds with many of his former comrades. The couple were again in desperate straits. Victor was unwilling to ask for help, but Ruth took matters into her own hands and wrote a begging letter to Keir Hardie on 29 November 1914:

Dear Mr Keir Hardie,

I know that you & my husband have had many differences, but I also know your good heart & I have nowhere to turn.

I am Victor Grayson's wife. I have brought him home from France, where he has been doing some special war correspondence … My landlord is calling for rent today at noon, and until some money comes for an article that will appear tomorrow, I haven't got any.

I got behind with the rent before Victor got this work at all & and it means turning out if I can't find it today.

I've got a sick husband & a baby … Will you, for God's sake, or anyone's sake, lend me £10 that we repay you £2 a week. Keep this letter as a written promise to repay. If you will, I promise you won't regret it. I cannot tell you how I shall bless you, Victor does not know of this letter & must not.

Will you send me the money if you'll let me have it, by my messenger, who is quite trustworthy.

Yours desperately
Ruth Grayson[17]

A fortnight later, in December 1914, a small advert from Grayson appeared in several newspapers asking for work, with the strict instruction that it should contain 'no politics'.

11

To Passchendaele

When you got beyond a certain line on your way up, that was the end of the world you came from and you just didn't bother to think about what was laid before you. You just did your job, and with any luck you came back. It's difficult to try to tell other people what it was like. It's not an easy thing to do. The salient was unimaginable.

Lyn Macdonald [1]

Well aware that they would have weak, if any, artillery cover, Haig ordered his ragged armies up for another attack, which would be known as the First Battle of Passchendaele. They were given two days to prepare. The ensuing battles would thus rely on pure hope over hard experience. The commanders cast precedent aside, as if the lessons of Loos, the Somme, Gheluvelt and even the immediately preceding Poelcappelle, so profligate with soldiers' lives, were worth nothing ... As the British official historian concludes, the task allotted the Anzacs on 12 October was 'beyond the power of any infantry with so little support'.

Paul Ham [2]

The stunt should never have been ordered under such conditions ... It was absolute murder. Corporal Harold Green, New Zealand Rifle Brigade.

Paul Ham [3]

In hindsight, the outbreak of the First World War might seem inevitable. Yet, to those who lived through that time, in the days before the conflict began Ireland seemed a more immediate cause for concern than did a European war. As Fenner Brockway later recalled,

The war of 1914 came suddenly. Ten days before it started I spoke at Oldham and my audience thought I was an hysterical scaremonger when I said we were near war … Irishmen in the crowd shouted 'Talk about Ireland, not Serbia.' The issue in the public mind was the con- stitutional crisis arising from the threat of Ulster to resist Home Rule.[4]

Almost in an instant, the project of European socialist unity crumbled. Only the major socialist parties in Ireland, Russia and Serbia opposed the war. Nothing highlighted this as starkly as the case of the German Social Democratic Party, which voted to give the Kaiser the war credits he needed to finance his country's aggression. German trade unionists had promised to lead a mass European-wide strike in the event of war, in order to end hostilities, seize the levers of power and fashion a socialist society. But events in Germany set the narrative for British trade union leaders:

No room for doubt remained [on the issue of war] when we learned that some of the most prominent German trades union leaders of this agitation against all war with their world-wide strike as a certain means of preventing it, were actually amongst the first men who took up arms in Germany and were in the ranks of the forces that swept down on Belgium, and helped in the raping of her.[5]

With Germany's course set, even some on the British left who had initially been anti-war – such as Arthur Henderson – swung their support behind military intervention. Keir Hardie and Ramsay MacDonald stuck to their pacifist positions, though anti-war socialists were firmly in a minority across the warring powers.

Grayson had initially jumped at the chance to report on the reality of war for his readers in Britain, relegating his speaking activities to a secondary occupation. After returning to England following his breakdown, Grayson took a few months to recover, but soon wanted to enlist. His two older brothers had been among the first to volunteer for service. At the age of 37, the Boer War veteran William Grayson enlisted on 11 August 1914. John Dickinson Grayson, a serving policeman, enlisted aged 35 on 3 September 1914. But Grayson was dissuaded from joining the infantry by Winston Churchill, now First Lord of the Admiralty, who saw that his ability could be put to better use as a recruitment speaker and in writing pro-war articles for newspapers.

In the spring of 1915, Ruth was offered a place in the Shakespearean Company which was set to tour Australasia. It provided her with an
opportunity to work and earn an income, whilst it offered Victor new
opportunities to aid the war effort. They set sail from England on 5 June
and arrived in Australia the following month, settling in Sydney. Extensive
preparations had been made on their behalf and the press were waiting for
the couple upon their arrival. Grayson was immediately offered work as
a journalist and, given that the Australian people had just re-elected the
pro-war Labour Prime Minister Andrew Fisher, he was certain of a good
hearing. As it was Churchill who had persuaded Grayson not to enlist,
it seems possible that he would also have played some part in Grayson's
passage to and warm reception in Australia. Grayson seemed to acknowl-
edge this in his first article for the popular *Mirror of Australia* newspaper,
which carried the headline 'Why I Think Winston Churchill is Great'. It
was an odd choice of topic for a socialist who had clashed with Churchill
politically and, even more so, granted that Australian troops were already
paying a heavy price for the calamitous Gallipoli campaign, for which
Churchill was widely held responsible. Nevertheless, after describing him
as 'an egotist of the first water', Grayson settled down to write a glowing
account of Churchill's role in getting the Royal Navy ready for war:

> At the time the so-called Army was in a hopeless muddle, and the
> encrusted fossils of the Admiralty were treating our Fleet as though
> they were the managers of a private ferry! Into this vortex of national
> insanity, the Prime Minister thrust Winston Churchill, whose genius
> was displayed in the wonderful way he concealed his purposes by smooth
> speech and drastic action. No-one except those with private knowledge,
> can have any conception of the odium into which Winston plunged
> himself by this unfashionable conduct. Titled ladies rose at him and
> snorted their rebukes, political leader writers of the 'proper' kind snarled
> at him ... back benchers and some of the front benchers of his own
> party cursed him ... But Winston proceeded to build up the Navy that
> we now possess.[6]

Grayson's hint that he had 'private knowledge' of Churchill's problems
suggests that he was closer to the former First Lord (failure at the Dar-

danelles led to Churchill's demotion to the position of Chancellor of the Duchy of Lancaster) than he was letting on. It was not the first time that he had called for strong armaments. As far back as 1908, Blatchford and he had visited Germany and brought back stories of a country preparing for a war of domination that could only be checked by Britain building up her army. This would have the added benefit of tackling the country's unemployment problem. Nevertheless, they had been ignored, at least by those on their own side of politics. Now, the article wound up in a crescendo of praise, with the writer turning prophet:

> Winston Churchill as Prime Minister of Great Britain is a conceivable and more than probable supposition ... He tried, and was hampered to an indescribable extent, to finish the present war by a brilliant and considerable 'coup'. He failed ... [but he] is certainly one of the most potent of the leaders and directors who will wipe German pride and Prussian brutality from the world's map.[7]

The next controversial article Grayson penned for the *Mirror* called for conscription to be introduced across the Empire. The case was carefully argued from a socialist perspective:

> We must have conscription. The word has a nasty taste and I admit that to be a conscript is a nasty thing ... When I ask for men however, I ask for them only on certain terms. Their duty to the State must be covered by an equivalent duty from the State to them ... I also demand that every man and woman shall be assured by the State a decent minimum of living in return for their services.[8]

This was Grayson's firmly held belief from the onset of the war. Every man and woman should be mobilised to defeat Germany and in return should be promised a fairer post-war Britain where class and privilege would be relegated behind work and sacrifice. It was a vision that a Labour government would eventually begin to implement, but only after another catastrophic conflict.

The Graysons stayed in Australia for a few weeks short of a year and, for the first time since they were married, Victor and Ruth enjoyed a comfortable lifestyle. Ruth spent a total of 30 weeks in Sydney and Melbourne with Wilkie's Shakespearean Company, while Victor convalesced and passed his time writing articles and even pondering a book on Australia, though there is no evidence that this project ever got off the ground. Of note is his obituary of Keir Hardie, who died on 26 September 1915. Hardie had been an early political idol for Grayson and the two were for a while on friendly terms. But their relationship had fractured because of Hardie's pursuit of the democratic road to socialism. Grayson, whose criticisms of his old colleagues in the British Labour movement reached a crescendo in this period, wrote with mixed feelings of his former colleague:

So Keir Hardie has passed away. His name has been anathema to many people who did not understand him. I do understand something of Keir Hardie, and have had unique opportunities of studying quite impartially his complex personality …

For a period he had to lead the Labour Party in the House of Commons. He turned out to be the poorest and feeblest leader that any party could possess. But his failure consisted of his abhorrence of tact. In spite of his general unpopularity and his constant and insidious persecution in Parliament, he played as brave a part as circumstances would allow. He has gone, and in spite of his unpatriotic utterances in the latter days of political and international confusion, I must raise my hat in recognition to the world's loss of a good, brave, and misguided soul.[9]

Grayson was understandably bitter about his treatment in Britain and, looking at matters from afar, he could be forgiven for giving voice to his own prejudices. Even so, to attack Hardie, even gently, was a dangerous move. The latter was someone whom the socialist movement regarded as a near-saint. Grayson must have realised that if his article made its way back to Britain, any future prospects within the country's Labour movement would be fatally damaged.

When Wilkie's Shakespearean Company left for New Zealand in August 1916, so too did the Graysons. Ruth's work involved travel and shortly after their arrival, what should have been a routine journey from Auckland to Wellington on the SS *Tongariro* turned into a near-fatal disaster when the ship hit a rock and sank. Thankfully, the passengers were rescued shortly before the ship went down, but it was an inauspicious start to their life in New Zealand, which, for Victor, would in any case prove more challenging than in Australia. Australia had a well-established Labour Party and a Labour Prime Minister, Andrew Fisher, who had just won his third successive election. His government was committed to the war and had no doubt put plans in place to ease Grayson's arrival. In New Zealand, on the other hand, the Labour movement was much more rudimentary. The New Zealand Labour Party (NZLP) had only been formed a month before Grayson's arrival. Whereas the British Labour movement had already seen some of the measures for which it had campaigned enacted by a Liberal government, the NZLP still had a long way to go. In this sense the New Zealand socialists were more radical and militant than those Grayson had encountered in Australia, and were excited that the man elected as a revolutionary socialist in Britain was to tour their country. He was paid handsomely by the NZLP, which saw the chance to use Grayson's name to win more members for their new party.

He was an instant success and his meetings revealed something of the Grayson of old, in Manchester and the Colne Valley. There was even a return to the theological element that had often characterised his earlier oratory. Gone was the reluctance shown in Australia to preach too much socialism. In New Zealand he was freer to speak his mind and he duly ratcheted up his oratory to suit his audiences. The *Auckland Star* of 16 August 1916 reported him saying that there was

A bigger war than the present one to follow – the war of poverty, the war of the labourer for the right to live in proper comfort, the war of the small but powerful cliques against the workers' emancipation. All things would change after the war, for it was essentially a workers' war. Was it Asquith and Lloyd George, or was it the workers who had produced Britain's present great army, and had poured out munitions in miraculous quantities? But the war had taught Labour such tremendous lessons that it would never rest content with things as they were. The day was dawning when Democracy would demand its right share of the comfort and beauty and ease of life … It would be the destiny of Labour to take control of society and re-mould it nearer to the vast desire.

During the remainder of 1916 Grayson's lectures included 'Christ or Caesar', 'The State of Mammon', 'The War and Labour's Destiny' and 'The Coming Revolution'. The general thrust was that Britain and the world could not revert to the pre-war capitalist system after such a sacrifice by working men and women. Instead, the opportunity was there for the workers to take hold of the levers of power.

Grayson's positive start in New Zealand was about to come under pressure. Although a majority of the workers, as in Britain, supported the war effort, there was a vocal minority that opposed both the war and Grayson's views on conscription. The *Maoriland Worker* opposed the war in its entirety as a capitalist conflict, but began by giving Grayson the benefit of the doubt. It published an interview in which Grayson was veering towards the sort of language he had last used in Britain and which demonstrates that he was well aware of the differences between the socialist movements in New Zealand and Australia. He talked of the war opening up the possibility of the overthrow of capitalism and suggested that the soldiers 'who had reaped the experiences of the trenches would come back trained to use guns and bayonets, and to act unitedly … they would never again be satisfied with the old life of unemployment and want and hardship'. The editorial team at the paper viewed Grayson with suspicion and were unimpressed that he seemed to be gaining popularity amongst the New Zealand socialists. The *Worker* began publishing letters questioning Grayson's views on conscription and performed an intellectual somersault by suggesting that Grayson could in fact be an enemy of the workers because his pro-war stance was shared by the German generals and others who were anti-worker. Harry Holland, the editor of the *Worker*, was thought to have been passed information by a government employee which suggested that Grayson had made two pacts before beginning his lecture tour. The first, with the leaders of the NZLP, was not to talk about conscription or make his views on the issue publicly known. The second, that he was in New Zealand with government backing to shore up support for the war and thereby blunt the hostility towards government-imposed conscription amongst the workers. The latter point would have been especially embarrassing for him, though it was not revealed at the time.

Grayson continued to attend packed meetings across New Zealand which were largely successful apart from the conscription question. Ruth proved a popular attraction, often opening the evening for her husband with a poetry recital. But at the final meeting of Grayson's lecture tour in Christchurch on 12 November, he was clearly shaken. We cannot now be sure what was said but we do know that soldiers in the audience sought to shut down the meeting. They were not successful, thanks to Grayson's skilled intervention, but he appears to have made a commitment from the platform to enlist. Caught between two sets of demonstrators, pacifists and soldiers, he publicly chose the latter.

The *Maoriland Worker* saw things differently and published accusations that Grayson had borrowed large sums of money from working men and failed to repay them. Though his health had improved in Australia, the more febrile nature of his New Zealand tour led him to begin drinking to excess once more. The paper's reports that Grayson had promised that an English banker (probably Ruth's father) would make good his debts and that Ruth was doing the begging on his behalf do, sadly, ring true, as Ruth's begging letter to Keir Hardie the previous year confirms. The paper went on to allege that Grayson had only signed up to avoid prosecution for fraud and later attacked him for delaying for two years before signing up to fight. On the latter charge Grayson was innocent. Churchill had encouraged him to work for the war in other ways. But on the charge of fraud it seems likely that there was some substance to the claim, though no direct evidence survives.

Victor Grayson was accepted to serve as a member of the Expeditionary Force on 26 November 1916. He had a ten-week wait before being posted to start his intensive training which lasted a further ten weeks. On 26 April 1917, Grayson embarked on the *Turikana* at Wellington to begin the three-month return voyage to England. The journey was not as grim as it may at first seem. Many of the men had never before left New Zealand and were filled with excitement. The ship made frequent stops at ports in Australia and Africa and the troops were allowed to go ashore. There was a good deal of humour on board and a ship's journal was produced, on the editorial board of which Grayson served. He also gained a temporary promotion from private to lance corporal for the duration of the journey.

On 20 July the ship finally docked at Devonport, near Plymouth, and the men disembarked to Sling Camp on Salisbury Plain, where 4,000 New Zealand troops were housed. There, they spent six weeks acclimatising and getting back into shape after their long journey. Then, on 5 September, Grayson set sail for France, destined for the Western Front.

Throughout 1917, boatloads of British and Dominion troops arrived at the French ports ... On arrival in France [they] found themselves in the 'bullring', one of the vast training camps that stretched from Le Havre to Etaples ('Eat Apples', as the Tommies called it), and from Calais to Boulogne: hectares of canvas tents and Nissen huts, officers' messes, canteens, hospitals, lecture theatres and training areas. They stood in lines of thousands, waiting to be counted off into battalions and marched off to their regimental base.

To call the Etaples camp notorious would be to understate its dark history. Both fresh troops and veterans were housed at the camp, which was intended to toughen the men up for the front, but the harsh conditions, in particular the brutality of the instructors – most of whom had not seen action themselves – created an atmosphere of fear and resentment. Whether the men were raw recruits or seasoned veterans, they were put through the same rigorous routine in an area known as the 'Bull Ring'. They were exposed to intensive gas warfare training, bayonet drills and long sessions of marching, with often barbaric treatment. Stories abounded that wounded men preferred returning to the front injured, rather than remaining at the camp. Private Bradfield from King's Lynn recalled that '[e]very man who passed through the Bull Ring so hated the staff that I wouldn't have given them a cat's chance if they'd come up the line. They were bastards all of them.' Another veteran confirmed: 'I can truthfully say that I had moments there as unpleasant as any on the Western Front. I was never so angry elsewhere.'[10]

Thanks to this particularly brutish behaviour on the part of the English officers, which no doubt reflected class prejudice, New Zealand and

Scottish troops formed a particularly strong bond. We have no record of Grayson's experiences, but he had preached at his recruitment drives that the war had brought the classes closer together in a common struggle. He must have been bitterly disappointed with what he saw at Etaples. The war poet Wilfred Owen had spent time in the camp the previous year and wrote of his experience to his mother:

> I thought of the very strange look on all the faces in that camp; an incomprehensible look, which a man will never see in England, nor can it be seen in any battle but only in Etaples. It was not despair, or terror, it was more terrible than terror, for it was a blindfold look and without expression, like a dead rabbit's.

The day Grayson arrived at the Etaples camp on Sunday, 9 September, a mutiny erupted that would take a week to suppress and a month for tensions to properly subside. Grayson only spent a week at Etaples, instead of the mandatory two, as New Zealand troops were rushed to the front to get them out of the way. Our knowledge of the mutiny is not helped by the fact that most records were destroyed by the British authorities following a thorough investigation after the war. In fact, only in recent decades has something of the truth surrounding the Etaples mutiny been revealed, thanks to painstaking research by determined historians. However, just because Grayson was present we should not assume, as some have, that he was in any way a leader of the mutinous behaviour. If he played any role – and there is absolutely no evidence that he did – it would have been more likely that he would have tried to calm tensions. Some 50 men were subsequently court-martialled, with one man shot. Grayson was not one of them. Further, the fact that Grayson went on to work for the British government after his active service would suggest that he played no part in the mutiny.

Throughout early September 1917 the British Army was preparing for an assault on a small raised area of land known as Passchendaele Ridge. But the weather was appalling. Grayson had entered Etaples camp just as storms blew down tents and rendered more than two thousand beds unfit for use. The wounded were being tended in the rain. Meanwhile, at the front further up the road in Ypres, the mud was limiting troop and supply movements to the Menin Road, while German artillery wreaked havoc. Despite the misgivings and protestations of the now British Prime Minister, David Lloyd George, as to the likelihood of success, the military were determined to make another push on the Western Front, a third battle of Ypres. Grayson was part of the nine British and Anzac divisions given to Field Marshal Haig with the aim of finally taking Passchendaele Ridge in the battle's last phases. As the men made their way up the Menin Road, word was spreading of another mutiny, this time amongst the Russian troops further along the Western Front. Ten thousand Russians serving in Champagne had overthrown their superior officers and set up soldiers' soviets (councils). They were surrounded by French cavalry, infantry and artillery, refused to surrender and shelled and machine-gunned into submission for 36 hours.

It is all but impossible for the words of historians to do justice to the carnage of what became known as the Battle of Passchendaele. All that now remains are vast cemeteries. One of the largest is Tyne Cot, a kilometre from Passchendaele, which contains 11,956 graves, 8,366 of them unnamed, and the Tyne Cot Memorial to the Missing. Upon this immense wall are the names of 35,000 men whose graves are unknown, 1,179 of them New Zealanders who served alongside Grayson in October 1917. For many, there never was a better argument made for the futility of war than Passchendaele and to visit Tyne Cot today – in all its silence and with views of the green ridges, soaked with the blood of a generation of Europe's manhood – is a haunting experience.

It took a full six days for the 23,000 New Zealanders to march to the Ypres battle-front. The men reached the ruins of Ypres and were confronted with what looked like a 'city of the dead'. Then they arrived at the front line. One New Zealander recorded that

The ground is covered with shell holes as close together as pebbles on the beach; the dead from the last two pushes were being buried at half a dozen places en route, but were still lying about the battle front in large numbers, a dreadfully gruesome sight, and the smell struck one forcibly when at least two-and-a-half miles away.[11]

Another ANZAC recalled that the front was 'nothing but desolation, not a blade of grass or tree, here and there a heap of bricks marking where a village or farmhouse had once stood, numerous "tanks" stuck in the mud, and for the rest, just one shell hole touching another'.[12] Three months of continuous shelling had destroyed the natural drainage of the area. The Germans held the high ground, so enjoyed what drainage there was as they sat tight. It was the New Zealanders who would have to drive forward in what was described as 'a porridge of mud'. Roads and supply lines were largely impassible, despite the heroic efforts of engineers. The men were up to their knees in mud most of the time, with no hope of keeping dry. Each man only had one blanket, one pair of boots and two pairs of socks and, despite the rum ration, the men's health and morale entered a downward spiral. Nevertheless, initial attacks were a success, thanks to ample preparation and artillery support, and the New Zealanders struck a hammer-blow against the Germans on 4 October. But the generals wanted more and Haig in particular, knowing the low esteem in which Lloyd George held him, wanted to continue the drive against the German lines.

The weather, however, continued to get worse and the preparation that had allowed previous success was missing in a further push on 9 October. It was a dismal failure. More than 13,000 Allied casualties, of which more than 5,000 were Anzacs, were incurred to gain just 500 yards of ground. Incredibly, Haig thought it 'very successful' and wanted the attack immediately renewed with even greater objectives. Another attack was planned for the 12th, but the men knew that plans were being rushed. The officers had little time to share their plans of attack with the men, the issuing of equipment was late and the usual artillery barrage was absent. The latter was particularly important as it often destroyed the maze of barbed wire through which the men would have to pass to reach their objectives. Added to this, the supply lines suffered as the weather continued to worsen. Artillery shells had to be transported by pack animals and veterans recalled seeing donkeys laden with shells sucked into the mud, never to surface again.

The day before the attack, Grayson was tasked with the unenviable job of helping supply the forward troops:

I found myself one of a party detailed to carry up rations to the front-line trenches through a dual barrage. We all knew the boys up the line were to hop over at daybreak the following morning, but we were not aware until the sergeant-major told us that they had been without rations for twelve hours. As much as the mud would permit our pace was speeded up, and we were soon in line upon the duckboards, myself and my immediate companions each laden with two petrol tins of water. The front-line was about two miles away. Every flare seemed to me to have the sole motive of the discovery of my overwrought form to the enemy.

After half an hour of well-nigh hopeless wandering a shrieking shell exploded so close to me that the concussion lifted my steel helmet from my head and almost blew me off my feet. At the same moment, I tripped over something and fell – between two dead soldiers. They had fallen facing each other, their arms extended. For a moment I envied them their pain-free sleep. An inscrutable Providence, rather than a conscious effort on my part brought me to my dank but welcome dugout. My comrades were hugely relieved at the sight of me, for they had counted me among the fallen.

Grayson then had somehow to get some rest before the attack at daybreak:

Before we advanced at Passchendaele we spent a night of unspeakable discomfort in a bog-bound field. Intermittent showers of rain had drenched us to our skin, and the Boche was so near to us that we dared not cough nor light a longed-for cigarette. As the shrapnel-mist began to rise I could perceive the tangled wire of the enemy lines tumbled in scattered heaps, and I realized that my increasing loneliness was being caused by hidden fire from some concrete structures to my left. The noise of artillery was deafening, the mud and water-logged shell holes made advance a work of art, and the bullets whistled past on every side.[13]

At that point, at 5.30 am on the morning of 12 October, Grayson and his comrades were ordered over the top. Grayson was wounded when a shell exploded and knocked him off his feet, lodging a piece of burning shrapnel in his hip. When he came to, concussed, he had to crawl to safety away from the front line. He wrote of his experience a few weeks later:

> After the terrible experience of crawling – wounded – out of the fighting line, I succeeded in reaching the advanced dressing station. This was an old Boche 'pill-box', completely surrounded by wounded comrades awaiting the services of a dresser. Unfortunately the dresser had been killed and his associate severely wounded, and our next hope was a dressing station three miles distant, beyond an over-shelled waste of mud which varied in depth from one to five feet.

Grayson's life was saved by a stretcher bearer who managed to get him to a muddy road and then by two anonymous artillery drivers who were fetching ammunition with their horse.

> No pen can ever describe the heroism of these splendid fellows, who were already panting from the exertion of guiding their horse through the mud and the menace of bursting shells. They were covered from head to foot in clinging slime, but perceiving my plight, they suggested a 'ride'. Though I had never mounted a horse in my life I accepted that offer as a drowning man clutches at a straw. With inconceivable tenderness they lifted me on to the mercurial back of Maori, a spirited beast who quickly divined the ignorance and incompetence of his rider. He plunged, sank, lept and curvetted throughout the whole of that memorable journey, and when our driver was winded the other relieved him by leading the terrified horse with its desperate burden. When we passed our own batteries Maori became a circus horse, and his winded driver confessed; 'I'm almost as frightened as you are. Maori, so help me, I am!'[14]

After Grayson dismounted from Maori at a dressing station, he was taken to a field hospital. From there he spent time at Rouen hospital before being transported back to Brockenhurst, England, where the General Hospital for the New Zealand forces was located. Here, surrounded by men with whom he had served in France, Grayson seemed a changed man. Introverted, brooding and, despite his best efforts to put on a cheery demeanour, it was clear he was a victim of shell-shock. His army medical records note that he was suffering from neurasthenia – a catch-all term for nervous disorders, but particularly the condition that came to be known as shell-shock.

12

On Lloyd George's Service

I suggest that the posters be headed 'A Voice from the Trenches'.

Victor Grayson planning publicity for his speaking tour[1]

After Victor Grayson's enlistment in the New Zealand forces, his wife Ruth and daughter Elaine remained in the country as long as he did. Victor was earning a decent wage for a soldier, once boasting that he earned 5 shillings a day in the New Zealanders, whereas as a British Tommy he would have received only one fifth of that. It was certainly enough to live on comfortably and Ruth was able to give up working with the Shakespearean Company and still see Victor. But when he left on the troopship for Europe, Ruth and Elaine followed, arriving back in London in June 1917. From there, mother and daughter travelled north to Bolton to stay with Ruth's parents, John and Georgina Nightingale. Ruth was pregnant with her second child and no doubt appreciated the middle-class comforts in sharp contrast to the deprivation in which she and Victor had lived during her first pregnancy. It is telling to note that baby Elaine was never taken on the relatively short train-ride to Liverpool to visit her grandmother and other members of the Grayson family. Many years later, Elaine claimed that this was because Elizabeth Grayson was not, in fact, her real grandmother. It is, however, more likely that the Nightingales were worried about losing their granddaughter and perhaps any negative influence the Grayson family might have upon her. They had always believed that Ruth had married a wayward, troubled man and, in a Britain still riddled with class snobbery, the Graysons were seen as belonging to a very different and less respectable world. Elaine would never meet her father's family. It is a telling illustration of how little the Nightingales thought of the Graysons that Ruth, who as Victor's wife was also his next-of-kin, never thought to inform his mother that her son was safe and recuperating from his injuries.

The result was that Mrs Grayson read of Victor's condition in the newspapers and resorted to writing to the Prime Minister, Lloyd George, via her local Wesleyan minister, asking for news of her wounded son.

Grayson was not discharged from the army until March 1918, and considerable use was made of him in the meantime. The British establishment was terrified that the Bolshevik revolution would sweep across Europe from St Petersburg like a revolutionary virus. If the munitions factories and other industries stopped working, the war might come to an end before a German surrender could be secured. Winston Churchill had become Minister of Munitions the previous year, and it was of little surprise that he found use for Grayson, the man once elected as a revolutionary socialist, but now a valuable asset of the wartime government. In January 1918 he was interviewed at the Ministry of National Service in Whitehall, which arranged for him to go on a short speaking tour of the industrial heartlands of northern England, imploring the men to set aside their grievances and make one last push for victory. He joined up with Havelock Wilson, leader of the Merchant Seamen's League (MSL) and founder of the National Sailors' and Firemen's Union (NSFU) which campaigned against the brutal action of Germany's submarines, with the aim of cooling any potential industrial unrest and keeping the factories working. In 1917 the NSFU had refused to transport Ramsay MacDonald and Arthur Henderson to a socialist peace conference in Stockholm. Wilson was a former Liberal MP and respected trade union leader, who had been radicalised by the war. He had become a key ally of the government and often fronted the tours in which Grayson now featured. Churchill provides a description of how these tours were used in his memoir, *The World Crisis*,

On the Monday considerable numbers of men from the Seamen and Fireman's Union, many of whom had been submarined more than once, entered Coventry headed by Mr. Havelock Wilson and preceded by bands; and at the same time the organisation of the former Women's Suffrage Societies, under the fiery guidance of Miss Christabel Pankhurst, descended in a cloud of speakers, propagandists and canvassers. Patriotic meetings were held in all parts of the town. Under these varied pressures the strike collapsed, and by Tuesday night all Coventry was at work again.[2]

The tours served the purpose of a trouble-shooter, bombarding any area of unrest with a deluge of patriotic fervour until it complied once more. Grayson's work with Wilson was of this nature, with the addition of decommissioned tanks to use as props in which to tour the industrial areas and as a platform from which to raise funds for the war effort. At Hartlepool on 3 February 1918, Grayson attacked those workers in Britain who were demanding increased wages. He said that any strike action was akin to robbing a soldier of his ammunition just before he headed into battle. He then turned his fire on some old adversaries:

> When Ramsay MacDonald and Philip Snowden and other pacifist leaders talk to you about 'peace, peace, peace,' they are doing the same work in this country that Trotsky and Lenin are doing in Russia.[3]

In Middlesbrough, he called for Germany to be 'thrashed and then punished' for her conduct during the war. The next day he gave a similarly inflammatory speech in Sunderland, but shortly after this, his tour was cut short. Grayson received a telegram informing him that his heavily pregnant wife had been rushed to a nursing home and that there had been complications. He returned immediately to the couple's new home at 2 Vincent Square, Westminster, into which Ruth had recently moved from Bolton, then proceeded to the nursing home. Any happy reunion was short-lived. In a letter to the publisher, Grant Richards, Grayson described what happened:

> I returned from my northern tour – which was a really stupendous success – to find that considerable worry had been accumulating for me in my absence. On Tuesday evening-last my wife was removed to a nursing home, and on Wednesday gave premature birth to a girl-child – who died a few moments afterwards. My wife is now in a critical condition.[4]

Grayson asked Richards to send him money immediately as he would now face some considerable and unforeseen medical bills. Richards consented, agreeing to write off this advance against any future royalties that a proposed autobiography by Grayson might earn. Ruth, however, did not survive. She died in the nursing home at 42 Belgrave Road, London, on 10 February. She is buried at Kensal Green Cemetery in London and her headstone reads

> To the sweet memory of Ruth Grayson (Ruth Norreys), dearly beloved and only child of John W. and Georgina Nightingale. Born March 11th 1887. Died February 10th 1918.

The omission of any mention of Victor, or indeed of the dead daughter (of whom there's no surviving documentation), on the gravestone is very odd. It was ordered and paid for by John Nightingale who, whether out of grief or anger, made no reference to her husband. Furthermore, in the wake of Ruth's passing, Victor signed over custody of Elaine to the Nightingales. Why, is not entirely clear. The parties may have come to the mutual agreement that Grayson was in no position to bring up a daughter and, for their part, the Nightingales no doubt wanted to look after their only granddaughter as a living memory of their only daughter.

Grayson's life-story now becomes increasingly difficult to trace. He was certainly busy building a new career with a sense of purpose he had lacked since he was frozen out of the leadership of the British Socialist Party. And he made the most of his contacts from his pre-war career. One such was the publisher, Grant Richards (1872–1948), who had tried to interest Grayson in writing his memoirs as early as 1908. The two reached a deal for Grayson to write an explosive no-holds-barred account of his career. Richards was a well-known society figure with socialist sympathies who had previously published George Bernard Shaw and A.E. Housman. Richards expected that both he and Grayson would make a great deal of money from this venture, indicating that Grayson was still sufficiently in the public eye to expect large sales for his life-story.

He settled down and wrote a synopsis, along with drafts of the first few chapters, and came up with the title *My Search After God*. It was an intriguing title and suggested that Grayson, who now considered himself an agnostic, was either still looking for God or for a new movement that would replace the old religion. He wrote to Richards on 11 March 1918:

> I am personally certain concerning the book's selling power. I must, however, have at least an extension of six weeks of the contracted time for delivery of the completed manuscript. The loss of my wife has involved so much sorrow, worry, change – and the potent antidote of really important national work that I've had no time to settle down as I should like to, before beginning the actual writing.

Grayson had always preferred speaking from the platform to the arduous and sometimes monotonous task of writing and, despite his recent bereavements, he returned to the platform. His public speaking appeared to be going well, with Grayson putting in the type of performance that had left so many working-class communities across Britain spellbound a decade and more before. 'I've been very effective,' he told Richards, 'helping to keep production going on the Clyde and in various munitions areas.' Grayson's letter suggested that he was introducing an element of order and planning into his life. Whether he had secured an additional source of income, in addition to his work on behalf of the government, is unclear:

> I've now made an arrangement under which my pot will be kept boiling, my public work (for the next few weeks) be completed, and facilities for writing my book in a sweet Norfolk cottage, assured. My plans go something like this: -
>
> I proceed to Barrow-in-Furness and the Tyne ... I spend five days working on the book. I then go to Liverpool and the Mersey generally, for another week – administer my well-known fillip to the shipyard workers and public there – and return for another week to the 'Search ...' I then do the Bristol Channel and return for a couple of days to the Clyde – after which the object of my existence will be the completion of our venture ... Meanwhile, you may rest assured that no harm is being done to the circulation of the book by one's wanderings and orations in important and crowded communities.

It was certainly a busy schedule for a man who had previously suffered nervous breakdowns and who had just lost his wife and children. But Grayson had more mysterious calls on his time as he proceeded to explain, albeit obliquely, in his letter to Richards:

> I like to put all my cards on the table, as I think life is too short and uncertain … I shall spend the bulk of this week in helping an unliterary person to publish an important series of articles under his name. The articles may ultimately become a booklet – but I don't think you will consider my part in it a breach of contract. As a matter of fact, I have induced my … 'collaborator' to retain the publishing rights … and I think you would be interested in them. I can't say any more at present …[5]

Untangling precisely what Grayson was up to is a difficult task. He was probably alluding to having agreed to work with the National War Aims Committee (NWAC), a shadowy propaganda unit formed in August 1917 and run from 12 Downing Street. Furthermore, a series of 19 pamphlets was published under the title *Searchlights* and distributed without charge through Britain's largest newsagent chains, John Menzies and WH Smith. Could this be the 'important series of articles' to which Grayson referred? Only one of the articles appeared under Grayson's name, *Germany's Last Chance*, in which he called for a renewed effort against the Germans and, importantly, stated that industrial unrest at this time was tantamount to fighting in the Kaiser's corner.

> When this war is ended there will be a tremendous social problem to solve, and if I am spared I hope to co-operate in its solution. I shall stand for an equality of opportunity for every child born in these realms. It is because I yearn passionately for the attainment of this ideal that I want to beat the Boche. If he wins, the hopes of European democracy will perish. He is playing his last card – the card of 'industrial unrest'. Let us pack our present troubles in the old kit-bag until we have turned the mad dog out of the house.[6]

It is now widely forgotten just how close Britain came to revolution in 1918 and particularly in 1919. The Bolshevik seizure of power had alarmed European governments, and domestic revolutionaries and even trade unionists, so often dismissed by those in power, were now seen as a real threat. Civil servants drew up preparations to combat a wave of strikes that could bring about a revolutionary situation on Britain's streets. David Clark notes that

> the Board of Trade in 1918 collected the name and address of each trade union branch secretary in every town and village of the four countries of the UK which was then published in three volumes. The prime objective was to make available to the police details of individuals who might be considered as the most likely to be involved in revolutionary activity at a local level. The logic was impeccable and the effort was colossal.[7]

The above demonstrates just how worried and yet ill-prepared the British government was. In Grayson the authorities had a potential weapon to keep any revolution at bay. He had the necessary political stature, was of the working class and he had the contacts, information and inside knowledge that the government lacked.

His meetings continued but they did not always run as smoothly as Churchill's memoirs suggest. Harry McShane, the young ILP member who had followed Grayson enthusiastically into the British Socialist Party, recalled his experience of a Grayson meeting in 1918:

> By 1917 living conditions for the workers were becoming more and more difficult. Not only were they working fantastically long hours, but the money they earned bought very little. Prices had reached an impossible level ... Rent increases had stopped, but bad housing and shortages were everywhere. Everyone was getting sick of the war. The government tried all manner of tricks to counter the anti-war feeling. Victor Grayson ... was actually brought up to Glasgow to speak in his uniform. He was faced by a hostile audience and couldn't finish his speech, though Glasgow had always been a centre of support for him.[8]

The meeting to which McShane referred was held at Glasgow City Hall in late February 1918. John McGovern, a conscientious objector with communist sympathies and later a controversial Labour MP in the Grayson mould, also attended the meeting and recorded his experience of 'one notable Sunday evening':

> The speaker was Private Victor Grayson, who had formerly ... been a thorn in the flesh of the orthodox Labour leaders. His chairman was Sir Peter Mackie, Chairman of White Horse Whisky Distillers Ltd. When he rose to open the meeting there was no evidence of opposition. [As the meeting proceeded, a heckler] began a series of interruptions and fights broke out all over the hall, but the authorities did not make the error of trying to eject any of the interrupters. Grayson, who commanded a certain respect as a former Labour MP who had been wounded in battle, was given a fair hearing, but he indulged in comments about 'Kaiser Bill and his burglars' which did not please either the chairman or the platform party. Someone shouted out, 'You mean the capitalist burglars behind you on the platform.' To this Grayson replied, 'You should know that the burglars go out with a sack during the night and the capitalists go out with a little brown bag during the day.' Some of the faces on the platform were a study.[9]

Grayson went further in his Glasgow speech and elsewhere, by declaring that he would once again seek election to Parliament when the war was over. It would be his duty, he said, to ensure that the promises made to the working men and women who had sacrificed so much were honoured. Until then, he continued a busy round of platform work, including a series of meetings on Merseyside where he was well received. He gave his now standard arguments against industrial unrest and in favour of ensuring that the war was won:

> A man when he got that order [to go over the top] didn't say 'Just a moment. What about that twelve and a half percent bonus? What about my wages? What about my officer's pay?' No, the men went forward cheerfully because they knew they were out to beat the foulest enemy

humanity had ever had … the soil of freedom was absolutely dependent upon the victory of the British forces. If we lost this war, the advance of civilization was postponed for at least two hundred years.[10]

This meeting on Merseyside has been cited by historians as Grayson's last public act after which he disappeared from view. But that is not the case. It seems that Grayson became desperately ill and very nearly died. The cause remains uncertain, but it is worth remembering that from 1918 to 1920 the world suffered from the so-called Spanish Influenza pandemic, largely spread by soldiers returning home from the war. Nearly a quarter of a million British people died from the 'flu and perhaps 50 million worldwide. It particularly affected those in their twenties and thirties. In a letter written in May 1918 to his NWAC handler, Sydney Vesey, Grayson said he had 'been very ill for the past fortnight and am still confined to my room, though convalescent'.[11] In a further letter to his now long-suffering and evidently complaining publisher, Grayson wrote:

Dear Mr Grant Richards,

I have been ill – very ill – and worried over things. I will explain when I see you … I have nearly been at the door of death – but am just beginning to realise fresh energy. I have so many obligations that press – work – and some platform work – have been and are essential. The decease of my wife has involved me in worries – but the book will be done!

… I am not surprised that you think I have been treating you unkindly, and I am sorry to have made you think so. But I will 'deliver the goods'. I can very ill afford to wait, but I'm writing up. If you can ring me up and make an appointment, I will be obliged.

The sting of your note lies in its charming brevity. But I'm quite sure that we shall not quarrel.

The letters to Vesey and Richards were sent from 131 Harley Street, London. This was the address of Dr Von Sawyer, a German lady in her late fifties. Grayson had so often found comfort, support and consolation in the company of older women. In a letter to his sister, Augusta, Grayson described his situation:

> I am in a beautifully sumptuous house at present, until I get on my feet again. My doctor friend is not charging me for the apartment – nor nearly enough for my food and general attention and treatment. I don't think I will stay here very long, as I'm somewhat proud. Still, the world is very kind to me.[12]

Grayson received a further blow when he learned that his older brother, John, was killed in action in France on 28 June 1918, leaving behind his wife and five children. He seemed to disappear again from the public platform but the reason appears to be a simple financial calculation. For a public appearance, Grayson was paid no more than 2 Guineas (£2.10) by the NWAC, but for his writing they paid a much more lucrative £5.05 per 1000 words. Throughout the summer and autumn of 1918, Grayson turned out a series of what were labelled 'special articles' by the NWAC, ranging in content from his views on the political situation in Russia in *Kerensky* to his experience of war in *Preparing to Attack* and *Fight for Ridge*, and to attacks on growing industrial militancy in *Two Ways of Striking* and *A Soldier on Strikes*. It is also worth noting that requests for Grayson's work came from 10 Downing Street via J.T. Davies, Lloyd George's private secretary, which may indicate to us something of the former MP's importance to the war effort. Through the use of his pen, by mid-August Grayson was back on his feet financially and was able to move from Dr Von Sawyer's and into rooms at the superior Georgian House, Bury Street, London SW.1.

Now on a stronger financial footing and with his physical health improving, Grayson made a few final speaking appearances before the Armistice. The last newspaper reference to him on a public platform is from the *Hull Daily Mail* of 20 November 1918. Grayson had spoken the previous evening at the 'Lit and Phil' where he arrived characteristically late for the meeting and 'battered' in appearance. He told his audience that this was not due to wounds but 'falling down instead of using the lift', most likely the result of too much alcohol. He lectured the audience about his experiences during the war, stressing that he had gone out as a socialist and agitator, who 'had scars which he would carry to his grave, inflicted by the batons of British policemen'. Pacifists, he said, 'were impossible people' and he assured the crowd that he was going to return to politics to fight, because 'if politics could win a war against the mightiest foe, it would do other things. It might provide food, fuel, and shelter for children. In the problem of reconstruction the best brains of the Empire would be needed.' This was nine days after the Armistice and it is apparent that Grayson was set on a return to politics.

But then a curious thing happened. Grayson visited an old female comrade and handed her his annotated copy of his favourite book, *The Roadmender*. He then travelled back to London, never to be seen on a public platform again.

The remainder of Grayson's life is shrouded in mystery, not least because of an almost total absence of documentary evidence. This encourages a greater degree of speculation than the historian is generally comfortable in employing. But the final chapter of this book will offer an account of Grayson's last days that is at least compatible with such evidence that survives.

13
Towards the Truth

Never in my day in any country had a young man of twenty-six such a chance of making a great name for himself, and doing really fine work for his class and generation ... it seemed to me incredible that a sensitive, capable person of his natural turn for initiative could fail to see and to grasp the great opportunity which lay before him.

Henry Myers Hyndman [1]

The almost universal view, however, was that same-sex acts of whatever kind were unnatural, a deliberate perversion of what God intended (and most people believed in God). Any infraction or deviation should therefore be severely punished – and no distinction was drawn between sex between two consenting adult men and paedophilia.

Chris Bryant [2]

I am no longer a roadmender; the stretch of white highway which leads to the end of the world will know me no more ...

Michael Fairless [3]

Donald McCormick (1911–1998) was a *Sunday Times* journalist and prolific author with links to the right wing of the Conservative Party. He had no time for socialism or any of the causes for which Grayson spent his political life fighting. McCormick once said that he rated the 'British working classes as being about on a par with the lowest type of African tribe', which, coming from a supporter of the apartheid system, was meant as the worst kind of insult. But he had a journalist's eye for a good story. After failing as a writer of fiction, McCormick realised that the more he disguised his work as non-fiction, the better it would sell. From 1955 to 1976 he published a staggering 34 books ranging in scope from cannibalism to political biography via murder, espionage, UFOs and even erotica.

A common feature throughout his books was the use of interviews and of evidence to which only he was privy and which subsequently vanished when other researchers tried to access it. So important evidence, which often formed the basis of his work, such as key diaries and letters, was never seen by anyone else. When confronted, McCormick claimed on more than one occasion that these papers had been sold at auction – of which there was no record – or simply destroyed. It may then seem surprising that such a man was taken at all seriously as a historian, but he was, and his fraudulent account of the last months of Victor Grayson's life has fooled researchers for half a century.

McCormick's *Murder by Perfection* (1970) accuses the flamboyant fraudster and Lloyd George fixer, Maundy Gregory (1877–1941), of murdering Victor Grayson. To build his narrative, McCormick supplied verbatim interviews with Robert Blatchford from 1931 (when McCormick was barely out of his teens) and key witnesses including Private Walter Adams, who is presented as an old army friend of Grayson's. There is also a letter from the artist, George Flemwell, who describes Grayson entering the home of Maundy Gregory, from which – we are told – he never left alive. McCormick also tells us that Grayson was working to expose Gregory in a series of articles on political corruption and the illegal sale of honours. McCormick states that Grayson returned to political campaigning in 1919 to reveal the identity of 'a monocled dandy' who was behind the scandal. The problem is that none of this bears close scrutiny. Not a single document can be found indicating that Grayson was investigating the honours scandal or working to expose Gregory. Grayson's relationship with Blatchford does not appear to have survived his relationship with Winnie Blatchford. When we note that Blatchford made not a single reference to Grayson in his autobiography, and that he refused to speak about Victor to Reg Groves, his supposed openness with a young McCormick looks very suspicious. Private Adams, the key witness to the enmity between Grayson and Gregory and the resulting mysterious goings-on, has never been found. Despite the attempts of several researchers, including David Clark, no such Private Adams has been found in the ranks of the New Zealand Expeditionary Force. The most important piece of evidence, however, is the letter from George Flemwell. According to McCormick, Flemwell stated that he had witnessed Grayson and another man mooring an electric canoe on the Thames outside 'Vanity Fair', the home of Maundy Gregory. Flemwell was supposedly sketching on the riverside at Thames Ditton on 28 September 1919 when the two men passed him. He immediately recognised one of them to be Grayson, whose portrait he had painted before the war. Flemwell later visited the house to ask after Grayson. However, a 'handsome woman of bohemian appearance' denied all knowledge of Grayson and the incident that Flemwell described.

George Flemwell died in 1928, though it was not until 42 years later in 1970 that his alleged sighting of Grayson was revealed. McCormick, the only person to see the letter from which this entire scenario is reconstructed, was contacted by David Clark when he was researching his biography of Grayson. McCormick claimed to have auctioned the letters at Maples a few years previously, though the firm had no record of this. McCormick died in 1998, but the author Andrew Cook managed to interview his widow in November 2000. Eileen McCormick claimed to have been 'deeply involved' with her late husband's work and Cook asked her about the Flemwell letter. He questioned how Flemwell could have been sure that he had seen Grayson when he was on the opposite side of the Thames, and recounts Mrs McCormick's response and his own subsequent conclusions:

> She immediately responded that it had been an Indian summer, sunny with clear blue sky, and that Flemwell had a perfect view of the river ... I approached the Met Office archive to see if this could be confirmed. The weather report for that date, 28 September 1919, was however cloudy, overcast sky with poor visibility. While reading the report, I noticed that 28 September 1919 was in fact a Sunday, which prompted me to check Hampton Court Palace records. I discovered that Barge Walk, the north bank of the Thames on which Flemwell was allegedly sitting while painting, is owned and controlled by the Palace, and was in fact closed to the public on Sundays – how then could Flemwell have been there? The balance of evidence not only suggests he was not, but points to the whole scenario being fabricated by McCormick in order to knit together two unrelated stories ... to create his 'Murder by Perfection' book.[4]

Tellingly, when Cook asked her about other parts of the story, including the role of Private Adams, Eileen McCormick responded that her late husband 'often used his imagination to flesh things out a little', a classic case of British understatement. McCormick understood how to cater to his audience. He knew that, at least since the Zinoviev letter, paranoia about state and establishment manipulation and cover-ups has run through the British left. He had fashioned a story of a fallen hero, who, on the brink of exposing Maundy Gregory to reveal state corruption, was murdered by this corrupt stooge of the Liberal and Conservative Parties. McCormick's tale fed his readers' appetite and for five decades the story was widely accepted as fact. McCormick's 'research' and, indeed, *Murder by Perfection* as a whole may be dismissed as pure invention. But a second explanation of Grayson's disappearance also merits attention.

When researching his biography of Grayson, David Clark located the manageress of Georgian House, where Grayson is reported to have lived from late 1918 to September 1920. Hilda Porter was 13 years Grayson's junior and had travelled to London from her native Ipswich to work as a receptionist. She had proved so able that she quickly became the manageress of a block of flats at Vernon Court, opposite the stables of Buckingham Palace. She recalled that in early 1918 Grayson came and booked a suite of rooms and that his wife intended to join him after she had given birth. He later returned 'distraught' to inform her that his wife had died. Months later she met Grayson again, but this time at the superior Georgian House in Bury Street, Piccadilly. It was here that Grayson lodged, in suite 42 on the fourth floor. Her recollections are important because, prior to the publication of Clark's biography, much of this information was unknown. The discovery of Grayson's letters to Grant Richards validates Porter's story that he briefly stayed at Vernon Court, around the time of his wife's death, before moving on. This suggests not only that Grayson knew Porter but that her story – despite the six decades between the events and her recollection of them – was reliably accurate. As a result, Porter's subsequent revelations have to be taken seriously.

During his stay at Georgian House, Grayson kept out of the public eye. There are no reports of newspaper articles or pamphlets being published under his name, nor did he appear on any public platform. Yet, despite this, Porter tells us that Grayson spent the majority of his time shut away in his rooms at his desk, writing. We know that he was not publishing under his own name and, according to his letters to his publisher, Grant Richards, his autobiography had not progressed past the first two or three chapters by mid-1918. We also know from their correspondence that Grayson was writing on behalf of others, including an 'unliterary friend', and that he was, given his personal circumstances, well paid to do so. So, for whom was he writing?

According to Porter, Grayson received a regular set of visitors – all of them men – including Horatio Bottomley, Havelock Wilson and Maundy Gregory. All three were pro-war with strong links to the Liberal Party and the coalition government headed by Lloyd George. Grayson and Bottomley were well acquainted, having sat in the Commons at the same time. Indeed, Bottomley had crossed the floor to approach Grayson during his unemployment protest in an attempt to calm him. Now Bottomley made his living as a newspaper proprietor and had involved himself in dubious financial initiatives, including selling his own form of war bonds. Grayson had written for Bottomley's *John Bull* newspaper throughout the war, so it is not inconceivable that he was now writing copy under an assumed name. Bottomley commanded substantial fees and was known to sub-contract much of his work. Havelock Wilson and Grayson had shared platforms in early 1918 fundraising for the war effort. Many of Wilson's activities in 1918 were carried out under the banner of the British Workers League which, under his stewardship, would become the National Democratic and Labour Party (NDP) at the end of the year. The NDP attracted pro-war elements of the old Clarion movement, Lloyd George-supporting Liberals and dissidents from Grayson's former party, the British Socialist Party. It was openly hostile to Ramsay MacDonald, Philip Snowden and the rest of the pacifist block within the Labour Party and was partly funded by coalition Liberals as a means of splitting the Labour vote. When Grayson spoke of standing again for Parliament in the December 1918 'coupon' election, it is almost certain that this would have been under the banner of the NDP. There are several reports of him attending Labour Party meetings as a journalist immediately after the Armistice but, as no journalism resulted, it seems likely that Grayson was either spying on elements within Labour, researching for clients or recruiting for the NDP. The third man who visited Grayson regularly was Arthur John Maundy Gregory, a man infamous in his own lifetime as a charlatan, political fixer and crook, obsessed with his own image. He was a failed teacher and actor who had initially made his name as an impresario and theatre producer, before selling celebrity secrets to the police and publishing tittle-tattle in his own monthly magazine, *Whitehall Gazette*. Gregory would almost certainly have known Ruth Grayson and, through her, have met Victor. From early 1918 Gregory was one of several dubious figures whom Lloyd George employed to sell titles and honours in return for substantial political donations. He also reported on left-wing political activists to Basil Thompson, head of Scotland Yard.

In *Murder by Perfection* and in much of the commentary on Grayson and Gregory's relationship since its publication, Gregory has been presented as being employed to keep an eye on Grayson, with the suggestion that the latter was politically dangerous to the British establishment. During 1918 and 1919 the establishment feared that Britain might be on the brink of revolution. Tanks were deployed in Liverpool and Glasgow against striking workers, sections of the army were in open revolt and workers councils were formed. Despite leading Britain to victory in the First World War, Lloyd George was seen by many, including Churchill, as too soft on Bolshevism. Basil Thompson even believed he might be in league with Lenin and Trotsky.[5] Russian money was pouring into Britain to pay for pro-Soviet propaganda, not least in the *Daily Herald*, edited by George Lansbury, at the launch of which in 1912 Grayson had been a guest speaker. Grayson was no Bolshevik. He was still very much an English socialist in the Robert Blatchford, Edward Carpenter and William Morris mould. After all, Lenin had gone to the trouble of writing his own criticism of Grayson. That he was missing from the revolutionary activities of 1919 demonstrates that Grayson now saw his role lying on the other side of the political divide. It seems more likely, then, that Grayson was in fact informing on his former comrades and being paid handsomely for his efforts and possibly also for the propaganda he may have been writing. Porter recalled men dressed in livery, almost certainly employees of Gregory, delivering packages for Grayson every fortnight. It seems probable, then, that with Gregory acting as an intermediary, Grayson was feeding information to Basil Thompson of Scotland Yard and the recently established MI5. There is no other way to explain Grayson's income. He had entered the war penniless and came out of it only slightly better off. Yet suddenly, shortly after the Armistice, he was living in luxury with his rent paid without difficulty. But on Saturday, 20 September 1920, Grayson walked out of Georgian House, escorted by two unknown men who had spent the day in his rooms. It was the start of one of the great mysteries of the twentieth century. To Porter, to whom he had become so close that he even proposed marriage, Grayson whispered, 'I'll be back in touch with you', but he never was. Porter kept his rooms free for as long as she could but, eventually, she collected what was left of his papers and belongings and returned them to his mother, Elizabeth, in Northbrook Street, Liverpool.

There was another witness to this strange and sudden disappearance, Grayson's daughter, Elaine. Grayson had signed custody of her to Ruth's parents, John and Georgina Nightingale, shortly after his wife's death. Elaine lived with the Nightingales in Bolton and remembered that her father visited regularly after the war, until his disappearance. Victor would catch the train to Bolton on a Friday and usually stay for the weekend. So frequent were his visits that Victor kept his dog, Nunquam, in Bolton and even had his own room, in which he was caught hiding whisky under the floorboards. But one weekend Grayson failed to arrive. As Elaine later recalled:

> I had watched for him for three or four weekends and he hadn't come ... Then I asked why he hadn't come and they said he was busy. He didn't write and he didn't telephone and it wasn't like him. I cried and I asked Jane [the nanny], 'Why hasn't Daddy come?' and she said, 'He will never come again because he's going to travel. He's going a long way away and he won't be able to get back but he will never forget you. He'll always think about you and one day perhaps he may come back.' That was a worse shock to me than mother dying.[6]

Her father did not come back, though Georgina Nightingale and the nanny Jane seemed to believe for many years afterwards that he would.

Despite any misgivings they might have had about Grayson, the Nightingales developed a good relationship with him after Ruth's death and he was evidently welcomed into the family home. But there is no record that they raised the alarm when Grayson suddenly stopped visiting and failed to telephone or write. On reflection, it seems rather odd that the sudden disappearance of their son-in-law did not prompt a call to the police.

Reports of Victor's disappearance did not emerge until seven years later, in 1927. Until then it was believed that he had merely retired from public life. This was quite plausible as Grayson had disappeared from the public eye in Britain before. In 1916, whilst Grayson was touring Australia and New Zealand, Edward Carpenter, his friend and mentor, had lamented in his autobiography that Grayson's disappearance from public life was regrettable. Only when William Grayson called for an investigation into his brother's disappearance did the story gain traction. It is also worth noting that Grayson's mother was furious and asked that her famous son be left to live in secrecy, if that was what he desired. Then, bizarrely, it was revealed that in the 1921 annual report of Grayson's former Unitarian College in Manchester, he had been listed in the roll of the deceased. There is no evidence in the college archives to indicate why this was done, nor was anyone at the time able to explain why Grayson had been listed. The timing seems too coincidental to be a simple clerical error and too serious a matter to be based on hearsay. It would at least have taken a letter or the word of a respected person for Grayson's death to have been recorded, but, if such a document ever existed, it is now lost.

A significant and intriguing sighting of Grayson is alleged to have occurred in Maidstone, Kent, in 1924. This story has been mentioned in every Grayson biography, but new research gives it additional weight. John Beckett, then a young and rebellious Labour councillor in Hackney, touring the platform speaking circuit, was lodging in Maidstone with Ernest Hunter, later political editor of the *Daily Herald*, and Seymour Cocks, a future MP. On 23 August 1924 they held an open-air meeting near Maidstone prison. As John Beckett recalled:

Seymour Cocks opened the meeting, Hunter spoke, and I followed. After his speech, Ernest made off for refreshment; and after mine, a tall, rather handsome man said to me 'that was some speech sonny, I used to give them just the same stuff'. He invited Cocks and I to adjourn to the nearest hostelry. When we were settled he told us some interesting stories of Irish politics, and admitted connection with the Irish Secret Service. His name, he said, was Victor Grayson.

Furthermore, the man had talked about his time in the New Zealand Expeditionary Force and was in a nervous state, so much so that Cocks thought he might be suffering from shell-shock. He gave the men his address, but this was unfortunately lost. According to John Beckett's son, the historian and biographer, Francis, his father always believed that it really was Grayson whom he had met. Though Beckett had no knowledge of Grayson when he encountered the stranger in Maidstone, he later had the opportunity of inspecting photographs and reading about the former socialist hero and it is telling that he continued to believe that it was indeed Grayson who had approached him, until he died in 1964.[7] John Beckett wrote his autobiography, but it remains unpublished. His son has allowed access to this work which contains a small but significant piece of new information. After the Maidstone sighting, Beckett and Cocks went to visit Philip Snowden and Beckett recalled that

Snowden questioned Cocks and I closely concerning the incident. The description we gave appeared to convince him that the man we had in reality met was Victor Grayson. I have never been able to settle the matter satisfactorily in my own mind, but I can see no reason why the claim should have been made if it was not true. The stranger wanted nothing from us, indeed he entertained us well. He told us his name without any attempt to make a story or sensation from it, and when we made no comment, made none himself. The odd thing is that this is the only recorded sighting by anyone in the political world. My own view is that he stopped at the meeting, noticed a speaker of about the age he himself had been at the peak of his political career, and something in the atmosphere of an enthusiastic meeting touched his recollection and made him talk to us.[8]

It seems possible that Grayson was reminded of his younger self. Certainly, Beckett possessed a platform style and oratorical gifts that veterans compared with those of Grayson at his best. The similarities were striking and Fenner Brockway, who knew both men, wrote that 'Beckett was young, enthusiastic, dynamic ... By his energy, spectacular methods and ability to win people by his "rabble-rousing" oratory at street corners, he built up a huge following ... There was no policy in his speeches, just punch and hit. A boxer.'[9] Francis Beckett, speaking about his father's sighting, said: 'I have no doubt that he was certain the man he saw was Grayson.'[10]

Since himself becoming MP for Colne Valley in 1922, Philip Snowden had been making his own unsuccessful attempts to track down Grayson. If anyone could identify the missing man it would be Snowden. A century later, it seems entirely possible that the mysterious stranger was indeed Grayson. The fact that the man had spoken of his war record, his service with the New Zealand forces and, in particular, that he appeared to be suffering from shell-shock – not something that was publicly known – add credence. If, after long and careful interrogation of Cocks and Beckett, neither of whom previously knew anything of Grayson except his name, Snowden was certain the man was Grayson, then the case is surely strong. Snowden was a serious, even dour, man and not one to indulge in idle flights of fancy. The surprising fact is that, though Snowden writes in his autobiography about his attempts to find Grayson, he does not mention the Beckett incident which, at the time, was the best sighting of Grayson there had been and one that he could verify. The best explanation is that by 1934, when Snowden's autobiography was published, Beckett had embraced fascism and followed another of Snowden's enemies, Oswald Mosley, out of the Labour Party to form the British Union of Fascists. Understandably, Snowden did not want to give Beckett any sort of publicity by referring to him, an approach seen elsewhere in biographies and memoirs of Labour figures of the era.

Less verifiable sightings of Grayson continued. Old acquaintances claimed to have seen him, mostly around the London and Maidstone areas. Sam Eastwood, Grayson's election agent from the Colne Valley campaign, told an inquiring journalist in 1927 that Grayson had recently been in communication with him. Furthermore, he had an address for him in London but declined to share it, claiming that he was under a promise not to divulge it.[11] Eastwood was not the only witness. Vernon Hartshorn, the Welsh Trade Unionist and Labour MP who served in the first two Labour governments, was another friend of Grayson who claimed to know that he was still alive in the late 1920s and who expected him to one day reappear in public.

There is a particularly strange story involving a London furniture shop of which there are two versions. In 1963 Derek Forwood was investigating Grayson's disappearance and was given an odd piece of paper by an elderly former Grayson associate, Ernest Quarmby. It was an opened envelope from the Dale Manufacturing Co., furniture dealers at 473 Oxford Street, London. The company was owned by two men, Douglas Wood and Hartley Edward Batt, neither seemingly having any connection to Grayson. But printed on the envelope along with the company address were the words, 'Personal, Mr Victor Grayson'. At first sight, it appeared to be handwritten, but on closer inspection the text had been printed. Quarmby had been given this in either 1931 or 1932 and he had sent a letter to the firm, addressed to Grayson, asking if it was indeed his old friend. A response came back that there was a Victor Grayson at the shop, but not the once famous politician. The story took on another form in 1933 when George Deer, then Mayor of Lincoln and a future Labour MP, was contacted by a man who claimed to have seen Grayson on a London Underground train and to have followed him to the premises of a furniture firm on Oxford Street. A letter was brought back bearing the address of Dale's (possibly the same letter Derek Forwood was given in the 1960s). Ernest Marklew, a member of Grayson's 1907 by-election campaign team who would win Colne Valley back for Labour in 1935, then wrote a letter addressed to Victor Grayson at the Oxford Street address. Marklew received the following response 'It is true my name is Victor Grayson, but I am not the Victor Grayson you are looking for.' Marklew showed the letter to another old friend of Grayson's, Jess Townend, and to George Deer who each separately confirmed that the handwriting in the letter bore an uncanny resemblance to the missing man's. Marklew, who was then quite ill, is said to have gone down to the store to meet the Victor Grayson who claimed to work there. Unfortunately, he kept no written record of his trip and, when Deer and Townend visited his home in Cleethorpes, he had already been taken to a convalescent home, where he collapsed and died two days after an operation.

In the 1960s, Derek Forwood could find no connection between Grayson and the Dale Manufacturing Company and the matter remained a mystery to him. My researches indicate that Dales went bankrupt in June 1932 with debts of £119,300. The link to the envelope may be one of the key reasons that the firm became insolvent. In the twelve months before going under, Dales spent a staggering £50,000 (£3,500,000 today) on advertising alone, more than twice the company's total declared assets in 1933. Is this perhaps the link? Grayson was declared missing in 1927 and there had been a flurry of press reports and speculation about his whereabouts in the late 1920s and early 1930s. What better advertising gimmick could there be for a furniture store down on its luck and in desperate need of new business than to advertise that the mysterious and vanished Victor Grayson was working there? Or, did the real Grayson have something to do with the scheme? After all, looking at the spending, there would have been more to the advertising campaign than just envelopes. Dales may have disappeared, but its former owners' advertising stunt may have been the basis for the sightings and rumours that followed throughout the 1930s that Grayson was living in London and working in a shop on or around Oxford Street.

The next significant sighting was that of Sidney Campion on the London Underground, as mentioned in the Introduction. As a young ILP member in Leicester, Campion had idolised Grayson and, though they had only met once before, Campion claimed in 1963 that he could still model a lifelike bust of Grayson, so clearly etched on his memory was his face.[12] In a letter to Derek Forwood he wrote:

I have no doubt that I saw V.G. as described in the Press reports. It was not a question of later recollection. I made a statement immediately I reached the Parliamentary Press Gallery; I told several colleagues; naturally some of them considered it to be a good story and sent it to their papers. I never wrote anything at the time for the Press. Since then the subject has come to the surface time and again ... I know that when

I saw V.G. on the District Railway on my way to the Houses of Parliament I was almost overwhelmed, and I watched every expression on his face, tried to catch all he said. Of course he was a rehabilitated V.G., had forsaken the bottle, and possessed some of his former verve.[13]

Campion elaborated on what he thought had happened to Grayson after the war:

A few years later [after the Great War] when I moved to Lancashire I became very friendly with Charles Sixsmith, a Socialist textile manufacturer with mills near Bolton. He knew the father of Victor Grayson's wife, and he told me that he had learnt through the father that after the war in which he had served, V.G. was a disillusioned Socialist and turned Tory, and sought employment as a Tory propagandist. Bonar-Law was supposed to have been approached by V.G.'s father-in-law but I forget the outcome.[14]

This statement is intriguing. Campion is correct about Grayson's in-laws and their Bolton connection – something not widely known. We also know that Grayson had become disillusioned, as the old English socialism he had espoused became sidelined in the wake of the success of Bolshevism in Russia. We know, too, that he was writing pro-war propaganda – which included anti-union and anti-Marxist material – so it is not beyond belief that he might have turned Tory. After all, his old friend and comrade Robert Blatchford did just that.

During the Second World War, Scotland Yard carried out a thorough investigation into the disappearance of Grayson, after prompting from Grayson's sister, Augusta. Quite amazingly, given that the outcome of the war was still in the balance as the Battle of Stalingrad raged, a senior figure in the British government authorised police time and resources to be devoted to hunting for Grayson. What is more, Scotland Yard then spent decades denying that an investigation had ever taken place. This was the answer given to my own Freedom of Information request. Only after being shown press releases from the war where the police had appealed for information, did they admit that an investigation had taken place.

But they now insisted that the relevant files no longer existed. I asked what had happened to them. I was told that anything relating to a public figure would have been sent to the National Archives and that it was very rare for such papers to be destroyed. Predictably, the National Archives had received no such papers. There the trail ended. The original investigation must have been ordered by a member of the government. We know that officers combed everything from Grayson's school and college reports to his parliamentary records. Much was taken away and never returned and the archives still bear the scars of pages ripped out of minute books and reports. Why was Grayson of such importance to the wartime government?

One more piece of new information may shed a little more light. In 2018 I contacted Terry McCarthy who had been head of what was then known as the National Museum of Labour History in London in the 1980s. I asked him how the museum had come across the letters between Grayson and his male lover, Harry Dawson, which had always been described as from 'a private collection'. McCarthy revealed the true origin of the letters and how the museum came across them. The letters had originated from the papers of J.H. Thomas, a former Labour cabinet minister and Ramsay MacDonald loyalist. Thomas was Grayson's complete antithesis, always seen as a sensible democratic socialist, rooted in the trade union movement. As McCarthy explained:

> When I received the letters from Victor Grayson to Harry Dawson which emanated from the private papers of J.H. Thomas, I was somewhat taken aback that the release of the papers did not cause a stir within the official movement, in fact the opposite was true. I can clearly remember one senior trade unionist saying, 'do we really want to know?'
>
> Thankfully we now live in more enlightened times, although I don't have to tell you there will be many in the establishment who won't be too happy you are revealing this. I was asked not to reveal Thomas's papers were the source but enough time has now passed.[15]

The letters between Dawson and Grayson cover the years 1905 to 1911 and indicate a long relationship. A typical one reads:

My stricken darling,

Need I assure you although I have been out of your sight I have not been
out of your mind. I agree with you that absence makes cowards of us
all and is the thief of God's time, but you have no beastly right to rear
yourself on your hind legs and baste me for cold hearted negligence ... I
have had no communication from you. Month in and out I have pined
in my windy garret and left the canker – sorrow – eat at my melancholy
heart and whiten my damask cheek ... it's the droop of your moustache
that takes me; and anyhow, any man who's in favour of the nationalisation of the means of production, distribution and swap, needn't pass
238 The Katacombs in search of a friend. We'll burn a Player's Weight
to old therapeina the wizened goddess of reconciliation and fondly lick
one another's epidermis on the first convenient occasion. To blazes with
miawling and grump. Set the thing you call your heart at rest. I love you
as ever, with the same devouring passion and intensity and thickness.
Your handwriting always pulls the stopper out of my heart and makes
my affections to blubber and blub ...

Thine till Plutus claims his own, and after.
A.V. Grayson

Obviously, someone went to a great deal of time and effort to get hold of this
correspondence and it seems likely that the letters were used to blackmail
Grayson. Perhaps they explain why, after the war, Grayson suddenly disappeared and did not stand for Parliament in the 1918 General Election
as expected. At that time, Grayson was reaching levels of popularity he
had not enjoyed since before the war and Ramsay MacDonald and others
must once again have seen Grayson as an enemy who had the potential to
split the Labour Party as he had done before. To be publicly outed as gay at
that time would have meant the definitive end of his public life and career.
Any close colleague and supporter of Ramsay MacDonald in possession
of such ammunition relating to someone regarded as a political enemy
would surely have used it. I suspect this is why Victor Grayson went into
hiding at Georgian House and why the man once feared as the harbinger
of bloody revolution to Britain was never heard from again.

A Missing Piece of the Puzzle

There have been many theories of how, where and why Grayson disappeared. Some fanciful, some entertaining, and some bordering on the ridiculous. In the summer of 2000 a BBC Radio 4 play, *Antique Silver*, took a unique and contemplative twist on Grayson's life by weaving several theories together. In 1920 he leapt into the Thames and whilst swimming downstream the listener hears him recall the events of his life, before disappearing out to sea. Grayson reappears years later running an antique shop where nothing is for sale. It ends in an air-raid. Others are less glamorous. An old ILP contemporary of Grayson's, Walter Southgate, penned the following:

> In a drunken state he may have wandered and fallen into the pestiferous chemical waste and mud of the River Lea marshes. The place was well known as a death trap and had been misgoverned by seven local authorities each with rights there. Within a short time a body once trapped would rot without trace.[16]

Grayson has also attracted his fair share of Walter Mitty characters. In 1948 a Ms Felena Kennedy reported to her local Labour MP, Alice Bacon (Leeds North East), that her first husband, John Wilson, was actually Victor Grayson. On his deathbed, Wilson had apparently called for Ruth and intimated that his name was Grayson. The story made headline news but pictures of the two men bore no resemblance and neither did their handwriting. In 1967 a nephew of Victor's, George D. Grayson, wrote to the *Daily Mirror* after a flurry of letters about Grayson's disappearance:

> In 1949 I was working on a construction site in East Africa when a plant operator asked me if I was related to Vic Grayson, a mechanical plant fitter. This was my uncle's job before he entered politics. The man told me that he had just left a construction contract in South America where he had worked with a Vic Grayson. I wrote at once to my mother for a photo of Uncle Victor which she sent – one taken about 1919. My new

friend was convinced, allowing for the thirty-year time lapse, that it was, indeed the colleague he had left in South America.[17]

Letters were sent to Victor Grayson at the South American firm, which were received, but never replied to. However, it takes some stretch of the imagination to believe that Victor Grayson, now approaching 70, would be working in such an industry. The answer may be a lot simpler and closer to home.

Amongst the papers of Reg Groves is a note indicating that he managed to track down the retired Chief Inspector Arthur Askew, who had interviewed Groves when he led Scotland Yard's investigation into Grayson's whereabouts during the war. It reads simply: 'Grayson married – settled in Kent.'[18] Among all the sightings of Grayson, the majority of the most plausible occur in and around Maidstone, in Kent, and London. It is a further mystery as to why Groves did not include this information in his later biography. One must assume either that Askew asked him not to, or that Groves did not wish to reveal his findings. David Clark certainly got the impression that Groves had eventually discovered Grayson's fate, but that he did not wish to reveal it.

As Jeremy Corbyn has written in the Foreword, 'somewhere in some files from Scotland Yard or the Home Office, the truth is known'. Although this book has done much to dispel the myths and uncover the real man, until those files are released, we will never really know the ultimate fate of Victor Grayson.

At the time of his disappearance, Grayson was barely 39 years old. In our history books, he appears to us almost as an apparition from a distant generation of Labour figures. However, when we consider that he was six months younger than Ernest Bevin, who served with distinction as Minister of Labour and National Service in Churchill's war-time coalition government, then as Foreign Secretary in Attlee's post-war 1945 government, we realise just how comparatively young Grayson had been. We can then see why many of his contemporaries mourned his loss from both the Labour Party and British politics. They asked how different both could have been if Grayson was nurtured, not vilified, by some of his more experienced Labour colleagues. He was, after all, a genuine product of the British working class with the ability to move the masses. There are lessons for today, too, many of which the British left is yet to heed. That a dizzying array of parties on the left will never further the cause of socialism in Britain, that the Labour Party was formed to represent working people in Parliament, not to be an instrument of protest, and that strong party structures and organisation are the basis of electoral victory.

Whatever our opinions and retrospective takes on Grayson's turbulent and fraught existence, it is to be hoped that Chief Inspector Arthur Askew was right and that Grayson lived on and settled into a comfortable, quiet new life.

Notes

Chapter 1. The Boy from Liverpool

1. E.P. Thompson, *William Morris*, p. 2.
2. Letter from Augusta Greenwood to H.G. Wells, June 1946.
3. Max Arthur, *Lost Voices of the Edwardians*, p. 10.
4. Anthony Miller, *Poverty Deserved? Relieving the Poor in Victorian Liverpool*, p. 12.
5. Ibid., p.1.
6. Quoted in Tony Lane, *Liverpool: City of the Sea*, pp. 51–2.
7. *Liverpool Echo*, 4 October 1954.
8. Quoted in Jonathan Rose, *The Intellectual Life of the British Working Classes*, p. 368.
9. Emmet O'Connor, *Big Jim Larkin: Hero or Wrecker?*, p. 11.
10. The records show the ship was in fact captained by A. Rae, which sounds very much like Clay, and would suggest that the story is true, if a little varnished.
11. W. Thompson, *A. Victor Grayson M.P., England's Most Illustrious Socialist Orator*, p. 10.
12. *Liverpool Echo*, 29 December 2013.
13. Fred Bower, *Rolling Stonemason: An Autobiography*, pp. 78–9.
14. Letter from Fred Bower to Reg Groves, 23 October 1941.

Chapter 2. The Student Revolutionary

1. James Harding, *Agate*, dustcover.
2. James Agate, *Ego 9*, p. 237.
3. Percy Redfern, *Journey to Understanding*, p. 132.
4. Ibid, p. 132.
5. Bonar Thompson, *Hyde Park Orator*, pp. 72–3.
6. Redfern, *Journey to Understanding*, p. 132.
7. Thompson, *Hyde Park Orator*, pp. 73–7.
8. Redfern, *Journey to Understanding*, p. 133.
9. David Clark, *Victor Grayson: Labour's Lost Leader*, p. 23.
10. H.M. Hyndman, *Further Reminiscences*, pp. 278–9.
11. *Yorkshire Post and Leeds Intelligencer*, 2 August 1905.
12. *Manchester Courier and Lancashire General Advertiser*, 2 August 1905.
13. *Yorkshire Post and Leeds Intelligencer*, 2 August 1905.

14. *Manchester Courier and Lancashire General Advertiser*, 2 August 1905.

15. *Socialist and Labour Journal*, June 1905.

16. Ibid.

17. Philip Snowden, *An Autobiography*: Volume One, p. 163.

18. *Leeds Mercury*, 13 April 1906.

19. Leonard Smith, *Unitarian to the Core*, p. 73.

20. David Clark, *Victor Grayson: The Man and the Mystery*, p. 17.

21. Friedrich Engels, *Condition of the Working Class in England*, p. 69.

22. The *Clarion*, 26 July 1907.

23. *Gloucester Citizen*, 12 March 1927.

24. Quoted in Martin Pugh, *Pankhursts*, p. 123.

25. *Leeds Mercury*, 23 July 1906.

26. Hannah Mitchell, *The Hard Way Up*, p. 118.

Chapter 3. The By-Election

1. *Leeds Mercury*, 18 December 1905.

2. Kenneth O. Morgan, *Labour People*, p. 64.

3. *The Worker*, Colne Valley Election Special, 1907.

4. David Brooks, *The Age of Upheaval*, p. 92.

5. H.V. Emy, *Liberals, Radicals and Social Politics 1892–1914*, p. 19.

6. Michael Foot in *The Labour Party: A Centenary History*, ed. Brian Brivati and Richard Heffernan, pp. xiii –xiv.

7. David Dutton, *A History of the Liberal Party*, p. 17.

8. The Taff Vale judgment ruled that a trade union could be sued and compelled to pay for damages inflicted by its officials. In practice, it threatened to make strike action impossible.

9. Sir James Sexton, *Agitator: The Life of the Dockers' MP*, p. 149.

10. David Clark, *Colne Valley: Radicalism to Socialism*, p. 17.

11. Colne Valley Labour Party, *Jubilee Souvenir*, p. 20.

12. Letter from Wilfred Whiteley to Derek Forwood, 30 August 1963.

13. Will Thorne was an early member of the SDF and was taught to read by Karl Marx's daughter, Eleanor. He helped to organise the great London Dock Strike of 1889 and to found the National Union of Gas Workers and General Labourers, now part of the GMB union. He was elected to Parliament in 1906 for the West Ham South constituency.

14. 'England Arise' is a socialist hymn penned by Edward Carpenter in 1886 and was particularly popular before the First World War.

15. *Huddersfield Chronicle*, 23 December 1905.

16. Letter from Jess Townend to Derek Forwood, 27 March 1963.

17. Ibid.

18. Ibid.

19. David Clark, *Victor Grayson: The Man and the Mystery*, p. 28.

20. *Leeds Mercury*, 5 February 1907.

21. Report from Head Office, 24 April 1907, p. 52 (LP/CAN/06/2/39).

22. *Dictionary of Labour Biography* Volume II, p. 336.

23. Letter from Victor Grayson to J.R. MacDonald, 3 July 1907 (LP/CAN/06/2/53).

24. *Leeds Mercury*, 20 June 1907.

25. *Leeds Mercury*, 5 December 1906.

26. He was later elected to Parliament in 1909 for the Hawick Burghs constituency.

27. *Yorkshire Post and Leeds Intelligencer*, 1 July 1907.

28. *Leeds Mercury*, 19 June 1907.

29. *Leeds Mercury*, 20 June 1907.

30. *Aberdeen Journal*, Monday, 1 July 1907.

31. *Yorkshire Post and Leeds Intelligencer*, 1 July 1907.

32. *Aberdeen Journal*, Monday, 1 July 1907.

33. *Leeds Mercury*, 22 June 1907.

34. Jill Liddington, *Rebel Girls: How Votes for Women Changed Edwardian Lives*, p. 132.

35. Hannah Mitchell, *The Hard Way Up*, p. 168.

36. *Aberdeen Journal*, Monday, 1 July 1907.

37. Max Arthur, *Lost Voices of the Edwardians*, p. 369.

38. Liddington, *Rebel Girls*, p. 149.

39. Mitchell, *The Hard Way Up*, p. 149.

40. David Marquand, *Ramsay MacDonald: A Biography*, p. 70.

41. Letter from J.R. MacDonald to Ben Turner, 10 July 1907 (LP/CAN/06/2/62).

42. Reg Groves, *The Mystery of Victor Grayson*, p. 19.

43. Rowland Kenney, *Westering – an Autobiography*, p. 141.

44. Letter from J. Bruce Glasier to Francis Johnson, 3 June 1907 (I.l. 1907/59 – Glasier papers).

45. Letter from J. Bruce Glasier to E.G.F., London, 5 July 1907 (I.l. 1907/14 – Glasier papers).

46. Letter from J.R. MacDonald to E. Whiteley, 8 July 1907 (LA/PA/07/1/92).

47. Kenney, *Westering*, p. 141.

48. The *Clarion*, 27 July 1907.

49. *History in Quotations*, 26 April 1876.

50. Recollection of J.J. Mallon in *Northampton Mercury*, 24 December 1926.

51. Ernest Lockwood, *Colne Valley Folk*, p. 77.

52. F.R. Swan, *The Immanence of Christ in Modern Life*, pp. 218–19.

53. Stanley Pierson, *British Socialists: The Journey from Fantasy to Politics*, pp. 142–3.

54. Clark, *The Man and the Mystery*, p. 52.

55. Groves, *The Mystery of Victor Grayson*, p. 23.

56. The Jarrow by-election was won by Pete Curran.

57. Clark, *The Man and the Mystery*, pp. 54–5.

58. *The Times*, 18 July 1907.

59. *The Times*, 19 July 1907.

60. Thompson, *A. Victor Grayson M.P.*, p. 17.

61. Groves, *The Mystery of Victor Grayson*, p. 23.

62. Thompson, *A. Victor Grayson M.P.*, p. 17.

63. Ibid., pp. 17–19.

64. Fred Bower, *Rolling Stonemason: An Autobiography*, pp. 136–7.

65. Wilfred Whiteley interview with Cyril Pearce, *Society for the Study of Labour History*, Bulletin 18, p. 17.

Chapter 4. 'The Boy Who Paralysed Parliament'

1. Shaw Desmond, *Labour: The Giant with Feet of Clay*, pp. 89–90.

2. *Dictionary of Labour Biography* Volume II, p. 279.

3. Laurence Thompson, *Robert Blatchford: Portrait of an Englishman*, p. 189.

4. The *New Age*, 25 July 1907.

5. Roy Hattersley, *David Lloyd George: The Great Outsider*, p. 223.

6. A.J.A Morris, *C.P. Trevelyan: 1870–1958 Portrait of a Radical*.

7. *Daily Express*, 23 July 1907.

8. Thompson, *Robert Blatchford*, p. 22.

9. Jacqueline Dickenson, *Renegades and Rats: Betrayal and the Remaking of Radical Organisations in Britain and Australia*, p. 129.

10. Hannah Mitchell, *The Hard Way Up*, p. 168.

11. The *Clarion*, 26 July 1907.

12. Letter from F.H. Rose to J.R. MacDonald, 19 July 1907 (LP. GC 17/315).

13. Letter from F.H. Rose to J.R. MacDonald, 33 July 1907 (LP. GC 17/317).

14. Reg Groves, *The Mystery of Victor Grayson*, p. 30.

15. Fenner Brockway, *Towards Tomorrow*, p. 29.

16. S.G. Hobson, *Pilgrim to the Left: Memoirs of a Modern Revolutionist*, p. 114.

17. Ibid.

18. Edward Carpenter, *My Days and Dreams*, p. 260.

19. A.H. Moncur-Sime, *Edward Carpenter, His Ideas and Ideals*, p. 68.

20. Michael Bloch, *Closet Queens*, pp. 8–9.

21. Ibid., p. 224.

22. Ibid., p. 227.

23. James Morris, *Pax Britannia Volume 2*.

24. Only 17 years later there would be enough Labour MPs on those benches to form a minority Labour government.

25. W. Thompson, *A. Victor Grayson MP, England's Most Illustrious Socialist Orator*, pp. 26–7.

26. *Bolton Evening News*, 1 August 1907.

27. *The Times*, 27 July 1907.

28. *Kentish Mercury*, 2 August 1907.

29. Thompson, *A. Victor Grayson MP*, p. 23.

30. The Chairman of the NUDL was James Sexton, another Liverpool ILP contemporary of Grayson's.

31. Emmet O'Connor, *Big Jim Larkin: Hero or Wrecker?*, p. 24.

32. Ibid., p. 27

33. *Irish Times*, 8 August 1907.

34. *The Times*, Friday, 16 August 1907.

35. *Irish News and Belfast Morning News*, 8 August 1907.

36. HC Deb 8 August 1907 vol 180 cc346-50 (Belfast Labour Disputes).

37. Ibid.

38. Ibid.

39. Previous biographies wrongly assert that this speech took place a week earlier, which would have Grayson making his comments BEFORE going to Belfast, which is not the case.

40. Frank Wright, letter to *The Times*, written 19 August 1907, published 20 August 1907.

41. *The Times*, 14 August 1907.

42. Ibid.

43. Reg Groves, *The Strange Case of Victor Grayson*, p. 54.

44. *The Times*, 19 August 1907.

45. Groves, *Strange Case*, p. 54.

46. Thompson, *Robert Blatchford*, pp. 204–5.

Chapter 5. Member for the Unemployed

1. Laurence Thompson, *The Enthusiasts*, p. 156.

2. Glasier Papers, University of Liverpool.

3. HC Debate 07 February 1908 vol 183 c1229.

4. Ibid.

5. HC Debate 10 February 1908 vol 183 c1361.

6. Unemployed Workmen Bill Hansard, 13 March 1908.

7. Ibid.

8. Ibid.

9. Ibid.

10. Labour Party constitution 1918.

11. *Manchester Courier and Lancashire General Advertiser*, 14 March 1908.

12. *London Evening Standard*, 14 March 1908.

13. David Clark, *Victor Grayson: The Man and the Mystery*, p. 35.

14. Carole Anne Naomi Reid, *The Origins and Development of the Independent Labour Party in Manchester and Salford, 1880–1914*, p. 945.

15. Reg Groves, *The Strange Case of Victor Grayson*, p. 61.

16. Ibid., p. 62.

17. Winston Churchill, *Complete Speeches*, Manchester, 28 January 1908, p. 874.

18. *Sheffield Evening Telegraph*, 22 April 1908.

19. Groves, *Strange Case*, p. 60.

20. Manchester Clarion Scouts Demonstration, WCML/Labour Party Archive, 335.1 F37 Box 10.

21. The *New Age*, 17 October 1908.

22. Will Thorne, *My Life's Battles*, p. 176.

23. HC Deb 15 October 1908 vol 194 cc495-7.

24. *Exeter and Plymouth Gazette*, 10 September 1921.

25. The *New Age*, 24 October 1908.

26. HC Deb 16 October 1908 vol 194 cc614-34.

27. Robert Blatchford in The *New Age*, 24 October 1908.

28. The *New Age*, 24 October 1908.

29. Ibid.

Chapter 6. 'England's Greatest Mob Orator'

1. H.M. Hyndman, *Further Reminiscences*, p. 280.

2. *Western Daily Press*, 15 November 1935.

3. Shaw Desmond, *Labour: The Giant with Feet of Clay*, p. 89.

4. H.W. Lee and E. Archibold, *Social Democracy in Britain*, p. 174.

5. The *New Age*, 10 October 1908.

6. Desmond, *Labour*, p. 12.

7. Mayne stood in Falmouth in 1880 and came bottom of the poll. He was also Advocate General of the Madras Presidency.

8. Was this the inspiration for Harry Perkins in Chris Mullin's *A Very British Coup*?

9. John D. Mayne, *The Triumph of Socialism*, p. 2.

10. Ibid. p. 3.

11. Ibid., p. 4

12. *Dictionary of Labour Biography* Volume VI, pp. 83–9.

13. Laurence Thompson, *Robert Blatchford: Portrait of an Englishman*, p. 203.

14. Ibid., p. 204.

15. Ibid., p. 202.

16. Reg Groves, *The Strange Case of Victor Grayson*, p. 80.

17. S.G. Hobson, *Pilgrim to the Left: Memoirs of a Modern Revolutionist*, p. 116.

18. Fred Bower, *Rolling Stone Mason: An Autobiography*, p. 215.

19. James Griffiths, *Pages from Memory*, p. 16.

20. Harry McShane, *No Mean Fighter*, p. 38.

21. Thompson, *Blatchford*, pp. 196–9.

22. Letter from Sidney Campion to Derek Forwood, 18 March 1963.

23. Ibid.

24. Campion's copy of Grayson's pamphlet, *God's Country*, is now in the author's archive.

25. Letter from Campion to Forwood, 18 March 1963.

26. George J. Barnsby, *Birmingham Working People: History of the Labour Movement in Birmingham, 1650–1914*, p. 352.

27. EC report 5 December 1908 in Barnsby, *Birmingham Working People*, p. 354.

28. Barnsby, *Birmingham Working People*, p. 354.

29. Ibid., p. 355.

30. Lee and Archibold, *Social Democracy in Britain*, p. 173.

31. Nan Milton, *John Maclean*, pp. 44–5.

32. The *New Age*, 10 October 1908.

33. Lee and Archibold, *Social Democracy in Britain*, p. 174.

34. John Saville, *The Communist Experience: A Personal Appraisal*, Socialist Register 1991.

35. *Dictionary of Labour Biography* Volume VII, p. 240.

36. Ibid., p. 241.

37. Ibid., p. 242.

38. Desmond, *Labour*, p. 10.

39. Victor Serge, *Memoirs of a Revolutionary*, p. 33.

40. *Prisoners Awaiting Trial in Spain* (Hansard, 19 October 1909).

41. Ibid.

42. Ibid.

43. *Sheffield Evening Telegraph*, 19 October 1909.

44. Edward Carpenter, *My Days and Dreams*, p. 260.

45. *Northampton Mercury*, 24 December 1926.

46. Hyndman, *Further Reminiscences*, pp. 281–2.

47. Ibid., p. 282.

48. Ibid., p. 282.

49. Ibid., p. 283.

Chapter 7. Revolution Delayed

1. Tony Cliff and Donny Gluckstein, *The Labour Party: A Marxist History*, p. 50.

2. Ibid., p. 144.

3. W. Thompson, *A. Victor Grayson M.P., England's Most Illustrious Socialist Orator*, p. 6.

4. Ibid., p. 10.

5. *Huddersfield Examiner*, 1 January 1910.

6. P. Jones, *The Christian Socialist Revival 1877–1914*, p. 332.

7. Ibid.

8 Letter from C.W. Gibson to Derek Forwood, 23 July 1963.

9. Hilaire Belloc and Cecil Chesterton, *The Party System*, p. 8.

10. Ibid., pp. 103–4. It is worth noting that this appears a decade before Donald McCormick claims that Grayson was murdered by Maundy Gregory for threatening to expose the sale of honours.

11. Letter from C.W. Gibson to Derek Forwood, 23 July 1963.

12. *Brixton Free Press*, 2 December 1910.

13. Ibid.

14. Jill Liddington, *Rebel Girls: How Votes for Women Changed Edwardian Lives*, p. 147.

15. *South London Free Press*, 9 December 1910.

16. *Dictionary of Labour Biography* Volume IV, p. 84.

17. In fact, Gosling had no official Labour backing and was supported only by the North London Liberal Association and his own union. The local ILP saw Gosling as an opportunist and were at pains to get this message across.

18. However, the only official police report of disturbance was a complaint from a Tory campaign worker who accused 'Radicals ... mostly Irish and Welsh elementary school teachers' of disrupting one of their meetings.

19. Letter from C.W. Gibson to Derek Forwood, 23 July 1963.

20. Harry Martin had been elected to the Executive Committee of the SPGB upon its formation in 1904, when the party adopted the theories of Marx and Engels, mixed with Chartist traditions and the politics of the First International. Perhaps unsurprisingly, considering his stance on Grayson, Martin saw socialist compromisers everywhere, even within the SPGB, which he was to leave in 1911. Undaunted, he led a one-man 40-year campaign for socialism until his death in 1951. He could be seen standing on an upturned crate in Brixton, 'speaking for the revolution against all compromises and against all legislation'. Until his death Harry Martin's cry was 'No compromise!'

21. *Brixton and Lambeth Gazette*, Friday, 2 December 1910.

22. David A. Perrin, *Socialist Party of Great Britain: Politics, Economics and Britain's Oldest Socialist Party*, p. 18.

23. *Brixton and Lambeth Gazette*, 2 December 1910.

24. *South London Press*, Friday, 9 December 1910.

25. *South London Press*, 9 December 1910.

26. Ibid.

27. The *Clarion*, 9 December 1910.

28. David Clark, *Victor Grayson: The Man and the Mystery*, p. 123.

29. Letter from C.W. Gibson to Derek Forwood, 23 July 1963.

Chapter 8. The Battle for a Socialist Party

1. Anthony Wright, *British Socialism: Thought from the 1880s to the 1960s*, pp. 40–1.

2. Walter Kendall, *The Revolutionary Movement in Britain 1900–21*, p. 37.

3. Thompson, *Robert Blatchford: Portrait of an Englishman*, p. 172.

4. B. and S. Webb, *History of Trade Unionism*, pp. 688–9.

5. Quoted in Tony Cliff and Donny Gluckstein, *Marxism and Trade Union Struggle; the General Strike of 1926*, p. 58.

6. *Official Report of the British Socialist Party*, p. 5.

7. Kendall, *The Revolutionary Movement in Britain*, p. 37.

8. Quoted in *Dictionary of Labour Biography* Volume VII, pp. 73–4.

9. Kendall, *The Revolutionary Movement in Britain*, p. 37.

10. Reg Groves, *The Strange Case of Victor Grayson*, p. 108.

11. David Clark, *Victor Grayson: The Man and the Mystery*, p. 132.

12. Harry McShane, *No Mean Fighter*, p. 38.

13. Ibid.

14. The *Clarion*, 25 August 1911.

15. Ibid.

16. Kendall, *The Revolutionary Movement in Britain*, p. 38.

17. H.M. Hyndman, *The First Annual Conference of the British Socialist Party*, Official Report, p. 3.

18. H.W. Lee and E. Archibold, *Social Democracy in Britain*, p. 178.

19. Ibid., p. 179.

20. Kendall, *The Revolutionary Movement in Britain*, p. 40.

21. Lee and Archibold, *Social Democracy in Britain*, p. 180.

22. McShane, *No Mean Fighter*, p. 38.

23. Rachel Holmes, *Eleanor Marx: A Life*, pp. 141–2.

24. Ibid.

25. Nan Milton, *John Maclean*, pp. 45–6.

26. The *Clarion*, 5 January 1912.

27. Kendall, *The Revolutionary Movement in Britain*, p. 40.

28. McShane, *No Mean Fighter*, p. 39.

29. Ibid., p. 40.

30. Ibid., p. 39.

Chapter 9. More Than Just a 'Cheap Orator'

1. Martin Pugh, *Speak for Britain! A New History of the Labour Party*, p. 69.

2. John Carswell, *Lives and Letters*, p. 38.

3. Philip Mairet, *A. R. Orage: A Memoir*, p. 52.

4. Ibid.

5. S.G. Hobson, *Pilgrim to the Left: Memoirs of a Modern Revolutionist*, p. 117.

6. *Dictionary of Labour Biography* Volume VI, p. 200.

7. Carswell, *Lives and Letters*, pp. 42–3.

8. Ibid., p. 43.

9. David C. Smith (ed.), *Correspondence of H.G. Wells* Volume 2, pp. 239–40.

10. Carswell, *Lives and Letter*, p. 44.

11. Deborah Mutch (ed.), *British Socialist Fiction, 1884–1914*, p. 125.

12. Ibid., p. 263.

13. Ibid., p. 264.

14. Ibid., p. 264.

15. William Gallagher, *The Last Memoirs*, p. 40.

16. F. Foan, *The 'Intellectuals'*, *Socialist Standard* No. 97, September 1912.

17. David Clark, *Victor Grayson: The Man and the Mystery*, p. 278.

18. *Daily Herald*, 8 November 1912.

Chapter 10. A Taste of War

1. Leon Trotsky, *My Life*, p. 232.

2. R.N. Berki, *Socialism*, p. 92.

3. Fenner Brockway, *Towards Tomorrow*, p. 29.

4. David Clark, *Victor Grayson: The Man and the Mystery*, p. 145.

5. Ibid.

6. Clark, *The Man and the Mystery*, p. 146.

7. S.G. Hobson, *Pilgrim to the Left: Memoirs of a Modern Revolutionist*, p. 115.

8. LSE Lansbury/7 1913–1917.

9. Clark, *The Man and the Mystery*, p. 150.

10. *Sydney Morning Herald*, 21 July 1915.

11. *Manchester Evening News*, 14 January 1914.

12. *Mirror of Australia*, 8 August 1915.

13. Ibid.

14. Ibid.

15. Clark, *The Man and the Mystery*, pp. 170–1.

16. *Hull Daily Mail*, 20 November 1918.

17. ILP/4/1914/411-482 Ruth Grayson to Keir Hardie LSE.

Chapter 11. To Passchendaele

1. Lyn Macdonald, *Passchendaele: The Story of the Third Battle of Ypres 1917*, p. 192.

2. Paul Ham, *Passchendaele: Requiem for Doomed Youth*, pp. 316–17.
3. Ibid., p. 323.
4. Fenner Brockway, *Inside the Left*, p. 43.
5. Sir James Sexton, *Agitator: The Life of the Dockers' MP*, p. 237.
6. David Clark, *The Man and the Mystery*, p. 175.
7. Ibid.
8. Clark, *The Man and the Mystery*, p. 178.
9. Ibid., p. 182.
10. John Fairly and William Allison, *The Monocled Mutineer: The First World War's Best Kept Secret: The Etaples Mutiny*, pp. 46–7.
11. Glyn Harper, *Massacre at Passchendaele*, p. 31.
12. Ibid., p. 31.
13. *Darling Downes Gazette*, 9 April 1918.
14. *Daily Mail*, 29 January 1918.

Chapter 12. On Lloyd George's Service

1. Letter from Victor Grayson to Sydney Vesey, 13 May 1918.
2. Winston Churchill, *The World Crisis 1911–1918*, p. 1344.
3. *Northern Daily Mail*, 4 February 1918.
4. Letter from Victor Grayson to Grant Richardson, 8 February 1918.
5. Letter from Victor Grayson to Grant Richards, 11 March 1918.
6. Victor Grayson, *Germany's Last Chance*, 1918.
7. David Clark, *The Man and the Mystery*, p. 225.
8. Harry McShane, *No Mean Fighter*, p. 96.
9. John McGovern, *Neither Fear Nor Favour*, pp. 49–50.
10. *Bootle Times*, 19 April 1918.
11. Letter from Victor Grayson to Sydney Vesey, 7 May 1918.
12. Letter from Victor Grayson to Augusta Greenwood, June 1918.

Chapter 13. Towards the Truth

1. H.M. Hyndman, *Further Reminiscences*, p. 281.
2. Chris Bryant, *The Glamour Boys*, p. 4.
3. Michael Fairless, *The Roadmender*, p. 55.
4. Andrew Cook, *Cash for Honours: The Story of Maundy Gregory*, p. 78.
5. Simon Webb, *1919: Britain's Year of Revolution*.
6. David Clark, *Victor Grayson: The Man and the Mystery*, p. 245.
7. Francis Beckett, *The Rebel Who Lost His Cause; the Tragedy of John Beckett, MP*, p. 31.
8. John Beckett, unpublished autobiography (1938), p. 45.

9. Letter from Brockway to historian Colin Holmes. Quoted in Beckett, *The Rebel Who Lost His Cause*, p. 83.

10. Email from Francis Beckett to the author.

11. *Portsmouth Evening News*, 11 March 1927.

12. According to Who's Who of 1962, one of Campion's pastimes was modelling portrait busts.

13. Letter from Sidney Campion to Derek Forwood, 16 March 1963.

14. Ibid.

15. Email from Terry McCarthy to author.

16. Walter Southgate, *That's the Way It Was: A Working Class Autobiography*, p. 106.

17. *Daily Mirror*, 7 March 1967.

18. MSS. 172/VG/16/8.

Bibliography

Agate, James, *Ego 9* (Harrap & Co., 1947).

Arthur, Max, *Lost Voices of the Edwardians* (HarperCollins, 2006).

Barnsby, George, J., *Birmingham Working People: History of the Labour Movement in Birmingham, 1650–1914* (Integrated Publishing Services, 1989).

Beckett, Francis, *The Rebel Who Lost His Cause; the Tragedy of John Beckett, MP* (Allison & Busby, 2000).

Beckett, John, unpublished autobiography (1938).

Bell, Henry, *John Maclean: Hero of Red Clydeside* (Revolutionary Lives) (Pluto Press, 2018).

Belloc, Hilaire and Chesteron, Cecil, *The Party System* (Stephen Swift, 1911).

Benn, Caroline, *Keir Hardie: A Biography* (Hutchinson, 1992).

Berki, R.N., *Socialism* (Littlehampton Book Services, 1975).

Blatchford, Robert, *My Eighty Years* (Cassell & Company, 1931).

—— *Merrie England* (The Journeyman Press, 1976).

Bloch, Michael, *Closet Queens* (Little, Brown, 2015).

Bower, Fred, *Rolling Stonemason: An Autobiography* (The Merlin Press, 2015).

Brivati, Brian and Heffernan, Richard (eds), *The Labour Party: A Centenary History* (Palgrave Macmillan, 2000).

Brockway, Fenner, *Towards Tomorrow* (HarperCollins, 1977).

—— *Inside the Left* (Spokesman, 2010).

Brooks, David, *The Age of Upheaval* (Manchester University Press, 1995).

Brown, Kenneth, *Labour and Unemployment, 1900–1914* (David & Charles, 1971).

Bryant, Chris, *The Glamour Boys* (Bloomsbury, 2020).

Campion, Sidney R., *Reaching High Heaven* (Rich & Cowan, 1943).

—— *Towards the Mountains: A Study in Autobiography* (Rich & Cowan, 1943).

—— *Only the Stars Remain* (Rich & Cowan, 1946).

Carpenter, Edward, *The Intermediate Sex* (George Allen & Unwin, 1908).

—— *My Days and Dreams* (George Allen & Unwin, 1916).

—— *Towards Democracy* (George Allen & Unwin, 1916).

Carswell, John, *Lives and Letters* (Faber & Faber, 1978).

Churchill, Winston, *The World Crisis 1911–1918* (Odhams, 1938).

—— *Complete Speeches*, Manchester, 28 January 1908, 1,874.

Clark, David, *Colne Valley: Radicalism to Socialism* (Longman, 1981).

—— *Victor Grayson: Labour's Lost Leader* (Quartet, 1985).

—— *Victor Grayson: The Man and the Mystery* (Quartet, 2016).

Cliff, Tony and Gluckstein, Donny, *Marxism and Trade Union Struggle; the General Strike of 1926* (Bookmarks, 1995).

—— *The Labour Party: A Marxist History* (Bookmarks, 1996).

Cole, G.D.H., *A Short History of the Working Class Movement, 1789–1947* (Allen & Unwin, 1948).

Colne Valley Labour Party *Jubilee Souvenir* (Slaithwaite, 1941).

Cook, Andrew, *Cash for Honours: The Story of Maundy Gregory* (The History Press, 2008).

Crick, Martin, *History of the Social Democratic Federation* (Keele University Press, 1994).

Desmond, Shaw, *Labour: The Giant with Feet of Clay* (Collins, 1922).

Dickenson, Jacqueline, *Renegades and Rats: Betrayal and the Remaking of Radical Organisations in Britain and Australia* (Melbourne University Publishing, 2006).

Dudden, Arthur Power, *Joseph Fels and the Single-tax Movement* (Temple University Press, 1974).

Dutton, David, *A History of the Liberal Party* (Palgrave Macmillan, 2004).

Emy, H.V. *Liberals, Radicals and Social Politics 1892–1914* (1973).

Engels, Friedrich, *Condition of the Working Class in England* (Oxford World Classics, 1999).

Fairless, Michael, *The Roadmender* (Collins' Clear Type Press, 1940).

Fairly, John and Allison, William, *The Monocled Mutineer: The First World War's Best Kept Secret: The Etaples Mutiny* (Souvenir Press, 2015).

Fels, Mary, *The Life of Joseph Fels* (Doubleday, 1940).

Gallagher, William, *The Last Memoirs* (Lawrence & Wishart, 1966).

Gilbert, Martin, *Winston S. Churchill. Vol. 4 1917–1922* (William Heinemann, 1975).

Grayson, Victor, *Germany's Last Chance, Searchlights* (National War Aims Committee, 1918).

Griffiths, James, *Pages from Memory* (Aldine Press, 1969).

Grigg, John, *Lloyd George: War Leader 1916–1918* (Allen Lane, 2002).

Groves, Reg, *The Mystery of Victor Grayson* (Pendulum Publication, 1946).

—— *The Strange Case of Victor Grayson* (Pluto Press, 1975).

Haigh, J. Lockhart, *Sir Gallahad of the Slums* (Liverpool Booksellers Company, 1907).

Ham, Paul, *Passchendaele: Requiem for Doomed Youth* (Doubleday, 2017).

Harding, James, *Agate* (Methuen, 1986).

Harper, Glyn, *Massacre at Passchendaele* (HarperCollins New Zealand, 2000).

Hattersley, Roy, *The Edwardians* (Little, Brown, 2004).

—— *David Lloyd George: The Great Outsider* (Little, Brown, 2010).

Hobson, S.G., *Pilgrim to the Left: Memoirs of a Modern Revolutionist* (Longmans, 1938).

Holmes, Rachel, *Sylvia Pankhurst: Natural Born Rebel* (Bloomsbury, 2020).

—— *Eleanor Marx: A Life* (Bloomsbury Publishing, 2014).

Hyndman, H.M., *Further Reminiscences* (MacMillan, 1912).

—— *The First Annual Conference of the British Socialist Party*, Official Report (1912).

—— *England for All* (Branch Line, 1974).

James, David and Laybourn, Keith, *The Rising Sun of Socialism: The ILP in West Yorkshire* (The West Yorkshire Archive Service, 1991).

James, David, Jowitt, Tony and Laybourn, Keith, *The Centennial History of the Independent Labour Party* (Keele University Press, 1992).

Jones, P., *The Christian Socialist Revival 1877–1914* (Princeton University Press, 1968).

Kendall, Walter, *The Revolutionary Movement in Britain 1900–21* (Littlehampton Book Services, 1969).

Kenney, Rowland, *Westering – an Autobiography* (J.M. Dent, 1939).

Kent, Willian, *John Burns: Labour's Lost Leader* (Williams & Norgate, 1950).

Lane, Tony, *Liverpool: City of the Sea*, 2nd edn (Lawrence & Wishart, 1997).

Lansbury, George, *My Life* (Constable, 1931).

Laybourn, Keith, *The Rise of Socialism in Britain* (Sutton Publishing, 1997).

—— *Philip Snowden: The First Labour Chancellor of the Exchequer* (Bradford Art Museums and Libraries Service, 1987).

Lee, H.W. and Archibold, E., *Social Democracy in Britain* (The Social Democratic Federation, 1935).

Liddington, Jill, *Rebel Girls: How Votes for Women Changed Edwardian Lives* (Virago, 2006).

Lloyd, Nick, *Passchendaele: The Lost Victory of World War 1* (Basic Books, 2017).

Lockwood, Ernest, *Colne Valley Folk* (Heath Cranton, 1936).

MacDonald, Lyn, *Passchendaele: The Story of the Third Battle of Ypres 1917* (Penguin, 2013).

Mairet, Philip, *A. R. Orage: A Memoir* (University Books, 1966).

Mann, Tom, *Tom Mann's Memoirs* (MacGibbon & Kee, 1967).

Marquand, David, *Ramsay MacDonald: A Biography* (Jonathan Cape, 1977).

Mayne, John D., *The Triumph of Socialism and How It Succeeded* (London, 1908).

McCormick, Donald, *Murder by Perfection* (John Long, 1970).

McGovern, John, *Neither Fear Nor Favour* (Blandford Press, 1960).

McShane, Harry, *No Mean Fighter* (Pluto Press, 1978).

Miller, Anthony, *Poverty Deserved? Relieving the Poor in Victorian Liverpool* (Liver Press, 1989).

Milton, Nan, *John Maclean* (Pluto Press, 1973).

Mitchell, Hannah, *The Hard Way Up* (Faber, 1968).

Moncur-Sime, A.H., *Edward Carpenter, His Ideas and Ideals* (Kegan Paul, 1916).

Monger, David, *Patriotism and Propaganda in First World War Britain: The National War Aims Committee and Civilian Morale* (Liverpool University Press, 2014).

Morgan, Kenneth O., *Labour People* (Oxford University Press, 1987).

Morris, A.J.A, *C.P. Trevelyan: 1870–1958 Portrait of a Radical* (Blackstaff Press, 1977).

Morris, James, *Pax Britannia Volume 2* (Folio Society, 1993).

Mutch, Deborah (ed.), *British Socialist Fiction 1884–1914 Volumes 1–5* (Routledge, 2013).

O'Connor, Emmet, *Big Jim Larkin: Hero or Wrecker?* (University College Press Dublin, 2015).

Pankhurst, Emmeline, *My Own Story* (Herpesus Press Classics, 2016).

Pankhurst, Sylvia E., *The Suffragette Movement* (Lovat Dickson & Thompson, 1935).

Pearce, Cyril, Wilfred Whiteley interview with, *Society for the Study of Labour History*, Bulletin 18, 1969.

Perrin, David A., *Socialist Party of Great Britain: Politics, Economics and Britain's Oldest Socialist Party* (Bridge Books, 2001).

Pierson, Stanley, *British Socialists: The Journey from Fantasy to Politics* (Harvard University Press, 1979).

Postgate, Raymond, *The Life of George Lansbury* (Longmans, 1951).

Pugh, Martin, *Pankhursts* (Vintage, 2008).

——*Speak for Britain! A New History of the Labour Party* (Vintage, 2011).

Purvis, June, *Christabel Pankhurst: A Biography* (Routledge, 2018).

Redfern, Percy, *Journey to Understanding* (Allen & Unwin, 1946).

Roberts, Andrew, *Churchill: Walking with Destiny* (Penguin, 2019).

Rose, Jonathan, *The Intellectual Life of the British Working Classes*, 2nd revised edn (Yale University Press, 2010).

Rowbotham, Sheila, *Edward Carpenter: A Life of Liberty and Love* (Verso, 2009).

Russell, A.K., *Liberal Landslide: General Election of 1906* (David & Charles, 1973).

Saville, John, *The Communist Experience: A Personal Appraisal*, Socialist Register.

Schneer, Jonathan, *Ben Tillett* (University of Illinois Press, 1983).

Serge, Victor, *Memoirs of a Revolutionary* (NYRB Classics, 2012).

Sexton, Sir James, *Agitator: The Life of the Dockers' MP* (Faber & Faber, 1936).

Shepherd, John, *George Lansbury: At the Heart of Old Labour* (Oxford University Press, 2004).

Sloane, Nan, *The Women in the Room: Labour's Forgotten History* (I.B. Taurus, 2018).

Smith, David C., *Correspondence of H.G. Wells Volume 2 1904–1918* (Pickering & Chatto, London, 1998).

Smith, Leonard, *Unitarian to the Core* (UCM, 2004).

Snowden, Philip, *An Autobiography: Volume One* (Nicholson & Watson, 1934).

Southgate, Walter, *That's the Way It Was: A Working Class Autobiography, 1890–1950* (New Clarion Press, 1982).

Stewart, William, *J. Keir Hardie: A Biography* (Independent Labour Party, 1921).

Swan, Frederick. R., *The Immanence of Christ in Modern Life* (James Clarke, 1907).

Thompson, Bonar, *Hyde Park Orator* (Jarrolds, 1936).

Thompson, E.P., *William Morris* (The Merlin Press, 2011).

Thompson, Laurence, *Robert Blatchford: Portrait of an Englishman* (Gollancz, 1951).

—— *The Enthusiasts* (Littlehampton Book Services, 1971).

Thompson, W., *A. Victor Grayson M.P., England's Most Illustrious Socialist Orator* (The Worker Press, 1910).

—— *Victor Grayson: His Life and Work: An Appreciation and a Criticism* (J.H. Bennett & Co., 1910).

Thorne, Will, *My Life's Battles* (Lawrence & Wishart, 2014).

Thorpe, Andrew, *A History of the British Labour Party*, 4th edn (Red Globe Press, 2015).

Torr, Dona, *Tom Mann and His Times: Volume One: 1856–1890* (Lawrence & Wishart, 1956).

Trotsky, Leon, *My Life* (Wellred, 2004).

Tsuzuki, Chushichi, *H. M. Hyndman and British Socialism* (Oxford University Press, 1961).

—— *Tom Mann 1856–1941: The Challenges of Labour* (Clarendon Press, 1991).

Tsuzuki, Chushichi, *Edward Carpenter 1844–1929: Prophet of Human Fellowship* (Cambridge University Press, 2008).

Webb, B. and Webb, S., *History of Trade Unionism* (Longmans Green & Co., 1950).

Webb, Simon, *1919: Britain's Year of Revolution* (Pen & Sword, 2016).

Wright, Anthony, *British Socialism: Thought from the 1880s to the 1960s* (Longman, 1983).

The immense *Dictionary of Labour Biography*, currently up to Volume XVI, is an invaluable resource and all volumes have been utilized in some way.

Doctoral Thesis

Carole Anne Naomi Reid, *The Origins and Development of the Independent Labour Party in Manchester and Salford, 1880–1914* (1981).

Archives

The Reg Groves papers are at the Modern Records Centre at the University of Warwick.

Two main resources of Victor Grayson papers are housed at the University of Huddersfield and the Labour Party Archive in the People's History Museum, Manchester.

Papers relating to the National War Aims Committee are at the National Archives.

The letters from Victor Grayson to Grant Richards are in the Rare Book and Manuscript Library at the University of Illinois.

Papers relating to Katherine and Bruce Glasier are held at the University of Liverpool.

The Derek Forwood papers are in the author's possession but copies will be deposited to the Labour Archive at the People's History Museum, Manchester.

Acknowledgements

Victor Grayson has been a part of my life for nearly 15 years and so it is not surprising that the book that you hold in your hands has grown with me. Through numerous house-moves, relationships, job-changes, marriage, children etc. this book has slowly evolved. The people who deserve the most thanks are my wife, Hannah, and our boys, Arthur and George, for their patience and fortitude, particularly after hearing me say 'it's nearly finished' more times than I would now dare to count.

Archivists seem to rarely get the thanks they deserve and so I put on record my gratitude to Darren Treadwell at the People's History Museum, Claire Berman at the University of Illinois, Meirian Jump at the Marx Memorial Library, Lindsay at the University of Huddersfield, Liz at the Modern Records Centre, University of Warwick, and Lynette and Lindsey at the Working Class Movement Library. There are undoubtedly others I have missed and I thank them too.

Old friends have also been very accommodating. Ian Dinning gave up the sofa-bed in his Hackney flat at the drop of a hat when I needed to visit archives in London. Ben Bentley followed up leads for me at Liverpool Central Library. Kevin Hickson always asked the right questions and accessed some useful archival materials for me. David Dutton has been incredibly kind in reading and re-reading various drafts of chapters and plugging the gaps in my knowledge of Edwardian politics, as well as condemning my poor use of the English language. I dread to think how much red ink he has used on this project and any errors that remain are of course my own.

This project has also been the basis for new friendships. David Clark, without whom so much of our knowledge of Grayson and the politics of the Colne Valley of that era would have been lost, has been beyond helpful and kind. This book is only possible because of the years of work he has put into unearthing and preserving the political history of Labour's early pioneers. It has been exciting to share new information with him and I hope that we will one day discover the whole truth. When I visited Colne Valley in March 2017, Julie Ward contacted me and spent a day driving me around the constituency as Grayson knew it, pointing out landmarks and locations that I was writing about but had never seen. Julie's father, Mike Shaw, shared with me his theories, ideas and archival material collected over a lifetime with me, whilst also giving this project some early press attention. I am sorry that he did not get to read this. David Hanson also read the manuscript and made some useful suggestions.

My thanks to Jeremy Corbyn for agreeing to write the Foreword. During the last 18 months of his Labour Party leadership, I escorted him to and from events in the West Midlands. To see the genuine hope on the faces of those he inspired and feel the raw energy of members of what had been previously written off as an a-political generation came as a shock at first. So too did the open hostility and sheer hatred of others. Throughout those moments, I often reflected on how young Grayson was when he was unwittingly catapulted to a similar level of public attention, affection and loathing, particularly when he had no party apparatus or staff to shield him.

To David Castle and all the staff at Pluto, thanks for taking a chance on me.

And finally to my Dad and Mum. I did it.

Dedicated to Derek Forwood, a man I never knew but who is now a part of the story of Victor Grayson.

Revolutionary Lives

Revolutionary Lives is a series of short, critical biographies of radical figures from throughout history. The books are sympathetic but not sycophantic, and the intention is to present a balanced and, where necessary, critical evaluation of the individual's place in their political field, putting their actions and achievements in context and exploring issues raised by their lives, such as the use or rejection of violence, nationalism, or gender in political activism. While individuals are the subject of the books, their personal lives are dealt with lightly except insofar as they mesh with political concerns. The focus is on the contribution these revolutionaries made to history, an examination of how far they achieved their aims in improving the lives of the oppressed and exploited, and how they can continue to be an inspiration for many today.

Series Editors:
Sarah Irving, King's College, London
Professor Paul Le Blanc, La Roche University, Pittsburgh

Also available

Index

note: *n* refers to a note; VG refers to Victor Grayson

Thanks to our Patreon Subscribers:

Lia Lilith de Oliveira
Andrew Perry

Who have shown generosity and
comradeship in support of our publishing.

Check out the other perks you get by subscribing
to our Patreon – visit patreon.com/plutopress.
Subscriptions start from £3 a month.

The Pluto Press Newsletter

Hello friend of Pluto!

Want to stay on top of the best radical books we publish?

Then sign up to be the first to hear about our new books, as well as special events, podcasts and videos.

You'll also get 50% off your first order with us when you sign up.

Come and join us!

Go to bit.ly/PlutoNewsletter